Coming Out to the Streets

The publisher and the University of California Press Foundation gratefully acknowledge the generous support of the Anne G. Lipow Endowment Fund in Social Justice and Human Rights.

Coming Out to the Streets

LGBTQ YOUTH EXPERIENCING
HOMELESSNESS

Brandon Andrew Robinson

UNIVERSITY OF CALIFORNIA PRESS

University of California Press
Oakland, California

© 2020 by Brandon Andrew Robinson

Library of Congress Cataloging-in-Publication Data

Names: Robinson, Brandon Andrew, author.
Title: Coming out to the streets : the lives of LGBTQ youth experiencing
    homelessness / Brandon Andrew Robinson.
Description: Oakland, California : University of California Press,
    [2020] | Includes bibliographical references and index.
Identifiers: LCCN 2020014432 (print) | LCCN 2020014433 (ebook) |
    ISBN 9780520299269 (hardback) | ISBN 9780520299276 (paperback)
    | ISBN 9780520971073 (ebook)
Subjects: LCSH: Sexual minority youth—Texas. | Homeless teenagers—
    Texas.
Classification: LCC HQ76.27.Y68 R635 2020 (print) | LCC HQ76.27.Y68
    (ebook) | DDC 306.760835—dc23
LC record available at https://lccn.loc.gov/2020014432
LC ebook record available at https://lccn.loc.gov/2020014433

Manufactured in the United States of America

27 26 25 24 23 22 21 20
10 9 8 7 6 5 4 3 2 1

To LGBTQ people looking for a place to call home

Contents

Acknowledgments

Every time that I return to this book, I think not only about the amazing and loving youth who fill its pages, but also about the many other people who helped touch my life and my thinking. I am profoundly grateful to so many of you. And I owe you so much more than an acknowledgment. Please know that this book would have been impossible without you.

My gratitude begins with Gloria González-López. Gloria fervently supported this project from the moment that I told her that I wanted to study LGBTQ youth homelessness. Gloria's unwavering championing of my work gave me the strength and confidence to do this research. In wanting to be a part of a new generation of sexualities scholars who promote human rights and progressive social policies, I could not have asked for a finer mentor. Gloria has told me since day one to do work that is urgently needed and to do work that matters. I hope this book lives up to that motto—a motto that I will take with me throughout the rest of my life.

Deb Umberson coming into my life was also a game changer. Deb is an exemplar sociologist and mentor. I am grateful for all the time and feedback Deb has spent on bestowing to me her indispensable expertise. Deb has a far-reaching impact in our field, and this impact includes her mentorship and training of the next generation of scholars. Thank you, Deb, for everything. I've grown so much as an academic and as a person because of you.

For Salvador Vidal-Ortiz, there are no words to express my deep thanks and gratitude. As a mentor, a coauthor, and a friend, Salvador has supported and shaped me into the scholar that I am today. All my academic pursuits, including this book, are because of the foundation that Salvador has provided for me intellectually. I truly don't believe I would be where I am today without him. Thank you for seeing something in me and for guiding me all these years.

I am also thankful for other scholars who supported me while I was at the University of Texas at Austin. Thank you to Sharmila Rudrappa, Stephen Russell, and Amy Stone for working with me throughout the stages of this project. Thank you, as well, to Simone Browne for showing me how to be brave and fearless and to do work that leaves an impact on this world. For their intellectual and personal support, thank you to Christine Williams, Mary Rose, and Shannon Cavanaugh.

To my friends during my time in Texas, thank you for everything. Thank you to Emily Spangenberg, Chelsea Smith Gonzalez, Beth Cozzolino, Maggie Tate, Rachel Donnelly, Sam Simon, Esther Sullivan, and Laura Kaufmann for all the fun times and conversations. A special thank-you to Kate Averett, not only for her queer friendship but also for transcribing my interviews with the service providers. Thank you to Shantel Buggs for being one of the greatest friends a person could ask for and for your brilliance and heart. Thank you as well to Amy Lodge for being an amazing friend, for the memories, and for the many hours of hearing all my ideas, over and over again.

I owe many thanks also to my writing group—Anima Adjepong, Shameka Powell, and Joseph Ewoodzie—for the years of feedback on this book. Anima and Shameka have read every chapter of this book—sometimes more than once—and I am so grateful for all their labor in making this book better. I appreciate the academic and intellectual standard you both always hold me to. I also appreciate the feedback I received on various chapters and ideas from Michela Musto, Stefan Vogler, Susila Gurusami, Meg Neely, and Jen Delfino. To Bernadette Barton and Jason Wasserman, thank you for reviewing this book, for supporting this work, and for all the invaluable feedback. I am forever grateful, as well, to Rachel Schmitz, who has not only provided incisive comments on this book but has also been the best coauthor someone could ask for in this academic life of trying to make the world better for LGBTQ youth. I'm so thankful for that random elevator encounter at ASA that brought us together. I am also thankful for another ASA encounter that happened: meeting Julia Meszaros, who is now a dear friend. Thank you also to Tristan Bridges for all your support of my work.

This project would not have been possible without the financial support I received in conducting this research and in writing. The National Science Foundation supported the last leg of the fieldwork and interviews. The Equality Knowledge Project at Eastern Michigan University helped to support data collection and allowed me to present some early findings at their campus. At the University of Texas at Austin, thank you to the Sociology Department, the Center for Women's and Gender Studies, the College of Liberal Arts, and the Graduate School for their financial support.

I am also grateful for the University of California President's and Chancellor's Postdoctoral Fellowship program. Being a UC Chancellor's Fellow at the University of California, Riverside, gave me the time to truly read, think, and write. I am deeply thankful for my postdoctoral mentor, Jane Ward, and for Ellen Reese, who supported me during this time as well. A special thank-you to my postdoctoral colleague Brittany Morey, who made navigating the postdoctoral program the most enjoyable. Kimberly Adkinson is a godsend in all that she does for this program. Thank you to Mark Lawson for continuing to lead and advocate for such an important fellowship program and experience.

Moving to Los Angeles also changed my life. I am so thankful for my LA friends who have enriched my world in ways that they don't even know. Thank you to Christina Moses, Brian Haag, Victor Rico, Oliver Udom, Gerry Gorospe, Bari Sofer, Kiki Stevens, Amanda Kuehl, and Todd Gilchrist. Y'all have made Los Angeles an even better paradise than it already was. I am also grateful to have found an academic home in the Department of Gender and Sexuality Studies at the University of California, Riverside. Being among colleagues committed to feminist and queer social justice is a dream come true. Thank you to Juliann Allison,

Alicia Arrizón, Crystal Baik, Amalia Cabezas, Katja Guenther, Sherine Hafez, Tammy Ho, Anthonia Kalu, Jade Sasser, Chikako Takeshita, and Jane Ward. Sherine has been an amazing and supportive chair. Thank you as well to Jane and Crystal for all the love and support.

At UC Press, I am thankful for my editor, Naomi Schneider. I am also thankful for all the editorial assistants—Renee Donovan, Benjy Malings, and Summer Farah—who touched this book along its journey. Thank you, as well, to the rest of the UC Press team for shepherding this book through production. A special thank you to Gary J. Hamel for copyediting the book and to Jon Dertien and BookComp, Inc. for managing the production of the book. Thank you to Cathy Hannabach and Ideas on Fire for the index.

I presented many of the ideas in this book at various conferences and talks; I have also published some of the ideas in previous outlets. I am thankful to everyone who came to hear me discuss these ideas and for all the support and feedback that I received. Part of the chapter "Reframing Family Rejection" was previously published as "Conditional Families and Lesbian, Gay, Bisexual, Transgender, and Queer Youth Homelessness: Gender, Sexuality, Family Instability, and Rejection" in the *Journal of Marriage & Family* 80(2): 383–96. Likewise, part of the chapter "New Lavender Scare" was previously published as "The Lavender Scare in Homonormative Times: Policing, Hyper-incarceration, and LGBTQ Youth Homelessness" in *Gender & Society* 43(2): 210–32. I am also grateful to Jeffrey M. Poirier and Jama Shelton for their *Child Welfare* special issue on Sexual Orientation, Gender Identity/Expression, and Child Welfare and for their support and feedback on my article "Child Welfare Systems and LGBTQ Youth Homelessness: Gender Segregation, Instability, and Intersectionality" in *Child Welfare* 96(2): 29–45. Many thanks to Angela Jones, Joseph DeFilippis, and Michael W. Yarbrough for organizing the *After Marriage* conference and the subsequent edited volumes, and for their support and feedback on my chapter "'I Want to Be Happy in Life': Success, Failure, and Addressing LGBTQ Youth Homelessness" in *The Unfinished Queer Agenda after Marriage Equality*. Specifically, thank you to Angela Jones, who has always supported me in all that I do; I am grateful for the friendship we've built over the years.

A deep and special thank-you to Thrive Youth Center, without which this book would have been impossible. Sandra Whitley is a true angel.

Sandy galvanized me every week during this project, and I hope I can someday be half the person that she is. Lauryn Farris is a firecracker and an amazing activist. Thank you, Lauryn, for the many great and insightful talks. Thank you as well to Chelsea, Maria, and Ray for all that you do. Another deep and special thank-you to LifeWorks. Laura Poskochil was a fierce supporter and advocate for this project. Laura energized me every week in all her labor of love. Thank you to Liz Schoenfeld for also supporting this project and to Gaby and Caitlin for being social work warriors. Thank you to the Texas Department of Family and Protective Services (DFPS) for their support of this project. Catherine Farris was a fabulous point of contact within DFPS. Thank you as well to the Austin Children's Shelter and Aja Gair. I feel so fortunate for meeting all the wonderful people who are doing the daily work of trying to make the world a better place.

Margaret and Ballard Robinson, I love you. I feel so honored every day to still have my amazing grandparents in my life. They made me who I am and have always been my biggest fans. To my mom, Tamara Blair, thank you for the optimism, and to my dad, Fred Robinson, thank you for the life lessons. To Sheri and Floyd Mount, thank you being there for me. Thank you to my other grandma, Emma Welch, for taking me in when I needed another home. You are missed. Katie Beran has been an amazing, loving friend. I do not know that I have ever met a kinder person. You balance me, Katie. To my godson, Kaeson, and my nieces, Rylee and Sydney, you inspire me to always keep working for social justice and social change. To my best friend, Kristin Bird, I love you. You keep me human, honest, and alive. Bird, you make me a better person.

To the LGBTQ youth in this study, thank you for everything. Y'all touched my life in unfathomable ways, and I will be forever changed by each and every one of you. Thank you for sharing your stories and for your heartfelt humanity. I wish the world for all of you. You are the reasons I wrote this book.

Introduction

One day after my shift as a volunteer at a San Antonio shelter for lesbian, gay, bisexual, transgender, and/or queer (LGBTQ) youth experiencing homelessness, I opened my laptop and typed in the web address for Craigslist. During my volunteer shift the previous night, youth residing at the shelter had discussed seeing advertisements on the website by Camila and Zoe, two Hispanic heterosexual transgender women who, until recently, had been staying at the LGBTQ shelter. Staff had suspended them for doing drugs and missing curfew. I skimmed the personals section of the advertisements on Craigslist until I found their ad.[1] I found the following ad. It read: "Pretty Ts Girls—t4m (Downtown) Hi guys I'm Camila, with black hair, 22 5´8 and I'm Zoe, with red hair, I'm 19, 5´5. We're both transgender crossdressers. We trying to get a room for the night to chill, we're laid back and looking to meet some cute guys. Looking to meet guys with party favors. Both versatile bottoms looking to have a drink, smoke some bud and have some fun."[2]

I had met Camila and Zoe while conducting fieldwork on LGBTQ youth homelessness in central Texas. Zoe's story captures the complexities of youth homelessness. "I first started coming out to the streets whenever I was thirteen," Zoe began, as we sat down for an interview a few months

1

after she posted the Craigslist advertisement. Zoe grew up with a single mother. Her dad—whom Zoe called her "sperm donor"—went in and out of jail during Zoe's childhood. He abused Zoe as well. At age thirteen, Zoe started doing drugs. She explained, "The only reason I started doing dope was because I felt unwanted from my family. Gay was a big issue. Me liking boys was a big issue. I tried to kill myself by doing the dope—to hurt my family."

Zoe started taking hormones while living on the streets, but as her breasts grew, she wondered if she should continue. She feared how her family would react. "I didn't know how to come out to tell them that I want to be a girl. And I didn't know if they were going to accept me," she explained.[3] "Well, this is my life. I am who I am. And if God didn't want me to be this girl, he would've already tooken me." To emphasize her point, Zoe described a moment where she thought she might lose her life. "I tried to steal my grandfather's wallet," she recollected. "I was messed up on heroin. Then I smoked crack. Then I drank Sex on the Beach—a whole bottle. And I was intoxicated." She continued, "Well, [my grandfather and I] started fighting, and I busted out the windows in his truck. Knocked his AC [air conditioner] unit out. Called my *tia* and said, 'He's going to shoot me. Papa's going to shoot me.' Well, he got that gun. And boom, he got me."[4]

She credited God for keeping her alive. But along with this harrowing family life, Zoe faced challenges outside the home as well. One of the hardest was her peers' negative reactions to her expansive expressions of gender—expressions that clashed with dominant societal notions of masculine men and feminine women. "I would dress up like a gangsta boy—muscle shirt, basketball shorts," she explained. "And everyone thought I was a butch lesbian." People did not react well to this appearance. Choking up, she added, "[Smoking weed] numbed the pain from going to school. Numb the pain of people looking at me. People calling me a faggot. They don't realize how hurtful the word *faggot* is."

In response to this bullying, school staff recommended that Zoe's mom home-school her, which her mother had neither the time nor resources to do. In seventh grade, Zoe dropped out of school and started living on the streets. Eventually, she ended up in Child Protective Services (CPS). She told me, "I got tooken away 'cause of the drug problems I had," and the state then sent her to "a boy's ranch [that] was like a behavioral place." Set in a wilderness environment, the ranch used Boy Scout philosophy to teach "young men" to accept authority, take personal responsibility for their actions, and build successful skills to return to the community.[5] Zoe said she stayed at the ranch for about a year. Upon completing the program, she went back to living on the streets.

Street life, of course, came with its own difficulties. The police arrested Zoe "no more than fifteen times," often for prostitution and public intoxication. These arrests kept her continuously "going in and out of prison." And homelessness shelters provided no respite. "I'd have to shower in the men's [shelter bathroom]," she explained. "And I was afraid I was going to get raped. And [some of the men] would tell me that I don't belong in there 'cause I'm a girl. And I'm like, I have to be clean. I can't let these fucking men run me out of this fuckin' shower."

Such discriminatory experiences toward LGBTQ youth, especially toward transgender and gender-expansive youth such as Zoe, commonly transpire in shelters. Partly in response to these experiences, an LGBTQ shelter opened in San Antonio to give LGBTQ youth experiencing homelessness a safer space to sleep and shower and to provide them with specific LGBTQ services, such as hormone replacement therapy and helping them change their name and gender marker on their identification (ID) card. Acknowledging the importance of the LGBTQ shelter in her life, Zoe stated, "I think . . . every state—all around the world—should have an LGBTQ spot."

Although it served as a refuge, the LGBTQ shelter also came with rules and regulations. One evening, Zoe went on an "ice skating" binge—slang for getting high on crystal meth—with Camila. Later that week, the director of the shelter drug tested them. When the test came back positive, the staff suspended them from the shelter for thirty days, which sent the young women back to the streets. That was when they posted the advertisements on Craigslist, seeking sex, drugs, and a place to stay.

THE LIVES BEHIND THE STATISTICS

Zoe's story reveals the pervasive inequalities that exist in US society and that perpetuate youth homelessness. Generally, homelessness means lacking a fixed, regular, and adequate nighttime residence. People experiencing homelessness sleep in shelters, on the streets, in abandoned buildings, at bus or train stations, and on friends' couches, among other impermanent options.[6] One in ten—around 3.5 million—youth, ages eighteen to twenty-five, experience homelessness each year in the United States.[7]

LGBTQ youth comprise around 40 percent of this youth homeless population, despite only comprising 5 to 8 percent of the US youth population.[8] Furthermore, LGBTQ youth experiencing homelessness face a host of obstacles, including physical and sexual victimization and mental health challenges.[9] In one study, 58.7 percent of lesbian, gay, and bisexual youth experiencing homelessness reported victimization, and 41.3 percent of that population reported depressive symptoms, including suicidal ideation.[10] As captured in Zoe's account, these challenges are exacerbated for transgender and gender-expansive youth experiencing homelessness, who have to navigate the gender segregation of shelters and services while facing other obstacles such as trying to obtain an ID card and clothing that aligns with their gender identity and gender expression.[11]

The numbers and challenges paint a bleak picture.

But I wanted to learn about the lives behind the statistics. I wanted to know what feminists call "lived experiences"—the firsthand, everyday accounts of how marginalized people experience the world and the personal knowledge they gain from these experiences.[12] Specifically, I wanted to know about the perceived pathways into and experiences of homelessness for LGBTQ youth experiencing homelessness.[13] Learning about these lived experiences centers the youth's voices, foregrounding what they identify as the main issues affecting them and the solutions to helping them. To document the youth's lives and to learn from their lived experiences, I conducted eighteen months of ethnographic fieldwork in central Texas. I also interviewed forty LGBTQ youth experiencing homelessness and ten service providers who worked with the youth.

Through doing this research, I found that LGBTQ youth homelessness involves more complicated processes than the usual narrative of "coming out"—or disclosing an LGBTQ identity—followed by parental rejection. Instead, LGBTQ youth homelessness often involves complex issues around gender expression and is not solely about the rejection of a child's identity. LGBTQ youth homelessness involves the policing of expansive expressions of gender and how these practices intersect with sexuality, race, and class to influence the youth's lives. These lives are simultaneously often marked by familial abuse, bullying, rejection, relegation to state child custody systems, drug use, violence, sex work, mental health challenges, encounters with police, criminal records, failure to get an ID card, the lack of a safe place to shower and sleep, and a host of other cumulative disadvantages.

These inequalities begin in childhood. Like most youth in this study, Zoe grew up amid poverty and instability. She felt unwanted because of her attraction to boys, and she feared disclosing that she was a girl. Despite these trepidations, Zoe took hormones, knowing that her changing body would probably further strain her familial relationships, which were already tenuous, as she had stolen money from her family for food and drugs. In effect, the problems of poverty and instability were compounded by Zoe's feelings of being unwanted for her gender identity and expression.

LGBTQ youth homelessness, however, involves not only familial rejection, but also problems with other institutions and relationships. School peers bullied Zoe, using homophobic language. Instead of addressing the bullying, school staff put the onus on Zoe and her family to resolve the issue. Subsequently, state child custody workers sent Zoe to a residential behavioral center—the boy's ranch—which did not affirm Zoe's gender identity and expression.

Institutions often fail LGBTQ youth. Peers and authority figures, along with the gender-segregated layout of most institutions, often constrain and punish LGBTQ youth, particularly through gender policing and homophobia. These practices in turn create unsafe and violent spaces for LGBTQ youth. Poor Black and Brown LGBTQ youth, such as Zoe and most of the youth in this study, face the harshest consequences of these punishing practices, as structural racism and racial profiling exacerbate the surveillance and punishment that they contend with. Because of this punishment and bullying, youth such as Zoe ended up on the streets.

The punishment of gender expression and sexuality continues once the youth experience homelessness. Zoe said police profiled her as a sex worker, a common experience of transgender and gender-expansive people of color on the streets. This "trans profiling" led to police not only repeatedly stopping Zoe on the streets but also harassing her, ticketing her, checking her for warrants, and cycling her in and out of jail. Furthermore, social service organizations and governmental services for people experiencing homelessness often segregate sleeping and showering arrangements based on the gender binary. As a consequence, Zoe experienced violence in shelter bathrooms. To ameliorate some of these difficulties, she engaged in sex work and intimate encounters to obtain temporary shelter—often at a hotel—and to earn money and get drugs. Essentially, she used her sexuality and gender expression to obtain resources that society failed to provide to her.

While Zoe found respite from the violence of the streets at the LGBTQ shelter, staff regulated her and others' behaviors, including their sexual behaviors, their gender expression (e.g., how they dressed), and their substance use. Zoe had a safer place to shower and sleep, and she could meet other LGBTQ people, access hormones, and obtain an ID with her name and gender marker changed, but she had to deal with new rules. If she did not adhere to the rules, she went back to sleeping on the streets. This contradiction of the shelter as an LGBTQ refuge from the violence of the streets, yet also a regulating institution that policed sexual behaviors and gender expressions, kept Zoe and other youth cycling through unsafe environments, including the streets, shelters, and jails. The cycle of homelessness continued.

THE LIMITS OF RIGHTS AND IDENTITY

While Zoe was living on the streets and in shelters, many people in the United States celebrated certain gains in civil rights for LGBTQ people. During this study—in June 2015—the US Supreme Court federally legalized same-sex marriage. Five years earlier, the federal government repealed "Don't Ask, Don't Tell," allowing gay, lesbian, and bisexual people to serve openly in the military. Lawmakers in certain states and cities have also passed laws banning discrimination based on sexual orientation and/ or gender identity and gender expression with regard to employment and housing. How, then, can we understand Zoe's life and the lives of hundreds of thousands of other LGBTQ youth experiencing homelessness during an era of same-sex marriage and other LGBTQ civil rights gains?

The gains in civil rights have not benefitted all LGBTQ people equally. A few months after the US Supreme Court legalized same-sex marriage, the people of Houston—in November 2015—voted to repeal the Houston Equal Rights Ordinance, making Houston the largest US city without protections for LGBTQ people. A drive to repeal this ordinance involved fearmongering around transgender and gender-expansive people using public restrooms appropriate to their gender identity and/or expression. Other state and city legislatures have also introduced—and some successfully passed—"bathroom bills" to codify this public restroom discrimination against transgender and gender-expansive people, forcing youth like Zoe into bathrooms that make them more vulnerable to experiencing harassment and violence. And during this writing, the Trump administration has banned transgender people from serving in the military. A leaked memo has shown that the Trump administration wants to define gender as biological and immutable.

On a societal level, then, certain sexuality-based rights have advanced, but a backlash has occurred, especially against transgender and gender-expansive people. This backlash around gender identity and expression negatively impacts many LGBTQ youth experiencing homelessness. Moreover, rights guarantee neither tolerance nor acceptance. And tolerance and acceptance often only benefit people who assimilate to dominant societal values. For instance, LGBTQ people who conform to societal standards such as marriage, monogamy, and dominant gender relations may find acceptance within society. But people who have expansive expressions of gender and/or who publicly display their non-heterosexuality, such as a same-gender couple holding hands in public, may not. People see expansive expressions of gender as "too gay." People often see public displays of non-heterosexuality as "flaunting" sexuality, even when the behavior is similar to the behavior of heterosexual people. The message of tolerance communicates: you can identify as LGBTQ, but don't make a show of it. Rights and tolerance do not celebrate difference.[14]

A central tenet of this book is that to understand this unevenness between LGBTQ social change and the lived realities of LGBTQ youth experiencing homelessness, we need to move beyond notions of rights and identity. We need to focus on embodiments and enactments of gender and how gender expression intersects with sexuality, race, and class in intricate ways that we often miss in our emphasis on identity and single-issue (often sexuality-based) rights. The gender binary, on a structural level, and negative attitudes and behaviors toward transgender and gender-expansive youth, on an interpersonal level, work to render certain youth vulnerable. Hence, a focus on rights and identity overshadows the meanings of LGBTQ embodiment; how contexts shape these meanings; and how gender expression, sexuality, race, and class influence LGBTQ people's relations to others, and their experiences within institutions.

This book intervenes by foregrounding how gender expression and its intersections with other social categories shape the lives of LGBTQ youth experiencing homelessness both before and during their experiences of homelessness. As this book will show, people's responses to the LGBTQ youth's expansive expressions of gender often led to policing the youth's assumed non-heterosexuality. Hence, gender regulation always incorporates sexual regulation and vice versa. These regulations always incorporate policing race and class as well. These intersecting regulatory processes form the youth's pathways to the streets and affect their experiences of homelessness. In amplifying, then, how gender embodiments and enactments centrally influence people's lived experiences, and specifically the lived experiences of LGBTQ youth experiencing homelessness, *Coming Out to the Streets* proffers a new understanding of homelessness as shaped by processes of gender, sexuality, and embodiment, and shows that gender and sexuality always mutually interconnect through people's gender expression and its intersections with race and class.

GENDERING SEXUALITY

Zoe—a transgender woman of color attracted to men—looked like a "gangsta boy." She often wore baggy jeans, tank tops, and skater shoes. She even said that people thought she was a butch lesbian. Zoe dressed in ways many people might consider masculine, and hence, she challenged and expanded our ideas of womanhood (including trans womanhood). People's perceptions of this gender presentation, though, shaped their assumptions about her sexuality—that she was a lesbian, even though she identified as heterosexual. Many transgender youth in this study discussed how before they identified as a heterosexual transgender person, they identified as gay or bisexual (but not yet transgender). As their understanding of their gender changed, so did their understanding of their sexuality, showing a fluidity between these categories. During my fieldwork, many heterosexual transgender youth like Zoe would still refer to themselves as "gay" in many conversations. Gender and sexuality involve complex processes.

Part of grasping these complexities involves recognizing that gender means more than an identity or who we are. We also "do gender," which consists of the way we embody and enact masculinities and femininities. Doing gender also entails the meanings people assign to gender embodiments and enactments within various interactions and contexts.[15] The meanings of gender embodiments and enactments vary across time and cultures. Think about how some of the meanings around masculinity and femininity have changed from the 1800s to now. For instance, before the 1940s, in the United States, we used to dress girls in blue and boys in pink. People saw pink as a strong color and saw blue as delicate and dainty.[16] Boys also wore dresses, including President Franklin D. Roosevelt, who is photographed as a child wearing a dress. Or consider, do people embody and enact gender the same way at work as they do at home, as they do at the bar? Contexts and other people shape experiences of gender.

These experiences and meanings of gender intertwine with sexuality. Queer theory emerged as a field of inquiry in the 1990s to examine how power shapes experiences of gender and sexuality and how desires, behaviors, embodiments, and other modes of expression disrupt notions of stable identities. Queer theory also gave us the key concept of heteronormativity—how discourses and practices in society construct heterosexuality as superior to all other expressions of sexuality. Heteronormativity also relies upon and works to naturalize the gender binary of masculine men and feminine women.[17] Furthermore, many societies privilege people whose gender embodiments and enactments align with their assigned gender at birth and who desire—within this binary construction—the "opposite gender."[18] This binary system also privileges men and masculinity over women and femininity, and it devalues not only women and femininity but also people who challenge the gender binary such as gender-expansive people.

Notably, complex processes related to gender and sexuality play out daily on the interactional level. For example, enacting and embodying expressions of gender in a way not in line with one's gender assigned at birth threatens heterosexuality—especially in sexual situations—and the gender binary.[19] People objectify and scrutinize gender-expansive people and gender-expansive bodies because expansive expressions of gender challenge dominant social structures.[20] If someone embodies and enacts an expansive expression of gender, such as a boy wearing fingernail polish, many people view the child as gay (or as going to grow up to be gay).[21] Within a heteronormative society, many people often see being gay as negative. Thus, people might police this boy's gender expression—through acts such as bullying, calling the boy a fag or sissy, and taking away the fingernail polish—not only to make the boy conform to dominant notions of masculinity but also to try to prevent the boy from being or becoming gay. Gender policing entails regulating sexuality, as people gender-police other people to enforce expressions that conform to the dominant heteronormative gender relations within society. This gender policing through social sanctions such as bullying and physical violence aims to uphold the gender binary and heteronormativity as natural and correct. But the fact that we constantly monitor and police each other and ourselves to try to maintain these systems exposes that these categories are not natural and innate.

Re-gendering Sexuality

The lived experiences of the youth in this study involved messier processes and experiences than the categories and language we often use to make sense of people's lives. Some heterosexual transgender people in this study also thought of themselves as gay. And Zoe, who identified as a heterosexual transgender woman, dressed in ways deemed masculine; hence, people assumed she was a lesbian. Many of Zoe's experiences with people's negative reactions to her, including negative reactions to her sexuality, entailed negative reactions to her gender expression.

Sociologist C. J. Pascoe's concept of "gendered homophobia" illuminates this relation of sexuality and policing people's embodiments and enactments of gender. In her study, Pascoe examined how heterosexual boys in high school used homophobia to police each other's masculinity. If a boy did something that his peers deemed feminine, those peers policed the boy's gender by calling him a fag, even though the boy was presumably not gay. Moreover, the boys who used the epithet *fag* did not see themselves as homophobic and said they had nothing against gay people. Homophobia often pertains to policing gender—specifically to policing masculinity. Importantly, the gender-expansive, gay person in Pascoe's study—who *embodies* the fag—experienced constant harassment and dropped out of school.[22]

I want to magnify this last point.

In this study, I examine how gendered homophobia affects poor, gender-expansive LGBTQ youth, especially youth of color. I amplify how the policing of gender and sexuality intertwine to shape the lives of people who embody abject positions—people and bodies positioned outside of and challenging the dominant relations of gender and sexuality in society.[23] Particularly, in focusing on embodiment and policing embodiment, we see how sexuality *always* relates to gender and how homophobia always relates to sexuality *and* gender. This gendered homophobia occurs in ways that Pascoe documented. It also occurs in how a gay or lesbian couple experiences homophobia because two men or two women together challenge dominant notions of masculinity and femininity. For most of the youth in this study, the gender policing they faced was inextricably linked to policing (or trying to prevent) their non-heterosexuality. Indeed, most homophobic violence entails the perpetrator of this violence perceiving someone as gay because of the person's expansive expressions of gender.[24] Publicly disrupting gender often challenges heteronormativity more than same-sex desire does, or, for the sake of my point, more than a sexual and/or gender identity does.[25] In this book, I contend that separating gender and sexuality as analytically distinct fails to capture how gender and policing gender always pertains to sexuality and how sexuality and policing sexuality always pertains to gender.

This attempt at untangling gender from sexuality has been part of gay and lesbian assimilation strategies. As some gay and lesbian people assimilated and achieved social acceptance, they wanted to distance themselves from gender-expansive people. Certain gay and lesbian communities engaged in gender policing practices to distance themselves from historical discourses of "sexual inversion" that often linked same-gender desire to having inborn reversed gender traits.[26] Moreover, the category of transgender took hold in the 1990s partly to allow for certain gay and lesbian people to conform to dominant societal expectations and to engage in distancing from people who embody and enact expansive expressions of gender. The neat distinctions, though, between gender and sexuality, including gender and sexual identities, do not capture how these categories operate structurally, interpersonally, or individually in people's lives.[27]

To put it another way, we cannot study gender without studying sexuality. We cannot study sexuality without studying gender. The constant academic and political practice of separating gender and sexuality as analytically distinct (while still saying that they mutually constitute one another) needs a reexamination. Indeed, the fact that we have two separate words—*gender* and *sexuality*—fails to capture how people always experience these categories simultaneously in their lives. I have no easy solution to this language problem. But gender and sexuality actually do conflate in the ways many people experience these categories. As sociologist Karen Cuthbert argues, "[G]ender might *be* sexuality (and vice versa) in some contexts."[28] This separation of gender from sexuality as different fields of investigation and as different identity categories cannot account for people's experiences with these categories, especially certain poor LGBTQ people of color's experiences.[29]

Indeed, for many youth in this study, gender and sexuality interchanged—often were not seen as separate categories. One moment, a youth would identify as a heterosexual transgender woman, and the next moment as gay, or talk about "fagging out." They often also experienced people policing their sexuality through the policing of their gender expression. These elisions of gender and sexuality make the separation of the categories analytically problematic in capturing embodied, lived experiences. In turning to the youth's embodiments—and not just focusing on identity—we see the complexities and elisions of gender, sexuality, and other social categories. This move to examine embodiment and the gender and sexual regulations of abject body positions will show how people often experience gender and sexuality as the same thing. How the youth in this study experienced and discussed gender and sexuality in their lives creates a new departure in thinking about these social categories.

Gender, Sexuality, and Intersectionality

These experiences of gender and sexuality intersect, as well, with race and class. Intersectionality, as an analytical framework, examines how systems of power interconnect, shaping people's experiences of privilege, oppression, and their material realities. This framework originally began through feminists of color—notably non-heterosexual women of color—describing and analyzing how women of color experience life differently than white women and men of color. Identity categories such as "woman" or "person of color" ignore intragroup differences and do not take into account that different axes of power and oppression forge the lived experiences of women of color.[30]

Furthermore, through historical processes and legacies of colonization and slavery, stereotypical images of Black women, such as mammies, matriarchs, jezebels, and welfare queens, live on today. Sociologist Patricia Hill Collins shows how these controlling images objectify Black women and work toward justifying the oppression of them. For example, the controlling image of the jezebel constructs Black women as loud, promiscuous, muscular, and aggressive, and hence, as not embodying and enacting socially idealized white, middle-class femininity.[31] Notably, these controlling images always entail stereotypes around race, gender, sexuality, and class. People often depict the mammy as loyal and asexual; whereas, people see and depict the jezebel and the welfare queen as poor and hypersexual. Other stereotypes, such as Latinas as sexually exotic and passionate, also serve to objectify and position Brown people and bodies outside of the white, middle-class relations of gender and sexuality in society.[32] These processes also uphold white, middle-class enactments and embodiments of gender and sexuality as the dominant relations in society.

The same sort of objectification holds for men of color. Controlling images of Black men, especially of poor and working-class Black men, often casts them as criminals, hypersexual, and violent.[33] The dominant relations of masculinity—called "hegemonic masculinity"—rely on marginalized masculinities, such as Black and working-class masculinities, to uphold its relation to middle-class whiteness.[34]

Class matters too. In a study of high school girls, sociologist Julie Bettie documented how middle-class girls positioned themselves against the working-class girls. The middle-class girls saw the working-class girls' heavy makeup and tight clothes as low class, oversexed, and tawdry. Gendered class differences, hence, were sexual class differences.[35] In effect, people of color experience processes around gender and sexuality differently than white people. These processes largely work to subordinate people of color and privilege white people. Class also shapes these meanings, negotiations, and processes, subordinating working-class and poor people's enactments and embodiments of gender and sexuality to those of middle-class people.

LGBTQ people of color such as Zoe also experience and negotiate their life by virtue of the intersections of gender, sexuality, race, and class. In her work on "sexually nonconforming" Latinas, sociologist Katie Acosta documents how mothers could accept the non-heterosexuality of their Latina daughters yet the mothers wanted their daughters to embody and enact dominant expressions of femininity. The mothers feared that expansive expressions of gender or expressions of masculinity would mark their daughters as visibly non-heterosexual, and hence, make their daughters' lives more difficult—lives already difficult as marginalized women of color.[36]

Along with gender, race and class also shape experiences of homophobia. Poverty makes it harder for poor LGBTQ people of color to avoid violent contexts, whereas middle-class and/or white LGBTQ people have resources to access safer spaces. LGBTQ people of color also experience violence as an attack on multiple aspects of their identity, not just their sexual and/or gender identity. For example, LGBTQ people of color often perceive homophobic violence from other people of color, as punishment for "betraying" their racial group.[37] Race and class always constitute gender and sexuality, and the intertwining of these categories and their social processes have material effects on everyone's lives, with detrimental effects shaping the lives of LGBTQ youth experiencing homelessness.[38]

Coming Out to the Streets depicts how LGBTQ youth homelessness often involves the policing and punishing of young people who embody intersecting abject positions—namely, the poor, Black and Brown, gender-expansive, and non-heterosexual (or presumably non-heterosexual) positions. Many issues facing LGBTQ people, especially LGBTQ people of color who are poor, are not directly or solely about sexuality or sexual identity. LGBTQ people often do not disclose their identities. Embodiments, then, centrally shape—more so than identities—many LGBTQ people's lives.

In a simple sense, this book continues the legacy of queer theory and queer of color critique to call into question categories and identities and to map the complexities and messiness of gender, sexuality, race, class, power, oppression, and resistance. In doing so, this book documents how when a youth is "down and out"—to use language from studies of homelessness—gender expression and its embodied intersections with other social categories often affect people more profoundly than their identities. This examination of LGBTQ youth experiencing homelessness will also show how these categories always work together and that many people cannot or do not separate these social categories, including gender from sexuality (or race and class from sexuality and gender), in their everyday lives. Often they also do not have the resources to control how others see and treat them because they are unable to access contexts and spaces that accept their embodiments. In the end, trying to contain categories as having separate meanings analytically produces dull understandings of people's lives and the issues that affect them, and this is especially true for LGBTQ youth.

THE LIVES OF LGBTQ YOUTH

"Pigs!" The flaming queens shouted, as they flung beer cans at police. Bricks, rocks, and garbage cans flew overhead, as shattered glass rained down with the smashing of the bar's windows. Many stories exist about that night. Perhaps, some exaggerated. But what is certain is that on June 28, 1969, poor, marginalized, non-heterosexual, and gender-expansive people had had enough, and they fought back against a police raid of the Stonewall Inn. Tired of police harassment and angry about gay bar raids, they resisted. And along with the Cooper Do-nuts and Compton Cafeteria riots a few years earlier, the Stonewall riots would launch a national LGBTQ movement. Nothing would be the same again.

A year later, Marsha "Pay It No Mind" Johnson and Sylvia Rivera founded the Street Transvestite Action Revolutionaries (STAR). As women-of-color activists—whom many might today also consider transgender (though the word *transgender* did not exist as part of the lexicon in 1970)—Johnson and Rivera started STAR to foreground and advocate for issues that concerned gender-expansive people of color within the gay liberation movement. As part of their advocacy, they opened the first known youth shelter for people we now call LGBTQ. This shelter started as a trailer truck in Greenwich Village. After someone towed the trailer truck, Johnson and Rivera got a house in the East Village.[39] The stories go that Johnson and Rivera hustled at night to support the shelter, and during the day they worked with street youth on their reading and writing. Although STAR only lasted for a few years in the early 1970s, Marsha P. Johnson and Sylvia Rivera left a legacy of advocating and providing for non-heterosexual and gender-expansive street youth of color.

The history of LGBTQ people in the United States is a story about LGBTQ youth homelessness. Street kids comprised an essential part of the Stonewall riots. They were a central part of starting the LGBTQ movement. LGBTQ youth homelessness, then, is not a new phenomenon.

But the political rights gained over the last few decades, along with media visibility of more LGBTQ people, has reshaped the landscape of LGBTQ youth homelessness. Today, approximately eleven million people in the United States—more than the population of Georgia, the eighth-largest state—openly identify as LGBTQ.[40] The average age of coming out as lesbian, gay, or bisexual has dropped significantly to around thirteen years of age. A quarter of transgender people also come out as transgender before the age of eighteen (though they often come out earlier as gay, bisexual, or another marginalized gender and/or sexual identity before coming out as transgender).[41]

Despite LGBTQ youth coming out earlier into an environment that they might perceive as more accepting, a great deal of inequality endures. Policies often do not protect LGBTQ youth from bullying in schools. Discrimination in employment, housing, and public accommodations continues. And as young people come out earlier, they confront adults' and peers' attitudes and reactions for longer periods of time. If a parent or guardian does not approve of their child identifying as LGBTQ, conflict often occurs.[42] The home, schools, neighborhoods, religious communities, and child custody systems remain sites of prejudice and discrimination for many LGBTQ youth. In turn, some youth flee these spaces or are pushed out of them.[43] A paradox occurs. Within this historical moment of visibility and advancements of rights, youth come out earlier, but they still come out into an unwelcoming climate and an unequal society for LGBTQ people.

Consequently, this narrative surrounding LGBTQ youth homelessness circulates: LGBTQ youth come out younger and younger; some parents reject their LGBTQ child; so the youth has nowhere to go but to the streets. Within this framing, discrimination and prejudice against a youth who *identifies* as LGBTQ are the predominant reasons why LGBTQ young people experience homelessness. But negative reactions toward youth with expansive expressions of gender often get eclipsed from this discussion about identity, along with the complexities of race and class and how the intersections of social categories influence the policing of gender, sexuality, and embodiment. People who embody gender expansiveness might face discrimination their whole life, whether or not they come out or identify as LGBTQ. Moreover, little to nothing is known as yet about poverty and its relation to LGBTQ young people, especially LGBTQ youth of color.

By foregrounding how gender expression and its intersections with other social categories shape experiences of LGBTQ youth homelessness, I provide a better understanding of how certain LGBTQ youth—mainly poor Black and Brown gender-expansive LGBTQ youth—experience and negotiate gender and sexuality today. I offer up new ways of understanding gender and sexuality in these times, as well as a new understanding of urban poverty and homelessness. These new ways of seeing gender, sexuality, poverty, and homelessness help us address the complexities of social inequalities and how these inequalities interconnect to devastate certain lives.

THE NEW HOMELESSNESS

At the LGBTQ shelter in San Antonio, I met Emmanuel, a twenty-one-year-old gay Latino, who liked to say that he looked like the Disney character Aladdin. Emmanuel's wage labor experiences partially illuminate the structural underpinnings of homelessness today. A few months after moving to the shelter, Emmanuel, who had been diagnosed with schizophrenia, got a job at a McDonald's. This job paid $7.50 an hour on weekdays and

$8.50 an hour on weekends. Emmanuel exhibited a great deal of excitement to have this job. When he got his first paycheck, he proudly showed the check to everyone at the shelter, but he had no idea what to do with the check, as he had never seen a paycheck before. The director of the shelter worked with Emmanuel on how to open a bank account and accumulate savings. Eventually, Emmanuel moved out of the shelter and into an apartment. A month later, he was back at the shelter. He had missed some days at work, and a supervisor had suspended him. Without the income, he could not afford his rent. A few months later, the cycle repeated itself: Emmanuel got another job, moved out of the shelter, and then a landlord evicted him. The last time I saw Emmanuel, he was living on the streets, hoping to get back into the LGBTQ shelter.

Cycling between the streets, shelters, housing, and jails was common for the youth in this study. Although many people hold stereotypes about a person experiencing homelessness—drunk, mentally ill, unclean, lazy— it is the political economy that produces most homelessness. In 2015, when this study began, the fair market rent for an efficiency apartment in the San Antonio metro area was $551, and for an efficiency apartment in the Austin metro area it was $681.[44] Assuming Emmanuel worked forty hours a week, he would maybe gross $1,200 a month. McDonald's, however, never gave him forty hours, so he had a lower income. As Emmanuel's hours changed every week—often the case in the service industry—he could not really secure a second job to fit into this changing work schedule and make up the difference in his salary. In effect, around half (if not more) of Emmanuel's income might go to rent, which set him up to experience housing instability or homelessness.[45]

This scenario of low income, high rent prices, and housing instability creates economic insecurity for many and homelessness for some. Increased poverty due to the expanding role of the private sector in economic affairs and the shift to a service economy shapes homelessness today. These changes were concurrent with the retrenchment of social welfare policies and diminished affordable housing.[46] Over one million single-room occupancies (SROs)—one of the biggest forms of low-income housing—went away from the 1970s into the early 1980s, often because of gentrification.[47] Gentrification occurs when developers and city officials redevelop urban neighborhoods for affluent people moving back to urban centers. This redevelopment raises property values and displaces low-income people. Along with gentrification and the decrease in affordable housing, the decline in manufacturing jobs that resulted from globalization and the deindustrialization of US society moved the economy into a service industry, whereby wages became low and stagnant as inflation continued to grow.[48] At the same time, welfare reform slashed poverty assistance, and lawmakers dramatically reduced the federal budget for subsidized housing.[49] The amount of people experiencing homelessness grew because of these larger economic shifts in US society, *not* because more people have become alcoholics or have mental health challenges than in the past—which many people assume causes homelessness.[50]

Furthermore, race, gender, and age influence how these economic changes stratify certain groups of people as more vulnerable to experiencing homelessness. Black and Brown people experience employment discrimination, face police and other agents of the state targeting them, confront racist practices that prevent them from accumulating wealth, and have their housing options severely limited through practices such as redlining.[51] Denying people of color jobs, locking them up, and restricting their wealth and housing accumulation disproportionately pushes them into poverty and to experiencing housing instability.[52]

Likewise, single mothers of color disproportionately experience poverty. Through welfare reform, poor women have lost benefits and have had to accept low wages and menial work.[53] Black women also disproportionately experience eviction, which makes finding another place to live difficult, exacerbating the problems of poverty.[54] In effect, single mothers of color disproportionately live in poverty and experience housing instability.

Youth, as well, often have low-paying jobs that many people see as only for youth to do while they attend college, even though many who work these jobs are not in college. Racial profiling has also funneled Black and Brown youth into carceral systems.[55] The marginalization and subjugation of youth of color from impoverished backgrounds positions them to experience high rates of poverty and housing instability. These factors, combined with the shifts in the US economy, showcase how and why people of color, women and their children, and unaccompanied youth now comprise substantial portions of people experiencing homelessness in the United States.[56]

This rich structural conceptualization of the causes of poverty and housing instability, and in some cases homelessness, shifts the burden of responsibility away from individuals to the larger political economy and its intersections with other forms of social inequality. This work, however, has not
fully captured how heteronormativity and the gender binary shape pathways into and experiences of homelessness. For instance, Black single
mothers who are heterosexual also experience marginalization through heteronormativity for failing to or refusing to live up to the white, middle-class
nuclear family ideal.[57] Black single mothers also disproportionately experience poverty, housing instability, and homelessness. Because racial inequality and its link to economic inequality has locked Black men out of fulfilling
socially expected gender relations of hegemonic masculinity, such as being
the breadwinner, some Black men experience homelessness as an extreme
result. Moreover, women experiencing homelessness may try to embody
and enact dominant notions of femininity by having a child and/or appear-
ing dependent and vulnerable so that they might access certain services and
shelters such as family shelters. Thus, heteronormativity and dominant
gender ideologies, including ideologies about the white, middle-class
nuclear family, shape pathways into and experiences of homelessness.[58]

This study documents how these processes unfold for LGBTQ youth
experiencing homelessness. Heteronormativity and the gender binary, as
intersecting with other forms of social inequality, push certain LGBTQ youth
to experience homelessness and shape their experience of homelessness—
through practices such as gender-segregated shelters, "family" shelters, and
the policing of non-heterosexuality and expansive expressions of gender.
These processes and experiences further contribute to the cycle of homelessness for certain youth. In this book, then, I show how gender, sexuality, and
their intersections with other social categories shape processes of homelessness. At the risk of sounding cliché, I will queer how we think about urban
poverty and homelessness today.

STUDYING LGBTQ YOUTH HOMELESSNESS

I framed this study around three objectives: (1) to document what the
LGBTQ youth perceived to be the pathways that led to homelessness;

(2) to show how the LGBTQ youth's lived experiences illuminate the needs and challenges of experiencing homelessness and being LGBTQ; and (3) to examine how the youth regard the ways in which services providers, peers, police, and other people treat them for experiencing homelessness and being LGBTQ.

To carry out these objectives, I immersed myself into ethnographic fieldwork from January 2015 to June 2016. I conducted fieldwork primarily at two sites. In Austin, Texas, I volunteered at a drop-in center for youth experiencing homelessness. In San Antonio, Texas, I volunteered at a shelter specifically for LGBTQ youth experiencing homelessness. In addition to fieldwork, I interviewed forty LGBTQ youth experiencing homelessness and ten service providers who worked with the youth. As I address in the methodological appendix, I also conducted other field work that informs this study, such as going to a transitional living program associated with the Austin field site, interviewing youth at a Child Protective Services shelter, participating in Point-in-Time Counts, and attending national conferences. I also discuss in the appendix the methodological quandaries of being a volunteer researcher.

Why Texas?

Before I outline the details of my field sites, I must address one question: Why Texas? During this study, San Antonio was the seventh-largest city and Austin was the eleventh-largest city in the United States.[59] San Antonio was the fastest-growing city among the top ten largest cities in the United States from 2000 to 2010.[60] And Austin was the fastest-growing city in the country from 2011 to 2014.[61] As San Antonio expanded, most people moved outward from the downtown area, leaving downtown San Antonio underutilized and underdeveloped.[62] Not far from downtown, San Antonio opened a twenty-three-acre campus for people experiencing homelessness. The campus centralized services for people experiencing homelessness to one site, a novel approach that created a social service "ghetto."[63] The idea seemed to try to keep people experiencing homelessness confined to one part of town—where they could get services. People not in that part of town had a hard time accessing services.

Austin addresses homelessness differently. It has gentrified its downtown area, and during this study, gentrification took place on the "East Side," an area historically occupied by low-income and Black and Brown residents.[64] Affordable housing shrank in Austin, and this lack of affordable housing made life increasingly difficult for working-class and poor people who live there. During my fieldwork, Austin was the most economically segregated major metro area in the United States.[65] Segregation reflects the effects of high unemployment and economic insecurity, which manifest in a growth in homelessness.[66] Likewise, services for people experiencing homelessness in Austin did not centralize in one place as in the campus in San Antonio. In Austin, people often had to walk (in the Texas heat) and/or pay for public transportation to get to various service providers in the city.

Moreover, one in three LGBTQ adults lives in the South. In fact, more LGBTQ people live in the South than in any other region of the United States, yet no southern state has statewide non-discrimination protections for them. Lawmakers in the South have also introduced more anti-LGBTQ legislation than any other region. LGBTQ southerners also disproportionately experience poverty.[67] Fascinated by the cultural and economic landscape of the urban South and how these landscapes shaped the lives of LGBTQ youth experiencing homelessness, I focus on the particularities of LGBTQ life in Texas—a state with an intriguing religious, social, and political setting that research on LGBTQ people often overlooks.

The Field Sites

To design this project, I decided to access LGBTQ youth experiencing homelessness through organizations. "Hanging out" at organizations that serve hard-to-reach populations is a good approach in making initial contacts with marginalized people.[68] Most youth in this study lived fairly solitary lives on the streets. Hence, locating LGBTQ youth experiencing homelessness out on the streets—instead of through organizations—presented difficulties. But by accessing people through organizations, I would miss youth who did not access services. Research has shown, however, that non-heterosexual youth experiencing homelessness access street outreach services more than their heterosexual counterparts.[69] Accessing LGBTQ youth experiencing homelessness through organizations can be fruitful in recruiting a main part of this population.

In Austin, Texas, I volunteered at a street outreach drop-in center for youth experiencing homelessness. This center opened three days a week from 12:00 p.m. to 3:45 p.m. The center located itself in the basement of a church on "The Drag"—a nickname for a street that runs along the western side of the University of Texas at Austin campus. The center served as one program within a larger organization in Austin that advocates for youth and families who seek a path to "self-sufficiency." The organization's website stated that the drop-in center provided a "safe space" for LGBTQ youth and had a "zero tolerance" policy for bullying.

At the drop-in, the organization and staff provided a clothing closet, food, case management, laundry services, medical services, transportation services, access to educational services, hygiene supplies, computer access, on-site counseling, and a place to socialize and get off the streets for a few hours. Staff at the drop-in center served people who gave ages anywhere between ten and twenty-three years, though most people accessing the center said they were eighteen to twenty-three years old.[70] Staff at the drop-in center served about twenty to thirty people each day the center opened, and over two hundred different youth each year. I mainly volunteered in the clothing closet, where I would help youth find clothes for everyday wear, work, job interviews, or court.

Notably, no emergency shelter in Austin existed specifically for youth experiencing homelessness within the age range of eighteen to twenty-five—often the upper-range of youth homelessness. If the temperature in Austin dropped below 32 degrees (a rarity), then the drop-in center would convert into an emergency shelter. Although some youth transitional living programs throughout Austin existed, the youth in this study who lived in Austin mainly used the drop-in center as their resource for services. Many youth did not feel comfortable at the shelters for adults experiencing homelessness, so they lived and slept on the streets.

At the LGBTQ shelter in San Antonio, fieldwork proceeded differently, as my volunteer role and shifts functioned differently there. The shelter opened in February 2015 and billed itself as the first LGBTQ shelter to open in the South. The shelter was part of San Antonio's homelessness campus, which served over fifteen hundred people experiencing homelessness. The homelessness campus was located on the Inner West Side of San Antonio—a predominantly Hispanic neighborhood. The LGBTQ shelter provided case management, emergency shelter, education services, employment resources, transportation, life skills, hormone replacement therapy, legal services, medical care, and mental health services. Although the shelter ran as its own organization, the young people staying there had access to the larger array of services that the homelessness campus provided, including the cafeteria, ID recovery, clothing, and a host of other resources.

Eight young people could stay at the LGBTQ youth shelter at a time, and they had to be within the age range of eighteen to twenty-five, or seventeen if emancipated. The youth at the shelter all shared one large room (called "the pod") that had four bunk beds and a locker for each person. Ten LGBTQ adults experiencing homelessness (above the age of twenty-five) lived across the hall. All eighteen people shared the "all gender" restroom that had three stalls, three showers, and two sinks. Many of the youth did not feel safe staying in the outdoor courtyard on the larger homelessness campus, where many adults experiencing homelessness in San Antonio go to sleep and to access services. The young people in this study mostly lived on the streets until the LGBTQ shelter opened. I mainly did weekly overnight shifts at the shelter from 10:00 p.m. to 7:00 a.m., and I often worked alone as the only person there with the youth during these shifts.

I recruited the majority of the forty youth I interviewed through the two field sites: nineteen came from the San Antonio field site and fifteen came from the Austin drop-in center. Four came from a transitional living program associated with the Austin field site, and two came from a children's shelter in Austin licensed by Child Protective Services. Thirty of the forty youth identified as youth of color. Of my ten interviews with service providers, five came from the Austin field site and five from the San Antonio field site.

Throughout this book, I describe the youth's gender, sexual, racial/ethnic, and other identities using the language they used to identify themselves. For example, if I describe someone as a heterosexual Hispanic transgender woman, then these were the terms they used to describe their sexual, racial/ethnic, and gender identities. Some youth did identify as Latino/a instead of Hispanic, but none identified as Chicano/a, Latinx, or other terms that capture this heterogeneous population. To try to keep the identities of the youth confidential, I have changed all names to pseudonyms.

Everything in quotes in this book comes from the taped and transcribed interviews. To make the narratives flow more smoothly, I do not always add "they said" or "they claimed" to the quotes. Quotes and descriptions of the past come from the accounts that the youth told me. I could not verify most of these experiences, but at times, I found news reports and arrest records to verify some events. This book, then, comes mainly from the youth's perspectives, although I do use the service providers' voices to add validity to the youth's stories. The views of other social actors, such as parents, teachers, and police do not appear in this book. The youth's perceptions of their past and of their current lives shape how they view themselves in relation to others and the social world. As adults often erase youth's voices—even when trying to understand and address young people's social problems—foregrounding how young people understand their social world and what they see as solutions to the problems they face corrects these past mistakes.[71]

ON WRITING AND LANGUAGE

One evening in San Antonio, Lucas, a twenty-year-old white heterosexual transgender man, seemed exceptionally quiet for someone who often caffeinated by putting five packs of Sweet 'N Low in his coffee. Later that night, Lucas asked me what happens to people who die and have no one to bury them. He then proceeded to pull up his left arm sleeve and show me over forty fresh cut marks on his arm. I used the first-aid kit to apply antiseptic and antibiotics to the wounds, and I wrapped the cuts with gauze. I had to decide whether to call someone in case he harmed himself again. I decided not to call anyone but to stay up all night and keep an eye on him. When the assistant director arrived the following morning, I told her about the incident. But do I write about this moment in my field notes and in this book?

"Can the subaltern speak?" feminist scholar Gayatri Spivak asked in a piece titled the same. This question haunts my ethical approach to studying LGBTQ youth homelessness and writing about their lives. Spivak raised a concern about the representation of oppressed people and how Western intellectuals use images that they already have constructed of the oppressed in representing and speaking for them.[72] How do writers, researchers, and intellectuals represent marginalized populations without doing further harm? Do I write about incidents such as Lucas's mental health moment? In doing so, am I furthering stereotypes that people use to pathologize LGBTQ youth and people experiencing homelessness?

I do not wish to further stereotype and marginalize the young people in this study. I do not want to romanticize them either. I also want to avoid depicting them as "victims" whom we need to rescue or save. I sought, as well, to avoid the "jungle-book trope" of going to study a marginalized population as if marginalized people comprise some wild, unknown group who are dangerous to study.[73] Attempting to document the complexities of the youth's lives—without trying to pathologize them—I constantly reflected on my research.

Dilemmas arise, though. For example, drug use, sex work, mental health challenges, and violence arose as prevalent themes throughout my field notes and interviews. But did I write these behaviors in my notes because my preconceived notions about youth experiencing homelessness conditioned me to be on the lookout for these behaviors? Did the young people discuss drugs, violence, mental health, and sex work because the services they access often highlight those behaviors in their lives? I never asked a question about those behaviors, but they seemed to shape the young people's lives. I still struggle to know if they shape their lives because social services emphasize "rehabilitating" those behaviors, often already assigning a negative connotation to doing drugs, engaging in sex work, having mental health challenges, and engaging in violence. Those behaviors, among others, do appear in this writing. I caution the reader not to see these behaviors as inherently bad or negative. Rather, society constructs certain behaviors as bad or deviant and makes certain behaviors salient modes of how the young people in this study, and perhaps I, as the researcher, have come to see and understand their lives. In the end, I do have the representational authority. I decide how to frame and depict their lives in this book.[74]

I try to reflexively think about the language I use to describe the youth and their lives. I refer to them as LGBTQ youth *experiencing homelessness*, instead of as LGBTQ homeless youth. Some youth did refer to themselves as homeless. But homelessness often entails experiencing a particular situation—such as episodic or transitional homelessness—and is not necessarily who someone is. This people-first language emphasizes the youth as humans as well.

I use the term *gender-expansive* to describe embodiments and enactments of gender that go against the dominant relations of gender in US society. Of course, language always changes. I fear that maybe five years, a decade, or more after I finish writing this book that terms such as *transgender, gender-expansive, queer*, or other terms will be outdated. I tried to attend to the best practices at the time of this writing.

I do *not* use the word *cisgender* to describe the youth who did not identify as transgender. While the concept of cisgenderism gives us an important way to capture how structures privilege people's embodiments and enactments that align with their assigned gender at birth, most youth in this study had expansive expressions of gender. Yes, some of the youth benefitted from cisgenderism. However, their lives and experiences with gender entailed more complicated processes that labeling them as cisgender might eclipse, as many youth also experienced discrimination, at times, because of cisgenderism. I also am hesitant of a cis/trans binary that erases the more complicated processes of gender and sexuality that I found in this study. I know that identifying the transgender youth as transgender and not labeling other youth as cisgender potentially reifies people who are not transgender as the unmarked privileged category. Ultimately, I identify the youth using the words they used to describe themselves. If they described themselves as transgender, I do as well. If they didn't, then I don't. I do show, though, how complicated gender and sexuality were in all the youth's lives, while paying attention to how transgender youth experienced life differently than the youth who did not identify as transgender.

Lastly, I use the term *carceral systems* instead of criminal justice systems. This usage draws attention to the fact that carceral systems further injustice and inequality, and hence, are hardly just.[75] Building on this reasoning, I use the term *state child custody systems* to refer to child welfare systems. As I will show, state child custody systems do not protect the welfare of LGBTQ youth.

THE JOURNEY AHEAD

In the coming chapters, I will take us through narratives of the youth's lives before experiencing homelessness and then to the streets and shelters. In chapter 1, I focus on the youth's families of origin—the people often blamed for LGBTQ youth homelessness. I caution that this family rejection narrative could cast people of color and/or poor people as more prejudiced than middle-class, white people. In doing so, I complicate the family rejection narrative by showing how poverty and instability shaped the youth's lives and their strained familial ties. Specifically, I illustrate how families' negative reactions, including abusive behaviors, toward the youth's expansive expressions of gender and its assumed association with non-heterosexuality contributed to further strain and instability within marginalized families, wherein the ties were already fragile. In chapter 2, I continue to complicate the family rejection narrative by showing how other institutions—schools, state child custody systems, religion, and the workplace—discipline and punish expansive expressions of gender and sexuality. The youth in this study found that these practices pushed them to the streets and generated more barriers and instabilities once they were experiencing homelessness.

Once on the streets, the youth faced more difficulties. In chapter 3, I detail how the criminalization of homelessness and the youth's interactions with police intertwine with policing and criminalizing the youth's gender and sexuality. These processes also intersect with racial profiling and the policing of poor Black and Brown people. From these policing practices, the Black and Brown transgender and gender-expansive youth kept going in and out of jails, which furthered the youth's experiences of instability and homelessness. However, the youth developed queer street smarts. In chapter 4, I show how the youth learned to navigate the ways in which gender and sexuality shape the streets and services for people experiencing homelessness. The youth found ways to avoid gender-segregated and other violent spaces. They also learned to navigate the gender-based and sexual-based violence of the streets. Sometimes, the youth used sexuality and their gender embodiment and expression to obtain resources while living on the streets. For the youth in San Antonio, the LGBTQ shelter was also a respite from the streets. But as I show in chapter 5, life in the LGBTQ shelter came with rules and regulations, including regulating the youth's sexual behaviors and gender expression. Staff often suspended youth for violating these rules, which kept youth cycling back to the streets and jails. The cycle of homelessness continued.

In the conclusion, I present the youth's solutions to addressing LGBTQ youth homelessness and put the youth's solutions in conversation with the findings from this study and with other work on addressing homelessness. I discuss how policy needs to be more complex and holistic than just a focus on identity, rights, sexuality, and homophobia. Policy needs to also move away from putting the burden of solving homelessness on the backs of people experiencing homelessness.

In rooting this study with LGBTQ young people's voices and lives, I hope to spark an overdue conversation across disciplines and outside of the ivory tower. I wish for this conversation to lead to progressive social justice and social change in valuing and helping LGBTQ youth, including LGBTQ youth experiencing homelessness.

1 Reframing Family Rejection

GROWING UP POOR AND LGBTQ

"My dad was getting his suspicions about me being gay. And he did threaten to kill me. He said, 'I'm going to kill you, then I'm going to kill myself. Because I'd rather die, than people know that I have a faggot for a son.' So, I took the initiative. I ran away at seventeen." Prada, a twenty-three-year-old Hispanic heterosexual transgender woman, was discussing with me her life before experiencing homelessness. She said she grew up in Los Angeles, California, with her single father.[1] When she was sixteen years old, Prada—with the help of an aunt—was able to contact her mother, who lived in Laredo, Texas. "And I told [my mother], I really don't want to be here anymore [with my father] because I'm scared for my life because I would have to act straight." Prada used birthday money to travel to Laredo. Unfortunately, this arrangement did not last long, as her mother got into trouble with a drug dealer, who threatened their lives. "So, we just packed up what very little clothes that we had and took off—back to California," Prada told me.

Back on the West Coast, Prada moved around, staying with grandparents and then with her aunt and uncle, who were pastors in Palm Springs. The aunt and uncle read Prada's journal and found out that she had attraction toward men. Since Prada's family perceived her as a boy, they interpreted this attraction toward men as a sign of homosexuality. Prada said her aunt asked her, "'Is this true?' And I'm like, 'Yeah. I'm not going to change who I am for anybody. I'd rather die before I change myself to please anybody.' And then she's like, 'Well if you want to stay here, you can't be doing that.' I'm like, 'Okay. Pay for my bus ticket. . . . Send me back to Laredo.'"

Back in Laredo, Prada could not get a hold of any family members. She began living on the streets and cycling in and out of shelters and transitional living programs before ending up in San Antonio at the shelter for LGBTQ youth experiencing homelessness, where I interviewed her. Wearing punk-rock attire—an off-the-shoulder Hello Kitty shirt, cut-off jean shorts, and Converse shoes—Prada told me about her current relationship with her family. "They said I was a disgrace to the family name, and that I needed to change my name because they wanted nothing to do with me. Because they didn't want a disgrace in their family, or an abomination as they call it now."

THE FAMILY REJECTION PORTRAIT

In 2014, *Rolling Stone* published an article titled "The Forsaken: A Rising Number of Homeless Gay Teens Are Being Cast Out by Religious Families."[2] The article explores the hardships of some LGBTQ youth who are forced to live on the streets and in shelters because their religious parents kicked them out after they came out. The *Seattle Times* ran a 2015 opinion piece with a similar narrative, "Young, Gay and Homeless: Why Some Parents Reject Their Children," and in 2017, *Slate* published "Family Rejection Leaves Too Many Transgender Americans Homeless."[3] This predominant framing depicts family rejection as *the* cause of LGBTQ youth homelessness.

As Prada's story shows, family rejection plays an integral part in the lived experiences of many LGBTQ youth who come to experience homelessness. Prada ran away from her father, and later, from other family members who refused to accept her as she was. According to a 2005 study, 73 percent of gay and lesbian and 26 percent of bisexual youth experiencing homelessness report that parental disapproval of their sexual orientation was what led them to their current situation.[4] A 2012 study found that service providers who worked with LGBTQ youth experiencing homelessness report that 68 percent of the youth—whom the providers worked with—ran away or their families kicked them out because of the young person's sexuality and/or gender identity.[5]

But family rejection represents only a piece of the story. Prada grew up with a single father in an unstable environment in a society that does not provide enough resources for families suffering economic hardship. She also had to contend with a father who was intent on raising his Brown child to "act straight." Because Prada had to navigate the class and racial inequalities of US society, her father's gender-policing strategies may have been rooted in trying to protect her from further discrimination. But these gendered child-rearing strategies only served as points of conflict within the home, as Prada resisted them.

In effect, the portrait of family rejection obscures how poverty and economic instability shape the ways marginalized families—often families of color—negotiate practices around gender and sexuality within their households. This overarching rejection narrative also overshadows how reactions to a child's gender expression and assumed homosexuality (often more so than an LGBTQ identity) shape familial strain and conflict, and it frames youth as passive victims kicked to the curb.

This chapter reframes this rejection portrait and demonstrates how the oversimplified rejection paradigm erases the complexities of the youth's lives. This reframing also challenges the narrative that puts too much blame and burden on the families of the youth and highlights how society and other institutions also maintain and enforce heteronormativity and the gender binary. Family rejection is a factor, but it exists in the intersections of systems of oppression in relation to poverty and racial inequality.

Furthermore, because poor Black and Brown youth disproportionately make up LGBTQ youth homelessness populations, this family rejection paradigm greases the slippery slope of depicting poor families and/or families of color as more prejudiced than middle-class, white families.[6] The rejection paradigm does not allow us to see how class and racial inequalities shape how poor LGBTQ youth—mainly poor Black and Brown LGBTQ youth—say they negotiate and navigate gender and sexuality within their familial contexts. The rejection narrative also simplifies how experiencing homelessness often entails a long process, born out of inter-generational poverty, and how the marginalization associated with poverty reproduces social inequalities across generations. Instead, the family rejection narrative paints a picture that says homelessness and going to the streets happen overnight. Many structural inequalities, however, come into play, and these inequalities unfold over time, generating familial strain and loosening the ties that bind youth to their families.[7]

In reframing this rejection portrait, I document the meanings and contexts underlying the familial rejection of the LGBTQ youth in this study. I outline how processes around poverty, gender, sexuality, and race shaped the youth's experiences of family rejection. I also foreground how the policing of the youth's expansive expressions of gender constituted a salient part of the tension and conflict within the family. I show how families often rejected the youth because of their expansive expressions of gender and its association with homosexuality and how poverty and racial inequality exacerbated this rejection. In chronicling the youth's complex familial stories, this chapter serves as a class-based analysis to examine how poor LGBTQ youth—mainly poor Black and Brown LGBTQ youth—said they negotiated and navigated gender and sexuality within their families. The chapter also shows how policing gender and sexuality, along with racial and class inequalities, formed the youth's pathways into homelessness, particularly in relation to how policing the child's gender and sexuality related to experiences of familial abuse and strain.

POVERTY, INSTABILITY, AND INTERSECTIONALITY

Obadiah, a twenty-year-old white man who dates transgender women, often wore ball caps and cowboy boots whenever I would see him at the LGBTQ shelter. "I used to go to school with bruises all over me when I was little," he stated. "And my mom was a drug addict." Obadiah continued to tell me about his childhood experiences as we sat together on his bottom bunk at the shelter. "And I remember when I was little, me and my brothers had to literally frickin' take off the door knobs to the restroom—took it apart—and we found her in there shooting up with this guy, when my dad was in jail." He went on, "[My father] was always an alcoholic. He spent more times at bars than anything." At eight years old, Obadiah went into Child Protective Services (CPS) custody. He spent the next ten years bouncing around CPS placements, until he "aged out."[8] He then lived in his grandfather's shed for a year, before moving to the shelter in San Antonio for LGBTQ youth experiencing homelessness.

In this section, I show how poverty and instability upset the lives of the youth in this study and underlie the processes of experiencing homelessness. Obadiah's story offers a glimpse into the instabilities that *all* youth described in talking about their childhoods. Not a single youth in this study reported living in a stable environment. Most youth detailed growing up in poverty, and how poverty goes hand in hand with instability. For many youth, this instability includes parental romantic transitions, residential movement, changing schools, the incarceration of a parent, the fracturing of social ties, and other major stressors that accumulate across a child's life.[9] Poverty and instability—two sides of the same coin—have devastating consequences for families, generating stress, depression, and other mental health challenges, as well as drug and alcohol use, familial conflict and abuse, strained familial ties, and other disrupting family dynamics.[10]

Rather than providing enough support services, the state often punishes poor families. One punishment involves taking their children away. In a study of court cases, researchers found that state child custody agencies remove children from their families for "reasons of poverty." As the researchers documented, economic hardship resulted in state child custody agencies removing children from the home.[11] This removal from the home exacerbates strained familial ties. Obadiah said state child custody workers did not place him with his siblings; consequently, he did not see his siblings for years. As youth move through various foster homes and other CPS placements, they struggle to maintain contact with family members. In the next chapter, I also show how state child custody systems further the processes of rejection and instability for LGBTQ youth.

Some youth in this study also grew up experiencing familial homelessness. Jenna, an eighteen-year-old white bisexual youth, talked to me about her experiences of homelessness as a child. She told me that her dad "was always kind of abusive toward my mom," and over time, "the fights got worse and worse and worse." Her dad eventually left the family, Jenna

explained, "and [my mom, my siblings, and I] were left with no money—
nothing like that. And my mom needed support for being a victim of this
violence for nineteen years. So, we found a domestic violence shelter. And
we went there." Jenna said her family then moved around a lot. "[My
mom] would honestly get churches to pay for like hotel rooms and stuff
like that—when we were in between houses. She would try to find jobs.
But it's hard with little experience," she stated. "[My mom] gets food
stamps, though, so that's pretty much how we got food. And the hotel, the
electricity and water never get cut off, so that's fine. But it's hard because I
have four younger siblings, and we were staying in one hotel room."

Poverty and homelessness often afflict people across generations. Several
youth in this study, like Jenna, discussed experiencing homelessness with
their families before experiencing it on their own. In an Australian study,
almost half of the people who received homelessness assistance reported
having parents who also experienced homelessness.[12] In the United States,
poverty and instability also pass down through generations. Childhood
adversity, often also associated with poverty and instability, links to homelessness as well.[13] Like many women experiencing homelessness, Jenna's
mom had fled a domestic violence situation and, without safety nets, had to
rely on shelters and churches to help support her family. Jenna eventually
moved on her own to a transitional living program in Austin.

For most youth in this study, these experiences of poverty and instability
also intersected with their experiences as youth of color, as well as explicitly
with people rejecting them because of their sexuality, gender identity, and
gender expression. Justice was an eighteen-year-old Black "glamazon,"
"diva," heterosexual transgender woman whom I met at the same shelter as
Prada and Obadiah.[14] Sitting outside on a curb with me, Justice said her
grandparents raised her "because they didn't think my mom was suitable
for the job." She said she "felt safe and secure [with my grandparents],
where I didn't have to move around or anything." After her grandparents'
deaths, Justice—at age eleven—went to live with her mother. Justice told
me, "I don't really have any family now. My relationship with my mom—it
was always kind of rocky—up until I got to be like fourteen, when she got a
new boyfriend. And then, I guess, her boyfriend didn't really like Black
people—me being half Black, half white kind of bothered him, especially
because I was his girlfriend's daughter." The boyfriend's racism intersected

with other forms of prejudice as well. Justice added, "And he didn't like the fact that I was trans. He thought that faggots were going to hell—quote quote. So, he was just a very ignorant, ignorant man. He caused a lot of friction between me and my mom's relationship—a lot of the depression and stuff I was going through." At fifteen years of age, Justice went into CPS custody until she was eighteen, at which point she lived on the streets of San Antonio until the shelter for LGBTQ youth experiencing homelessness opened.

Research shows that youth experiencing homelessness come from backgrounds of poverty and instability.[15] These experiences generate strained family ties between parents and their children, and youth often leave or are pushed out of families that have little to hold them.[16] Curiously, the lives of LGBTQ youth experiencing homelessness do not get situated within this literature. The family rejection paradigm does not talk about poverty and instability as part of the LGBTQ youth's familial lives. At the same time, the work on youth homelessness, poverty, and family instability does not fully account for why poor Black and Brown LGBTQ youth disproportionately experience homelessness. Partly, this gap occurs because the work does not document how race, sexuality, and gender, including gender identity and expression, interconnect with experiences of poverty, instability, and strained familial ties.

Justice, for example, had a secure life until her grandparents died, which she said then pushed her into a situation of instability and hostility in the home. Justice had a strained relationship with her mom even before her mom's boyfriend generated further tension and conflict with his racism and use of homophobic slurs. Unlike white gay and bisexual men, who often experience violence and/or homophobia as an attack on *only* their sexuality, white lesbians and bisexual women often experience violence as an attack on their sexuality *and* gender, and LGBTQ people of color often experience violence directed at multiple aspects of their identity.[17] These compounding discriminatory experiences not only strained Justice's relationship with her mother, but also generated some of her mental health challenges. As the intersections of one's social positions shape experiences of poverty, instability, and familial strain, youth of color, non-heterosexual youth, and/or transgender and gender-expansive youth often have harsher experiences of poverty, instability, and familial strain.

GENDER EXPRESSION AND FAMILIAL CONFLICT

One main source of conflict and strain for the youth in this study was the parents' negative reactions to their child's expansive expressions of gender. These reactions related to policing the youth's assumed non-heterosexuality. "She's racist. She doesn't like Black people. She doesn't like gay people. She definitely doesn't like transgender people," Adelpha empathically stated to me in talking about her mother. "But [me liking boys] started getting more obvious to her when I would like—like the clothes I would wanna wear, and all that kind of stuff." Adelpha, an eighteen-year-old heterosexual transgender woman, described herself as Black, Mexican, and white. With a shaved head and wearing leather pants, red combat boots, and a jean jacket vest, Adelpha looked like the model, actress, and activist Amber Rose when I first met her at the LGBTQ shelter in San Antonio. Adelpha spent most of her childhood and teenage years in state child custody systems. She had intermittent contact with her mother during that time.

As a teenager, Adelpha got a job in fast food, and she gained a sense of independence to dress and present how she wanted. "I finally was, like, you know, fuck it," she explained. "If my family loves me, they'll accept me. And I was working, so I felt like I could support myself." She continued, "I started wearing makeup, getting my nails done, growing out my hair, getting wigs, and shopping girls' clothes and all that." Adelpha said that her mother probably knows that she is transgender because of social media. "I think she knows, 'cause on like Facebook—I transitioned on Facebook—on social media—and everything. I changed my name on Facebook—me in makeup, wigs, all dolled up." She went on, "And [my mother] finally unblocked me from Facebook, and she called me when I was working at Burger King. She was like, 'Hey, what's going on? What the fuck?' And starts cussing me out, talking shit." Adelpha said that her mom "was so pissed off, 'cause she was—she called me an embarrassment—because she grew up in a different lifestyle. She grew up in gangs and hood life in California with the Mexican gangs, so she has a lot of street cred. And my dad does too."

In everyday interactions, we often use gender expression to interpret people's sexuality. If someone has an expansive expression of gender, we often presume that the person is gay. Adelpha's gender presentation—the clothes she wanted to wear—became a noticeable signal of her non-heterosexuality as interpreted by her mother. Adelpha also said that her mother does not like gay or transgender people. With some money and a sense of independence, Adelpha resisted and started presenting how she wanted. On social media, Adelpha said her mother pushed back against her gender transition. Adelpha linked part of this conflict with her mother's past gang and "hood life," inasmuch as Adelpha's gender presentation contradicts Chicano gang masculinity—a marginalized masculinity that asserts itself through aggres-sive behavior and physical force—not through being "dolled up."[18] Adelpha's expansive expressions of gender challenged her mother's "street cred," as Adelpha rejected the masculine ideals that her mother and other people expected her to enact and embody.

Also, at the LGBTQ shelter, I met Jenelle, a twenty-one-year-old Hispanic heterosexual transgender woman, who talked with me as well about familial conflict around her gender expression. A turning point in Jenelle's relationship with her mom occurred when Jenelle came out at age twelve. "And you know how people say a mother's love is uncondi-tional? When I was twelve, I figured out that my mother's love was condi-tional." With bright red hair and piercings on the sides of her lips and on the bridge of her nose, Jenelle also described her father as a "bigot." "[My father] calls me by my birth name and uses 'his' pronouns. And it just—it was heavy on my soul. After a while, you just have to live your true self, and you can't deal with that bullshit anymore." She went on, "My dad is probably going to die a bigot. When I was sixteen, he basically looked me in the eyes, and he said, 'I love you. You're always going to be my son. But you know you are going to die of AIDS, right?' And I—I just—that's a hor-rible thing to say to your kid."

Another source of familial strain occurred when a neighbor raped Jenelle when she was seventeen years old. Jenelle said that her mother blamed her. "She said because you are dressed the way you are dressed, and you look the way you look, you obviously were asking for it," Jenelle explained. "And I was just like—I was wearing shorts, a tight shirt, and I had my hair red. Really?" Jenelle said her mom told her to cut her hair and quit "cross-dressing" or leave. Jenelle went into a deep depression. Her grades slipped at school. She eventually ran away.

Gay identity has historically had a fraught relationship with families of origin, given the heteronormative ideology that undergirds the myth of the nuclear family. As prominent historians and other scholars have documented, gay identity emerged around World War II, when people (mainly white men) with same-sex attractions and desires severed family ties and moved to urban centers to form gay communities.[19] During this time, many people saw "gay" and "the family" (in the dominant sense of families of origin) as mutually exclusive, even as LGBTQ people forged families of choice, friendships, and communities of their own.[20] Times have changed. Some families of origin accept their LGBTQ child and integrate them into their family. Many do not. The dominant ideologies and practices within society still stigmatize, marginalize, and discriminate against LGBTQ people, especially transgender and gender-expansive people. Coming out or being perceived as LGBTQ—often because of one's expansive expressions of gender—still generates a great deal of familial strain and tension for many people.

In implicitly or explicitly coming out, the youth in this study participated in an act of tremendous power, as this act disrupts the family's heteronormative assumptions. But youth still rely on their family for support and love. Jenelle, however, found this support and love as conditionally related to her not disrupting heteronormativity or challenging the gender binary within the household. Jenelle persevered and still lived her "true self," which generated constant tension with her parents' beliefs about LGBTQ people. Notably, the parents of the youth in this study come from a different generation, in which the HIV/AIDS crisis and many negative stereotypes about LGBTQ people circulated. Jenelle's father's linking of HIV/AIDS with death has been a common homophobic tactic since the rise of the epidemic. Furthermore, many parents of LGBTQ children hold a common fear and misconception of their child contracting HIV. Parents often internalize negative stereotypes about LGBTQ people within the larger society and/or do not have enough education and accurate knowledge about HIV and/or LGBTQ people and communities.[21]

Jenelle's parents' negative reactions to her gender presentation were points of contention within her family. Her father would misgender her through his use of the incorrect gender pronoun and calling Jenelle his "son." Misgendering, as a microaggression against transgender and gender-expansive people, is degrading. Jenelle's mother blamed Jenelle for being raped, specifically her feminine attire. The heart of this conflict consisted of negative parental reactions to Jenelle's gender presentation and behaviors within an already unstable family environment. Jenelle's family fought all the time and struggled to get by in the Rio Grande Valley—a place with the highest rates of poverty in the state of Texas, located by the border with Mexico—so her parents' disapproval of her gender expression only generated further conflict and tension within the household. Shortly after her parent's divorce, Jenelle left—to be herself, to escape the blame, and to separate herself from the conflict at home.

Despite familial conflict and strained ties, many youth in this study maintained contact with their families—another complexity usually erased from the family rejection narrative. These relationships remained tenuous and conflictual, often because of the families' negative reactions to the youth's gender expression. But some family connection still existed. Discussions about seeing family members occurred most prominently during major holidays, such as Thanksgiving and Christmas. The youth knew how they needed to present at holiday gatherings and often monitored their gendered selves during these family events.

For example, the day before Thanksgiving, Julian, a twenty-two-year-old Hispanic gay youth with bright red highlights in his black hair, dug through the clothing closet at the drop-in center in Austin to try to find something to wear. As I helped him look through the clothes, he told me that he would have to not dress too gay for the family dinner and that this would be a challenge, as all his clothes looked pretty gay. Indeed, Julian, who sometimes went by the name Bree, often wore makeup and dressed in rhinestone jeans, tube tops, and jeweled sandals. At Thanksgiving dinner, Julian said he would not dress how he normally did.

Families' negative reactions to youth's gender identity and expression often still generate familial strain, even after youth have left home. Some youth still tried to maintain a relationship with their family. This maintaining of ties, though, involves the youth doing the mental, emotional, and physical labor of monitoring and modifying their gender presentation and behaviors. Another example is Zoe, a nineteen-year-old Hispanic heterosexual transgender woman, who lived at the shelter in San Antonio. With the holiday season approaching, Zoe had saved some money from her job at a call center to help her mom pay for Thanksgiving dinner. Upon getting back to the shelter Thanksgiving night, Zoe said that her family had told her at dinner that they would not accept her as a woman. She now considered going off hormones so her family would accept her.

In contrast, Cookie, a twenty-five-year-old Black heterosexual transgender woman, gives us a "negative case"—that is, a finding that appears to go against the pattern. Cookie was one of the only youth in this study who did not discuss familial strain and did not see her family as a factor leading to homelessness. Her story does illuminate, however, the larger picture about the labor of monitoring one's gender expression and sexuality in relation to one's family in order to maintain certain ties. "I came out—Lord Jesus—after high school," Cookie said to me when we sat in her room at the LGBTQ shelter in San Antonio. "But I was away from home. When I would go home, I would not take my sexual life or my sexual preferences or anything like that back home with me. And I'm still kind of like that until this day." Growing up, Cookie said, "I kept everything undercover. I never came out. I had boyfriends when I was in high school, of course. But they were undercover boyfriends. Because I played all the male sports that any male could play—from football on up."

Cookie's participation in football allowed her to keep her sexuality and gender identity "undercover." Football serves as an exemplar sport for showcasing masculinity and, hence, heterosexuality. Playing football also signals successful Black masculinity. Because racial inequality and its intersection with poverty often locks Black men out of most forms of financial success, for some, sports becomes an avenue—albeit a limited one—to success. Notably, this engagement in masculinized sports and keeping one's sexuality undisclosed can entail forms of physical and emotional labor.

This labor takes on a different meaning for many LGBTQ people of color, whose ideas about coming out often differ from those of white people. Cookie, like many LGBTQ people of color, challenged the idea of "compulsory disclosure"—that one must come out to be LGBTQ.[22] As queer of color theorist Marlon Ross argues, the construction of the closet often remains most relevant for middle-class, white gay men. This construct does not work as well for poor people and/or people of color, who have different kinds of ties and relations to their families and communities. They may also lack the economic means to afford severing ties and moving to a large city, as many middle-class, white LGBTQ people do. Some also see their families as a refuge from racism in society. Hence, poor LGBTQ people and/or LGBTQ people of color negotiate their gender and sexuality within their families differently than the dominant mode of coming out of the closet.[23] Many youth in this study face two opposing paradigms: either come out publicly—the dominant way in the United States—or negotiate gender and sexuality differently within one's family. Class, race, culture, region, and other factors all influence how LGBTQ youth experience and navigate these decisions. Cookie saw no point in disclosing her gender and sexuality.

Many youth in this study who could not or did not choose to negotiate their gender and sexuality with their family in the same way as Cookie detailed more experiences of familial strain and conflict—both while growing up and currently if they still had contact with family members. One such experience of strain and conflict involved abuse.

ABUSE AND HETERONORMATIVE COMPLIANCE

Xander, a nineteen-year-old Black gay youth, whom I met at a CPS-licensed shelter in Austin, wore black plastic-framed glasses and sported an Afro, as he told me about his childhood. "[My] dad accused me of being a pansy. . . . My nickname was twinkle toes." Self-aware of his own femininity, Xander said he sometimes gets mistaken for a woman. He went on to describe growing up in a single-parent household and how his father's reactions to his effeminacy affected him. "I was in the fourth grade [when my dad started calling me 'twinkle toes']. I dealt with this stuff all my life. He had such a negative connotation for me that I have extremely low self-esteem because of it now." Xander then described how this bullying intensified. "I was picked on by my dad and my little brothers. They helped [him], 'cause they didn't want to be the ones in the fire. When I came out, things got even worse. That's when he started kicking me out."

Scholars have documented abuse as a common experience among youth experiencing homelessness and as one of the main pathways into youth homelessness.[24] For LGBTQ youth experiencing homelessness, previous research has documented that around 50 percent have experienced physical, emotional, and/or sexual abuse as a child.[25] In this section, I demonstrate how the policing of a child's gender and sexuality relates to these experiences of abuse and how the youth in this study perceived this abuse as leading them into homelessness.

I conceptualize this abuse as a form of "heteronormative compliance." Sociologist Gloria González-López defines heteronormative compliance as "the beliefs and practices of obedience established by parents, siblings, and other relatives with the purpose of policing and reproducing heterosexuality as the norm within families and society at large."[26] Heteronormative compliance rests on strategies of gender policing, as parents often see expansive expressions of gender as a sign of a child being gay.

For instance, some family members see gender-expansive boys as hypersexualized and abuse them as a form of punishment. They may also perceive the child as too vulnerable to disclose the abuse to anyone.[27] In an abusive household, family members may focus the abuse on a gender-expansive child. As a service provider told me, "I think it is understandable that [LGBTQ youth homelessness] would be kind of disproportionate if we're talking about families who are kind of prone to abuse or neglect. They're much more likely, if they have something to kind of focus that on, about the youth, where they are not accepting of the youth." As Xander acknowledged, his brothers joined in bullying him to avoid their father targeting them too. Thus, other family members will also police gender expansive and LGBTQ family members. Xander had no family support.

Moreover, the rejection and verbal abuse directed at Xander amount to a gendered homophobia—the use of homophobic language to police masculinity.[28] Xander's dad insulted Xander with "pansy" and "twinkle toes" to police Xander's gender expression and, in effect, his sexuality. Racialized processes shape experiences of gendered homophobia and heteronormative compliance as well. In her study of "sexually non-conforming" Latinas, sociologist Katie Acosta shows that mothers of Latinas police their daughters' gender behaviors, often because they cannot control their daughters' sexuality. The mothers engage in this gender policing because they believe if their daughters perform dominant ideals of femininity, the daughters might be able to attain some heterosexual privilege in society, despite their sexual nonconformity. As Latinas experience marginalization because of their race and gender positions within society, they have more to lose if they also embody gender expansiveness—that is, if people also see them as non-heterosexual.[29] Being gender expansive and/or non-heterosexual furthers the already marginalized status of a person of color. Therefore, the verbal policing of Xander's expansive expressions of gender and his sexuality works in tandem with policing his race—trying to uphold a certain form of Black masculinity in a racially stratified society that already demeans and subordinates Black boys.

Notably, experiences of abuse through heteronormative compliance and strained familial ties unfolded throughout the youth's childhoods. Xander experienced verbal abuse "all my life." Family rejection doesn't happen overnight. This rejection materializes through longer processes of negotiating gender and sexuality within already unstable, impoverished environments.

Arthur, a twenty-five-year-old Black gay man, also discussed with me his family's policing of his gender expression throughout his childhood. "[My dad and stepmom] made me play football. I didn't wanna play football. I wanted to be in cheerleading. I wanted to do other stuff, and [my dad] wouldn't let me. He was like, 'No, you gonna play football. A man is supposed to play football. They supposed to be tough.'" In pushing back against his father's demands, Arthur stated, "I was like, 'So, I don't wanna play football. Like, that's not my life. That's not something that I wanna do.' And he made me play football. So, I played football. And after football, I moved in with my mom. I'm not about to do this stuff no more. I'm moving in with my momma."

Sitting in a big conference room with me at the LGBTQ shelter in San Antonio, Arthur went on to discuss his life with his mother and coming out to her as gay. "My mom, first she was in there talking to me. She was like, 'You know, you can get AIDS and this and this and that. You got to use protection.'" He went on, "And then my mom called my dad. She was like, 'Well, your son is gay.' And then my daddy came over there, and he punched me. And then I punched him back, because I'm not—you're not gonna punch and hit me or whatever 'cause I'm gay." I asked him to elaborate. Arthur replied, "Yes, he punched me in my face. And we was fighting in the street. And I told him, 'You ain't gonna put your hands on me. Like you don't know my life. You don't know me. So, don't put your hands on me. And then after that he left and then he didn't talk to me no more."

Arthur's mother subsequently kicked Arthur out, saying, "You ain't gonna be in this house if you gonna be gay."

Society constructs Black men as positioned outside of dominant notions of masculinity, as hyper-aggressive and particularly suited for certain types of sports such as football. In a racially stratified society that limits financial success for many people of color, some see sports as one of the only ways to success for Black men.[30] As mentioned earlier, Cookie utilized playing football to keep her family from policing her gender and sexuality. But Arthur, who sometimes went by Isla Emerald when dressed in long black wigs, tight jeans, and high-heeled Timberland boots, resisted engaging in this sport. He moved in with his mother.

Like Jenelle's father, Arthur's mother linked homosexuality to AIDS. When this homophobic comment and Arthur's father's physical violence failed to enforce heteronormative compliance, Arthur was banished from the home. He ended up sleeping under a bridge.

Family members did not just police sons' masculinity. People policed girls' gender expressions as well. Alaina, a nineteen-year-old white Hispanic lesbian whom I also met at the LGBTQ shelter, talked extensively with me about her foster parents policing her behaviors. "[My foster parent] did not agree with the tomboy lifestyle. She just did not. And it was hard for me there because she always locked me in a room 'cause I was gay. And I would always say that [I was gay], and then eventually I just took off and ran away." Wearing basketball shorts and an oversize T-shirt, Alaina also told me about a previous foster placement, where her race and ethnicity had been policed as well. "The first foster home I went to because I always spoke Spanish. [My sister and I would] be thrown in the backyard in a dog kennel and [had to] eat dog food. And one day my caseworker came over unexpected, and she heard [my one-year-old sister] yelling and yelling and screaming and crying 'cause she was full of poop and hadn't had her diaper changed. And I had no diapers out there. So, she ended up . . . taking us away. Basically, they beat the Spanish out of me."

Between bouts with CPS, Alaina stayed with her grandmother and dad at one point. While there, Alaina said her grandmother read her journal and discovered that Alaina had an attraction to girls. "[My grandma] beat me with a broom because 'you're not supposed to be looking at girls like that,'" Alaina recounted. "Even after I left my dad and went back into

[CPS] care, I tried to come back [to live with my grandma and dad], but my grandma wouldn't let [my family] take me back because I was gay. So, I kind of just got stuck in [CPS]."

Alaina experienced heteronormative compliance through the policing of her "tomboy lifestyle." Although people may accept girls presenting as tomboys at a young age more often than feminine-presenting boys, this acceptance may not be so common for poor Black and Brown youth in state child custody systems. Alaina's presentation as tomboy is what influenced her foster parent to abuse and reject her. This policing through heteronormative compliance occurred after she had already experienced harrowing abuse for speaking Spanish. Outside of CPS, Alaina also faced abuse and rejection at the hands of her grandmother, who would not take her back because of her sexuality. For a Spanish-speaking gender-expansive young Brown woman living in unstable housing environments, these experiences of heteronormative compliance compounded with these other forms of instability and abuse. Alaina ran away from several foster home placements. When I met her, she was staying at the shelter in San Antonio until her caseworker could get her into a transitional living program for people who have aged out of CPS.

In another poignant picture of the link between heteronormative compliance, abuse, and the straining of familial ties, Naomi chronicled to me her life before experiencing homelessness. "I grew up in a Christian household, so being the way I was wasn't really—it wasn't okay," Naomi explained. "Like my dad, when he first found out, he was like, 'You like it in the ass?' And the way he put it was just so downgrading to me as a kid, and I was like twelve when I came out." An eighteen-year-old bisexual transgender Latina, Naomi often wore colorful purple or silver wigs and adorned herself in flashy jewelry. As we sat outside the LGBTQ shelter at a picnic table, Naomi lit a cigarette and continued her story. "I had to hide my makeup in the ceiling from him 'cause whenever I would come—I was in like middle school; I was in like seventh grade—and I would hide my makeup in the roof 'cause whenever he'd find it, he would just throw it away. I'd save all my lunch money, and I would go to the dollar store, and I'd get me makeup and eyelashes and all that. And I got a hold of my sister's extensions, and I glued them to my hair." One day, Naomi's father caught her wearing the hair extensions. "I remember one time when my dad first saw me with them, he tore them off my hair. Like grabbed me by the hair, and they were glued on to my scalp, so when he tugged that shit, it ripped off my scalp, and I was bleeding, and he like rubbed my face in the carpet," she said. "He was obviously stronger than me, so I couldn't do nothing about it. It was just—it wasn't okay. That's how I see it. It wasn't okay."

Naomi went to live with her mother. Life did not get better there. "My mom knew something was different about me, but she abused me as a kid. My family would see slap marks on me, and they wouldn't say nothing about it. And they already knew what she was doing." In a reflective moment, Naomi said, "But I honestly now, looking back, I honestly think she did that 'cause she knew that I had took away her son. What she wanted was a boy, and I felt like now, looking back, that's the reason why she beat me, 'cause she knew that I was going to end up being different, and she was worried about that."

Dominant societal values and power shape abuse—who perpetuates abuse and who the perpetrator targets. For example, patriarchy shapes men's domination of women. Likewise, generational authority and the adult/child binary shape parents' domination and, at times, abuse of children. For many LGBTQ youth, heteronormativity shapes abuse through parents' attempts to uphold the gender binary and heterosexuality as the only way of embodying and enacting gender and sexuality within the family. These values brought on the abuse Naomi experienced. She resisted this abuse through creative practices: saving lunch money to buy makeup and accessories, hiding items in the ceiling, and wearing her sister's hair extensions. Naomi's dad responded to these practices of resistance with more violence and punishment, trying to strip away parts of her identity, her expression, and things that brought her pleasure. Other family members condoned the abuse by not saying or doing anything. Naomi saw this abuse as a strategy to try to ensure that she would not be "different." She left her family and throughout this study did not speak to them.

CONDITIONAL FAMILIES

Elsewhere, I have written about "conditional families."[31] In my original formulation, I utilize the concept to capture how the multifaceted dynamics of poverty and family instability shape how certain LGBTQ youth experiencing homelessness—mostly poor Black and Brown LGBTQ youth—negotiate their gender and sexuality within their families of origin. Material conditions and racial inequality shape negotiations of gender and sexuality within families. Many poor families of color already fear the marginalization and discrimination that their child will face. Hence, they work to uphold heteronormativity and the gender binary to prevent any further marginalization. In turn, poor LGBTQ youth of color ambivalently navigate these familial relations. The tension around their families' negative reactions to their gender expression and sexuality often materialize as another conflict within an already unstable environment.[32]

I want to use the conclusion of this chapter, however, to expand upon my concept in relation to recent sociological work on transgender and gender-expansive children and youth. Sociological research has shown that middle-class, white parents have more leeway in allowing their children to experiment or express their gender in more expansive ways.[33] Middle-class parents often value and try to cultivate their children's talents.[34] In taking a child-centered approach to child-rearing, they see allowing their children to explore expansive expressions of gender as a way to cultivate self-expression.[35] Cultivating this self-expression of gender often takes a great deal of labor and resources. Middle-class families are not more caring and supportive toward their child than poor families. Rather, middle-class families just have more resources and other economic means to support their child and to show that they care—or, at least, care in the sense of how we often conceptualize parenting and care work.

As recent work on parents of transgender and gender-expansive children has shown, parents often have to gain "gender literacy"—learning an expanded vocabulary about gender and then passing this vocabulary on to their child.[36] A parent also often needs a certain degree of socioeconomic privilege to respond to and advocate for one's transgender or gender-expansive child within institutions such as schools, sports, and religious communities. Parents of transgender and gender-expansive children even do a great deal of emotional labor trying to manage their own fears and expectations and trying to keep their child safe. Parents need resources to access affirming professionals and advocacy organizations.[37] Most of the families in these other studies were white and middle-class—their material conditions often included privileges unavailable to the poor. Yet middle-class white parents also struggled—for a variety of reasons—to accept and provide for their transgender or gender-expansive child.[38]

To state it differently, putting care into action requires networks, resources, and other societal privileges. Given the larger social structures and institutional constraints that still invest in heteronormativity and the gender binary, supporting and advocating for a transgender or gender-expansive child takes a lot of labor. Families of color, poor families, and other marginalized families do not have the same societal privileges to support and advocate for a transgender or gender-expansive child. This is not to say, though, that all poor families or families of color fail to support their LGBTQ child; many do. And as explored in chapters 4 and 5, youth also form families of choice, who, without resources, still support and provide for one another.[39] But marginalized families of origin may have reason to fear that an LGBTQ child, especially a gender-expansive child, will face even more obstacles in life and further stigmatization. These families fear that their child will experience a hard life for "being different," as Naomi said about her mother's fear of her gender expansiveness. Marginalized families also do not often have as much access to resources and spaces that facilitate acceptance.

This chapter demonstrates, then, that family acceptance, rejection, and other types of familial processes in relation to LGBTQ youth need an intersectional analysis to understand how race and class complicate these processes. Also, family rejection as a factor in LGBTQ youth homelessness needs to be situated within the contexts of instability and poverty. This reformulation helps us to move beyond the slippery, pathologizing assumption that poor people and/or people of color hold more prejudiced views than middle-class, white people. By contextualizing the young people's lives within poverty and instability, the violence of marginalization due to racial inequality and poverty, rather than race and class itself, gives us a better way of understanding how rejection of a child's gender expression and sexuality unfolds within particular familial environments. Poor people often do not have the material and cultural resources to get help or sustain familial ties. Additionally, as the state places poor people under surveillance, it removes their children from the home more often. This process breaks up poor families and further strains familial ties.

As this chapter also has shown, these conditions of acceptance or rejection hinge on parental reactions to the child's gender expression. Gender expression often presents more visibly than sexuality. Hence, parents try to regulate gender expression as a way of also regulating the youth's assumed non-heterosexuality. Within already marginalized families, negative parental reactions to a child's expansive expressions of gender serves as a point of contention that worsens familial strain within families with already tenuous ties. Many of the LGBTQ youth in this study experienced abuse and violence specifically targeted at policing their gender expression—trying to force a type of heteronormative compliance to make the young people uphold the gender binary and heterosexuality within the family. The youth often experienced this abuse as simultaneously about controlling their gender and their sexuality, and they often used words describing gender and sexuality interchangeably in discussing these experiences of heteronormative compliance, such as not dressing "too gay" when around their families. Abuse and the heteronormative forms that it took created what many youth's perceived as their pathway into homelessness later in life. Heteronormative compliance within marginalized families—already suffering from poverty and strained familial ties—partly explains why and how certain LGBTQ youth end up on the streets.

Importantly, youth are not passive victims. The LGBTQ youth in this study resisted the heteronormative compliance that they faced in their families. The youth established creative strategies to engage in expansive expressions of gender and to affirm their lives. The family rejection narrative often overlooks this point. Youth actively take part in negotiating gender and sexuality within their families. Youth also resisted through running away. Because youth who grow up in poverty often experience adultification—taking on adult responsibilities at young ages such as getting jobs, fending for themselves, and protecting and caring for other family members—they are able to sense that they can, and perhaps must, be self-sufficient.[40] Poor LGBTQ youth often already have experienced more independence than other youth, and hence, take the initiative to leave. The consequences, such as experiencing homelessness, can be dire. Still, youth saw the streets, with all the violence that occurs with living on them, as safer than and preferable to the home.

My revisiting the concept of conditional families establishes, then, that larger structural conditions—poverty, heteronormativity, the gender binary, racial inequality—influence the conditions in which families of origin accept and reject their child. Even when some good conditions exist, such as in some middle-class, white families, heteronormativity and the gender binary still make raising a transgender or gender-expansive child difficult. Poverty, instability, and racial inequality exacerbate these difficulties. When structural inequalities have already strained family ties, certain youth—often youth most marginalized by the larger structural conditions—go to the streets. If we want to bolster unconditional love and care, we need to reexamine the larger structural conditions shaping acceptance, rejection, and belonging.

Families, though, are not the only people and contexts in which children and youth encounter and navigate their gender and sexuality. As the next chapter will show, young people navigate other social institutions—schools, state child custody systems, religious communities, and the workplace. These systems also punish and discipline LGBTQ youth, so when society systemically sets up certain families to fail, the LGBTQ youth in this study have nowhere to go but the streets.

2 Queer Control Complex

"I ran into the hill, where there is a bunch of trees. And I had no time to keep my flip flops on, so I was barefoot. There was a few inches of snow on the ground. It was like six degrees. I just ran as fast as I could up the hill." Jessie, an eighteen-year-old white gay gender-fluid youth, was telling me about his breakaway from an abusive Christian boarding school when he was sixteen years old.[1] He continued, "I was out there for eight hours. And I was really starting to freeze to death. My feet were black, although I couldn't see it. I didn't realize how bad they were 'cause it was so dark." Eventually, Jessie found some train tracks. "I just sat there," he recounted. "And I was praying, 'Please God, send a train.' And instantly—maybe two seconds after that—I hear a train come. And I take the jacket, and I wave it. I tried to get their attention. They stop. They come out. And they say, 'What's wrong?'"[2]

What *is* wrong? And how did Jessie get here—alone, running away from boarding school, barefoot in the snow? Jessie's fraught relationships with institutions such as schools began at an earlier time. As we sat together at the LGBTQ shelter—Jessie in white Etnies skater shoes and light-washed, form-fitting jeans—he told me, "The bullying kind of started in kindergarten. I'm just an effeminate person, so like the other boys in the school would call me a girl." In sixth grade, the bullying got worse. "People called me a fag and just nasty things—called me a cat molester and shit. And one girl—one time—came up to me and just poked me in my eyes. And I was like, what the fuck. I could not see. I didn't know if I was going to go blind or not." Jessie also said that in music class, "[a boy] would call me names. And make fun of my walk and make fun of my talk." For a host of reasons, including these conflicts at school as well as discord at home, Jessie's parents sent him to a Christian boarding school in the Midwest.[3] "They were very abusive [at the boarding school]," Jessie stated, "and very homophobic."

One form of abuse came from the boarding school's ranking and punishment system. "They have a level system. It's called white chip, blue chip, then red chip," Jessie explained. "White chip was like if you were doing really good. You got to play video games. And sometimes you get seconds on food. You got white chip privileges. Blue chip was just kind of middle. You still had free time. You just didn't get the extra things." Staff members, though, often placed Jessie on red chip. "Red chip—you had to sit in the corner and read a book. And they punish by food." For example, Jessie said the breakfast consisted of tasteless oatmeal made with water. He also said, "If you are on red chip, you couldn't have a pillow." Over time, he "got really depressed" and tried to give himself "ink poisoning." When Jessie informed a staff person that he wanted to die, more violence ensued. "[A staff member] came back with paint thinner. And he was like, 'So, you want to kill yourself? Here.' And he goes to pour it down my throat," Jessie recalled. "But out of nowhere he starts choking me. He just grabs my throat and just chokes me." Shortly after this incident, Jessie ran out into the snow to escape. After he flagged down the train, medical personnel arrived and flew him to a hospital.

QUEER CONTROL COMPLEX

On September 21, 2010, gay activist and journalist Dan Savage and his husband, Terry Miller, launched the It Gets Better Project to address the bullying that LGBTQ youth face in schools and other institutions. The goal of the project is to prevent suicide among LGBTQ youth. The premise is that if youth get through their teenage years—overcoming bullying and not killing themselves—life will get better upon graduating from high school. A variety of LGBTQ celebrities recorded YouTube videos detailing how their lives had gotten better as adults. President Barack Obama contributed to the campaign as well.

In this chapter, however, I am not concerned with whether life gets better for all LGBTQ youth after high school. (It does not.) Instead, I want to address the fact that LGBTQ youth should not have to wait for life to get better. Youth such as Jessie should not have to endure verbal and physical violence and should not have to run barefoot in the snow to escape brutality. To make life better for LGBTQ youth, we need to continue to understand how and why institutions drive some LGBTQ youth to kill themselves or escape to the streets.

I document, then, the stories of LGBTQ youth experiencing homelessness to investigate how they negotiated their gender and sexuality in relation to various institutions. I focus on how schools, state child custody systems, religious institutions, and the workplace discipline and punish LGBTQ youth, especially poor transgender and gender-expansive Black and Brown youth. I detail the challenges, struggles, and resistance that go on within these institutions, while showing the youth's perceptions of how these institutions contributed to and perpetuated their experiences of homelessness. In documenting these experiences, I provide an understanding of the role of institutions in forming pathways into youth homelessness and in perpetuating homelessness once young people begin to live on the streets. This documentation allows us to see what work needs to be done to change institutions so that LGBTQ youth do not have to wait for life to get better.

Specifically, I introduce the concept of the *queer control complex* to map how institutions and institutional actors police and criminalize expansive expressions of gender and signs of homosexuality. This concept builds on sociologist Victor Rios's "youth control complex," which he defines as "a system in which schools, police, probation officers, families, community centers, the media, businesses, and other institutions systematically treat young people's everyday behaviors as criminal activity."[4] In US society, we have embedded crime-control discourses and practices into many, if not most, institutions. Now, youth—notably Black and Brown youth—repeatedly face negative judgments and criminalizing interactions from institutional actors.

I define the queer control complex as a system in which institutions and their agents systematically police LGBTQ youth's behaviors, particularly their gender behaviors in relation to policing their assumed nonheterosexuality. Gender policing makes up a main mechanism of this complex, whereby transgender and gender-expansive youth often encounter negative judgments and interactions from others. This queer control complex aims to get youth to adhere to dominant notions of gender and sexuality. For instance, student peers called Jessie "a girl," "a fag," and "a cat molester." Jessie said this bullying came from peers' negative reactions to his perceived effeminate mannerisms and his perceived nonheterosexuality. This policing routinely works to try to socially control LGBTQ youth and their gender and sexuality.

Moreover, discipline and punishment work to socially control populations through establishing and exacerbating group differences. As social theorist Michel Foucault documents, discipline, as a mode of domination, seeks to produce what he calls "docile bodies." To achieve docility, institutional actors implement practices that compare individuals to one another and hierarchically rank and evaluate people. Disciplinary techniques reward people who embody and enact dominant societal practices—such as boys embodying and enacting masculinity—and punish people who do not—such as boys embodying and enacting femininity. Strikingly, after we internalize dominant societal ideologies, we alter our behaviors. Foucault uses the idea of the panopticon to theorize how, like a prisoner in a cell who thinks a prison guard is always watching (whether a guard is watching or not), we often feel someone is watching us and evaluating our behaviors. In turn, we self-regulate our behaviors to conform to dominant societal practices.[5] In Jessie's case, staff members compared him to other students. They evaluated Jessie with a red chip, as being not as good as the youth on white and blue chips. Instead of succumbing to this disciplinary apparatus, Jessie resisted by threatening suicide and finally running away.

In this chapter, I will show how discipline and punishment, through acts such as gender policing, work to shape the lives of LGBTQ youth. Jessie experienced bullying and gender policing essentially his whole life. These processes shaped how he understood himself as gay and gender fluid and his relation to institutions and other people. Importantly, punishing sexuality happens not only through regulating sexual acts, desires, and identities, but also through gender policing. These mechanisms of control interconnect throughout institutions—through the queer control complex. And significantly, because of how racial and class inequalities link to racial profiling, surveillance, and punishment, poor Black and Brown LGBTQ youth disproportionately bear the brunt of these disciplining and policing processes. The queer control complex often works to mainly target poor transgender and gender-expansive Black and Brown youth.

The notion of a queer control complex, though, complicates notions of one particular institution (often the family) being *the* pipeline into homelessness for LGBTQ youth experiencing homelessness. Instead, I will discuss in this chapter how institutions interconnect to discipline and punish LGBTQ youth, contributing to their experiences of marginalization and their understanding of themselves as LGBTQ. Yes, families make up part of the queer control complex by trying to enforce heteronormative compliance, as I documented in the previous chapter. But families are only one part of this larger complex of control. Beyond the family, the queer control complex pushes certain LGBTQ youth, often certain poor transgender and gender-expansive Black and Brown youth, into recurring punishments and a life on the streets.

SCHOOLS

Most youth in this study did not go to boarding school. Many of them described going to under-resourced public schools. Although there were not formalized ranking systems such as the chip system at Jessie's school, discipline and punishment operated in detrimental ways at these public schools, often through the processes of bullying, suspensions, and arrests.

"School was hard always," Justice, an eighteen-year-old Black heterosexual transgender woman, told me, as we sat outside the LGBTQ shelter. "Every kid is going to have problems being bullied." Justice continued, detailing her experiences of bullying, "I had kids push me in the hallways—from tripping me, to throwing spitballs at me, to throwing textbooks at me, to throwing their food at me. It was really hard—even boogers were thrown at me. It was so hard. It was to the point where I wanted to commit suicide, and I actually attempted suicide a couple of times. This is during middle school."

Justice said she began "dressing like a full-time girl" in high school. The bullying got worse. "I had to carry a knife to school because the school wouldn't let me carry pepper spray. So, I just upped it a notch. Because kids were trying to steal my purse and trying to beat me up on the way to school." Authority figures bullied Justice too. "I was even getting it from teachers," she stated. "I'd walk in class with a little bit too much makeup on. And I've literally had a teacher say, 'Go wipe that shit off your face. And go get a tardy pass.' And I couldn't get another tardy pass because I'd be in OCI [on-campus intervention] all day." For Justice, this routinized bullying constituted the meaning of being LGBTQ. She stated, "I just thought every gay person was getting bullied like this. And it was just part of being in school and being LGBT."

We often view bullying as an individual person acting mean toward another individual. But bullying is a social act. Children and youth learn how and whom to bully from social structures. People who bully often target marginalized people, such as people who challenge heteronormativity and the gender binary. And gender policing—as a form of bullying— devalues gender-expansive youth and serves to remind them of their lower-status position.[6]

Bullying, as an act of discipline, works to further punish people who do not conform to the gender binary and heteronormativity. In Justice's case, peers may have particularly singled her out for bullying because she is a large Black transgender woman, over six feet tall. People often watch, discipline, and punish Black and Brown youth more. And as most women in the United States are not over six feet tall, Justice's height could draw more attention to her being transgender. Furthermore, Black and Brown youth who challenge dominant notions of gender and sexuality such as Justice can also face more aggressive bullying. Being a fierce "diva"—by bringing a knife to school—Justice resisted this aggression.

Part of schools' "hidden curriculum"—or unintended lessons—is that heterosexuality and the gender binary are privileged as the standards for gender and sexual expression. Disciplinary practices, school curricula, student-teacher relationships, and school events uphold this standard.[7] The teacher punished Justice for wearing makeup by having her remove the makeup and get a tardy pass, resulting in her going to OCI for the day. OCI involves identifying what school authorities perceive as a student's disruptive behaviors and identifying alternative behaviors for the student to enact. OCI, as another disciplinary space, tried to get Justice to conform. In this way, hidden curricula and school regulations further legitimize bullying and disciplining LGBTQ young people, such that Justice found it to be simply "part of being in school and being LGBT."

School bullying, particularly gender policing, came up in almost every interview. "I would always hang out with the girls. I would never hangout with the guys," Prada, a twenty-three-year-old Hispanic heterosexual transgender woman, told me. "I never wanted to play sports or anything. I was more into cheerleading, more into the makeup, more into the hair. And I've basically been bullied since kindergarten." Prada's best friend, Winston, a twenty-four-year-old African American homosexual man, talked about bullying as well. "I would always get into fights—on a regular basis," he explained to me. "It was because people would always pick on me based on my sexuality—the way I dressed, the way I acted, the way I talked." Naomi, an eighteen-year-old bisexual transgender Latina, said her mom pulled her out of school her freshman year. "I was always going through shit at school. I got into a fight with some girl for calling me a tranny. And . . . the guys when I'd walk down the hallway would be like, 'Where's her dick at?'"

Many LGBTQ youth in this study described bullying as part of their experience of growing up LGBTQ. As criminologist Gail Mason argues, homophobia-related violence shapes how sexually marginalized individuals come to understand their realities and themselves. Violence is productive. Violence reestablishes hierarchal constructions of difference. For example, violence against lesbians objectifies them, labels them as disordered, and marks them as warranting scrutiny. A person recognizes a lesbian person as different and may respond with hostility. Violence has repercussions even if not experienced, because people alter their appearance and behaviors to avoid it. We can think of women who do not walk alone at night as a way that violence—or the fear of violence—constitutes the meaning of womanhood and how women navigate their lives and safety in the world. Violence, as an instrument of marking difference, maintains relations of domination and subordination.[8]

Bullying—as a form of violence—partly constitutes the meaning of LGBTQ youth. As LGBTQ youth challenge heteronormativity, bullying makes up a common experience of school life. This bullying through gender policing reinscribes the gender binary as the dominant mode of gender relations within society. Even if some LGBTQ youth do not experience bullying, the fear of experiencing it shapes how they view themselves in relation to others. LGBTQ youth alter their appearance and behaviors and conceal their gender and/or sexual identity to try to avoid experiencing bullying.

Race also shapes bullying, as people often monitor Black and Brown youth's behaviors more. This surveillance extends to their gender behaviors. Class and socioeconomic status shape bullying inasmuch as schools with fewer resources often don't have Gay Straight Alliances or other programs to support LGBTQ youth and address bullying. The queer control complex relies, then, on the threat of bullying or actual bullying to discipline and punish LGBTQ youth, especially poor Black and Brown LGBTQ youth. Winston and Naomi fought back, since school authorities failed to address the violence that the youth experienced. This fighting back has consequences, as Naomi's mom removed her from school.

Another consequence of fighting back may be that youth are sent away to alternative educational institutions or to jail. "I got into fights here and there," Camila, a twenty-two-year-old Hispanic heterosexual transgender woman, explained to me at the LGBTQ shelter. "I got put into an alternative school when I was in—I was fourteen. And I got kicked out of alternative school for fighting. And then I got put into boot camp. So, I don't know—a little further punishment than the alternative schools." When I inquired about her reasons for fighting, Camila replied, "Just people making comments about my sexuality."

Julian, a twenty-two-year-old Hispanic gay youth whom I met at the drop-in center in Austin also discussed fighting in school. "I beat the hell out of people at school. I was fighting all the time," he explained. When I asked why he fought all the time, Julian replied, "The people who are homophobic are dicks. And so, I just kicked their ass and got on with it. That's why I went to jail my first time was for assault."

Camila's and Julian's experiences with punishment show the expansion of carceral systems into schools. School administrators suspend or expel youth for violating school policies. These suspensions and expulsions push youth into jails and other carceral systems.[9] These policies disproportionately criminalize Black and Brown students and/or students with disabilities.[10] They also affect LGBTQ youth, especially LGBTQ youth of color. A recent national study has documented that LGB youth, particularly gender-expansive girls, are up to three times more likely to experience disciplinary treatment at schools compared to their non-LGB counterparts.[11] When LGBTQ youth fight back against bullying, school authorities blame and punish them for their own victimization, presuming their guilt instead of recognizing that they are trying to protect themselves. These authorities also fail to recognize how gender policing and anti-LGBTQ discrimination produce bullies who target LGBTQ people and why LGBTQ youth fight back. The structural causes of the bullying and of fighting back are ignored. This dismissal of or failure to understand the structural causes of bullying results in LGBTQ youth, especially LGBTQ youth of color, being pushed out of schools.[12]

In a telling example of bullying and the expansion of carceral systems into schools, Arthur, a twenty-five-year-old Black gay man whom I met at the LGBTQ shelter, told me, "I used to want to kill myself because people used to call me fag, gay, and this and that. Look at you with your faggot ass—stuff like that. It would make me depressed." One day, Arthur fought back. "I went to jail because I kicked this boy in the face with steel-toed boots on." In explaining to me why, Arthur said, "He called me a *puta* and stuff like that. And then he was like you fucking faggot. And I just hit him." Arthur went to jail for the charge of an "assault with bodily injury." The other person dropped the charges. Arthur dropped out of school.

Bullying affected Arthur's emotional state. A *puta* is an insult often used to discipline and control young women's sexuality in Spanish-speaking communities. This slur used against Arthur was seemingly intended to police and discipline his gender and sexuality. Arthur fought back, but fighting back sent him to jail, setting him off-track on his education.

By intersecting gay, gender-expansive, and poor with Blackness, bullying and punishment creates a queer Black "bad boy." In her study of race, punishment, and schools, sociologist Ann Ferguson documents how teachers and school administrators more harshly punish young Black boys' behaviors than young white boys' behaviors. School authority figures see white boys as engaging in "boys will be boys" play, yet they see Black boys as inherently criminal and engaging in behaviors that will send them to jail. Through school punishment, school authorities create Black "bad boys."[13] School authorities overly punish, discipline, and criminalize gender-expansive and/or non-heterosexual Black youth, such as Arthur and Justice, and Brown LGBTQ youth, such as Camila and Julian. These punishing processes constitute poor LGBTQ people of color as both criminals and deviants. This punishment creates what I call *bad queers* and funnels them through schools to jails and to the streets.

Through bullying, hidden curricula, and the expansion of carceral systems into schools, educational institutions discipline, punish, and criminalize LGBTQ youth, particularly through gender policing poor gender-expansive Black and Brown youth. Schools make up part of the queer control complex, and this complex works to produce bad queers. When LGBTQ youth resist and fight back, they experience more punishment and contact with carceral systems. These processes pushed some of the LGBTQ young people in this study out of schools. Dealing with experiences of heteronormative compliance within families—as documented in the previous chapter—and bullying and other disciplining processes in schools, youth often have nowhere to go. Other institutions, including state child custody systems, also interconnect to continue these detrimental processes.

STATE CHILD CUSTODY SYSTEMS

"I'm continuously on precaution, which is the stupidest thing ever. I hate precaution," stated Gwen, a seventeen-year-old Hispanic lesbian. When I interviewed Gwen, she resided at a Child Protective Services (CPS) licensed shelter in Austin. She was dressed in a tie-dye shirt and Chuck Taylor shoes. She kept her purple hair short and shaved on the sides. Gwen spent a great deal of the interview telling me about her current life in this shelter. "They check on me every fifteen minutes, when I'm in my room," she explained. "And they have to have you on LOV, which is 'line of vision,' when you're outside of your room. And so, they have to watch you. . . . It's just more added pressure to the person. And more people knowing, 'Oh hey, this person is on precaution. I wonder what they've been doing.'" Gwen said that staff members place residents on precaution when they seem to be hurting themselves.

"I had the cops called on me one day while I was here," Gwen continued. "Staff saw a bandage on my arm, and they kept asking to see my arm. And I kept saying no. It's my body. They don't need to be intruding on me. . . . The cops showed up, and they started yelling at me. Telling me— asking me if what I thought was going on was a joke. And then just saying that I must be cutting myself for attention."

Non-heterosexual youth disproportionately reside in state child custody systems.[14] A study conducted in Los Angeles found that LGBTQ youth make up 19 percent of state child custody residents.[15] Twenty-one of the forty youth in this study reported contact with state child custody systems while growing up.[16] State child custody systems often contribute to the further marginalization of youth. From Gwen's perspective, staff thought she was self-harming, and they put her on "precaution"—a label that classifies a person as experiencing mental health challenges. This label alerts staff members, but also creates a known stigma visible to Gwen's peers.[17] Gwen said she was always kept within someone's line of vision, which made her feel that people were always watching her (even if staff were not).[18] Staff, though, were sometimes watching and called in police when Gwen asserted her bodily autonomy. Police arriving at the shelter only furthered Gwen's stigma as different—as criminal. This contact with police also signifies to Gwen—a gender-expansive woman of color—that her behavior deserves punishment and police intervention. These processes work to constitute poor gender-expansive women of color as criminal deviants.

Obadiah, a twenty-year-old white man who dates transgender women, also discussed with me the disciplining and punishment he experienced in state child custody systems. Sitting on his bunk bed at the LGBTQ shelter, he described the residential treatment centers (RTCs) state child custody workers sent him to. "It's a lot of rules. Honestly, a lot of rules—strict. Like these lockdown facilities—the toilet's inside . . . your room—were literally like metal, like in jail," Obadiah stated. "There's this board on the wall in CPS—they have all your names—red, green, and yellow. Green is like the best. Yellow is all right. If you're on the [red]—it's an RLD—it's called red level drop. You can't do anything. But when you're on green you can hardly do anything." Obadiah also told of the use of medication in state child custody systems. "And I also didn't like—so many kids got put on medication in CPS, which I don't understand," he told me. "'Cause these people don't understand these kids are acting up 'cause they want a family. They don't have a family to care about them and love them. That's why—I don't understand why—everybody in CPS in the dorms were on meds."

Going into more details about state child custody systems, Adelpha, an eighteen-year-old Black, Mexican, and white heterosexual transgender woman, explained to me, "They locked me up in a RTC for six months in the middle of nowhere. And it's basically like this boot camp for CPS kids. And they treat—literally, it is worse than prison." Adelpha went on to tell me that state child custody workers "put everyone" on "mood stabilizers, depression medication, anxiety—everything." Adelpha said that, in her view, "the reason they put CPS kids on medication is they get paid more for you. And it's a business, 'cause the doctors—you're like a business. CPS kids are thrown into the doctor's office. And the government and all that is paying the doctors. And then the foster parents are getting paid more 'cause your disabilities and all that medication." From Adelpha's perspective, the Texas state child custody ranking system influenced the amount of money a foster parent received. "They say that they want you to be good, but they don't," she recalled. "'Cause there's level of care. There's . . . basic, moderate, and intense. The higher level you are, the more they get paid."[19]

The youth's descriptions of RTCs as being like jails came up as a prominent concern during this study.[20] Treating young people as criminals sets them up to view themselves as dangerous and to see no alternative paths in their future lives except going to jail.[21] Whether on red chip, on precaution, on red-level drop, or labeled as intense, authority figures monitor, rank, and label youth and discipline them accordingly. These processes criminalize the youth as aberrant. Adelpha's comments, however, note the paradox of this labeling process. Labeling a youth as "intense" ranks and evaluates them as having "severe problems."[22] From Adelpha's perspective, state child custody systems incentivize foster parents to take in youth whom the system has labeled as worse than the "basic" and "moderate" youth. Adelpha pointed out that this system does not reward good behavior, or at least from her perspective, a "good" youth doesn't get a placement in a foster home.

Likewise, in not acting how authority figures expected them to act, the youth saw medication as a main form of discipline or a way to control them. Indeed, as a service provider I interviewed stated, "There's also a huge connotation with a lot of kids coming out of CPS and foster care that anything that has to do with meds or counseling, they see it as some sort of form of control." Although CPS authorities probably do not put all youth on medication, Obadiah's and Adelpha's views are that child custody workers medicate everyone, showing their mistrust of these institutions. Medication, of course, does not provide love and stability. Many youth ran away from these systems, or staff members constantly moved them to other placements.

Youth saw eviction from CPS placements as another form of control. Alaina, a nineteen-year-old white Hispanic lesbian who also stayed at the LGBTQ shelter, spoke to me about how a foster parent's disapproval of her sexuality influenced her being placed in a psychiatric hospital. "'Cause I was with a girl still, [the foster parent] didn't want me there. She ended up putting me in a hospital in Dallas," Alaina explained. "Usually when we act up, and they don't want to deal with us no more, they put us in a hospital."

Adelpha also gave details about this eviction process. "Say a foster home doesn't want you there no more. They have thirty days—like your caseworker has thirty days to come get you. But if they send you to a mental hospital, it automatically relinquishes their rights to you. So, they don't have to wait that thirty days." Adelpha continued, "It's so easy to send somebody to a mental hospital. It's so easy for an adult to send a kid to a mental hospital. 'Cause they're not going to listen to you. They're going to listen to the adult."

Eviction in state child custody systems or constantly changing placements generated a great deal of instability for the youth in this study. One youth—Lola—told me she had forty different placements while in state child custody systems. Moreover, youth saw eviction as part of trying to control them. Alaina's foster parent used eviction to punish her for her sexuality. Part of this power of eviction comes from the adult/child binary. Within this binary, adults have more power than children. As Adelpha stated, people believe adults more than children. This binary normalizes adults' power to discipline and punish young people—even to the point of evicting them.

The punishment of the youth's gender and sexuality also influenced why youth in this study said they ran away from state child custody systems. Notably, the gender segregation of their placements shaped some of these experiences. "The shelter was divided girl-side, boy-side," stated Trinity, a twenty-one-year-old white lesbian, who told me about the CPS-licensed shelter that state authorities sent her to after school personnel reported her father's abuse to the state. "A staff said that I could not talk to any of the little girls," she continued. "And the reason being is because I was gay. Because they thought I would do something to them, which made no fucking sense, 'cause I never showed any history of that kind of crap. . . . But it made it seem like I was a pedo[phile]. And it made me feel very disgusted with the place, with myself." Trinity said she ran away from the shelter shortly after a caseworker placed her there.

Likewise, Justice—the eighteen-year-old Black heterosexual transgender woman who discussed experiencing bullying at school and rejection at home—also talked about her experiences in state child custody. "The placement where I was at, they weren't providing me some of the things that I needed, being transgender," she explained. "Placing me in the wrong dorm. Misgendering me a lot of times. They would deny me a lot of basic rights that the kids would need."

The gender segregation of state child custody systems contributes to isolation and stigmatization. As I have documented elsewhere, gender segregation of these systems exposes transgender and gender-expansive youth to violence and influences youth to run away from their placement. Gender segregation in state child custody systems furthers experiences of instability and marginalization for LGBTQ youth, especially for poor Black and Brown LGBTQ youth.[23] Additionally, negative stereotypes about LGBTQ people, such as being pedophiles, could influence staff to not allow LGBTQ youth to interact with other youth. Gender segregation, stigmatization, and isolation in state child custody systems produce LGBTQ youth, especially poor LGBTQ youth and LGBTQ youth of color, as inferior. Some youth, including Trinity and Justice, told me that they would creatively use the resources that state child custody systems provided. They would get food, bus passes, access to educational resources, and other benefits. Once they got what they wanted or needed, they would often leave again, as state child custody systems did not respect or provide safety for them.

Notably, for Trinity and Justice, such instability continued throughout several institutions. Trinity experienced physical abuse in the home, and, as documented in the previous chapter, Justice experienced verbal abuse and rejection in the home as well, specifically in her mom's boyfriend's negative reactions to her gender expression and sexuality. Trinity and Justice also experienced bullying at school, specifically for being LGBTQ. Like Justice, whom peers and teachers targeted, Trinity said peers targeted her in school because of her sexuality. She explained, "I would have groups of people jump me in gym class and the hallways between classes. Sometimes, when I'd go home from school—even in elementary school I knew I was gay—and on the way home, I'd get jumped by people." School officials did not address the bullying in Trinity's case, but they did report the abuse in her home. State child custody workers then removed Trinity from the home. Trinity and Justice also experienced rejection and instability in CPS for their gender and sexuality. Within the queer control complex, they had nowhere safe to live.

Talking with me while she had her dinner at the shelter, Adelpha further detailed how people policing her gender embodiments and enactments shaped her experiences in state child custody systems. At an RTC, Adelpha said, "I started wearing makeup and dressing really feminine. And they were like—they would come up to me—and they were like, 'You need to stop that. This isn't Dallas.'" She went on, "They would make me take off my makeup. And then, I was trying to grow out my hair there. And they were just like, somebody would be there every day—well, not every day, but I think it was every month—to cut hair, 'cause everybody had like a buzz cut. I was like, 'No, I'm not cutting my hair.'"

Aside from this gender policing, Adelpha learned about transgender people while at a gender-segregated placement. "I met this trans woman, and she was in CPS too," Adelpha explained. "I didn't know she was transgender, 'cause I didn't know nothing about that." Adelpha continued,

"I was like, 'Who are you living with?' 'Cause there was a whole bunch of different CPS kids in different foster homes. She was like, 'Oh those guys over there.' And I was like, 'Oh I didn't know girls and guys could be in the same foster homes together.'" Later, someone informed Adelpha that the woman was a transgender girl. State child custody workers housed this young transgender girl with boys.

Thus, gender segregation of state child custody systems marginalizes certain LGBTQ youth, places them into unsafe environments, and denies them dignity. This gender segregation also bolsters actions of gender policing. For example, staff members policed Adelpha's gender embodiment and behaviors through acts such as cutting her hair and through associating expansive expressions of gender with cities—Dallas—as if only people in cities embody gender expansiveness. At the state-level, the Texas Department of Family and Protective Services has no policies in place to ensure staff treat transgender and gender-expansive youth according to their gender identity. Nothing in the Texas residential childcare contract addresses LGBTQ children and youth.[24] Ironically, through the gender segregation of these systems, Adelpha met a young transgender woman and upon meeting this person and learning about transgender people, Adelpha began to explore her own gender identity more.

To fully capture state child custody systems, their disciplining and punishing of expansive expressions of gender and non-heterosexuality, and how state child custody systems contribute to youth's instabilities, I turn to Xander, who resided at the same CPS-licensed shelter as Gwen, with whom I opened this section. Wearing a black leather jacket, tight jeans, and black leather boots, Xander, a nineteen-year-old Black gay youth, sat with me in a private room at the CPS shelter and explained to me his situation, "Things were sort of complicated being in my previous placement. And I sort of lost it for a second. And then, I was put on a thirty-day notice, which is sort of like an eviction notice. They are kicking you out." When I asked what happened, Xander replied, "I stabbed a dude. I'm not going to lie. He was throwing caramel in my hair. My hair is one of my trigger points." Xander said he stabbed the other person "in the balls with my [hair] pick." Before this incident, Xander had already had problems at this placement. "I was gay. They didn't want anyone around me," he said. "I wasn't allowed to be with the boys. And obviously, I wasn't allowed to be with the girls." This segregation generated feelings of difference. "I felt like a zoo animal put on the stage around those kids," he recalled. "Just 'cause I was the only gay dude. 'What's it like being gay? Are you a male or female?'"

The policing of Xander's gender, sexuality, and race shaped his experiences in state child custody systems. Staff segregated Xander from everyone. This segregation could protect LGBTQ youth from violence, but for Xander, it simply marked him as different. Gender segregation produces transgender and gender-expansive people as objects of scrutiny—as "zoo animals"—by marking them as different for challenging the gender binary. This gender segregation also normalizes bullying. Furthermore, since hair has a significant political and personal meaning to Black people and communities, the attack—when someone threw caramel on his hair—seemed to also attack his racial identity. As Xander mentioned, this attack triggered him, and he fought back. His punishment entailed eviction. Staff members moved him to different placements, which further exacerbated his experiences of instability.

Along with families and schools, state child custody systems compose part of the queer control complex. State child custody systems rely on other institutions (e.g., RTCs, psychiatric hospitals), processes (e.g., eviction), and institutional housing arrangements (e.g., gender segregation) to assist in controlling and punishing the youth and their gender and sexuality. These systems continue the rejection, punishment, and abuse that the LGBTQ youth have already faced at home and at schools. They continue the production of bad queers, mainly by criminalizing poor Black and Brown LGBTQ youth, evicting them, and pushing them into jails and/or to the streets.

Perhaps this rejection of LGBTQ youth in state child custody comes from a longer history of not seeing child welfare as including LGBTQ people. Historically, many people saw the notion of "child welfare" as standing in opposition to LGBTQ rights: child welfare meant protecting children from LGBTQ people. This discourse of children versus LGBTQ people erases LGBTQ children and their welfare, leaving the notion of child welfare largely in the domain of anti-LGBTQ sentiments and movements.[25] State child custody systems still further these historical sentiments, as these systems do not protect the welfare of LGBTQ children. In Texas, no explicit policies protect or respect LGBTQ children and youth. In not protecting their welfare, state child custody systems produce LGBTQ youth as inferior and different. Many young people in this study ran away from state child custody systems or left the system when they turned eighteen. On the streets, though, some youth struggled to find services to assist them because of many services' religious affiliations. Religion makes up part of the queer control complex too.

RELIGION

"I've been to church, where I'm sitting there, and they talk very specifically about homosexuality. And it being a sin. And it being wrong. And I definitely don't agree with that at all," stated Audrey, a twenty-three-year-old Hispanic lesbian, whom I met at the Austin drop-in center and who dated Trinity. At the San Antonio LGBTQ shelter, Arthur told me similar things about sexuality and religion. "Once people started talkin' 'bout stuff in church, it just made me distance myself away from the church," he explained. "Because people made comments about gay people. And I was like, I don't feel comfortable. I don't want to be here no more because they are talkin' 'bout gay people. And it's a sin to be gay." For Lola, a twenty-year-old Hispanic bisexual woman whom I met at the Austin transitional living program, religion entailed a lot of rules, especially around sexuality. "Mostly not-to-dos," she called religion. "Everything is not to do this, not to do that. Not to like another female, not to have sex—that's sin. It's a sin. Everything's a sin. It already looked bad when I had two kids. She's a sinner. I was judged a lot." Xander—from the CPS shelter—told me, "[My dad] shoved Catholicism down my throat like it was water, and I was dehydrated, and I needed it to save my life. But I didn't. He tried to show me the light." Xander went on, imitating his father, "I'm going to show you the error of your ways. In this passage, it says you cannot be gay." Xander replied, "Bitch, it does not say that."

Many youth in this study discussed growing up learning about religion—mainly Christianity—and about a God who would punish them for their sins. They often said that one sin in particular they had learned about was homosexuality. Youth resisted these messages and rejected religion often because of religion's association with policing and condemning their gender and sexuality.

In general, many LGBTQ people have negative or ambivalent experiences with religion. For LGBTQ youth experiencing homelessness, these negative or ambivalent experiences have detrimental consequences. As the US government has defunded social service programs, faith-based charity agencies now serve as the main organizations that help the poor. Today, churches and religion play some of the largest roles in homelessness assistance. These religious-affiliated organizations or churches provide food and shelter to people experiencing homelessness in order to "witness" (or tell them) about God and Jesus Christ.[26] Because LGBTQ youth in this study experienced rejection and punishment from religious people and religious messages, they often hesitated to access many services for people experiencing homelessness. In not accessing these services, the youth do not receive as much help as other people experiencing homelessness, potentially making them more prone to continue living on the streets.

Religion arose as a salient theme during my fieldwork. Churches or church-affiliated organizations provided a main source of accessing food for people experiencing homelessness in Austin. Although the Austin field site did not have a religious affiliation, the drop-in center was in the basement of a church. This organization also held other big events (e.g., prom, Christmas party) at another church nearby. Importantly, during one of my interviews with a service provider at my Austin field site, this provider talked about how this religious affiliation of services erects another barrier for some LGBTQ youth experiencing homelessness. "I think that that limits, where they would get services for a while," she explained. "[The Austin drop-in center is] inside of a church. So, for them, even coming to us—which, we're not faith oriented or related—but you don't know that when you just see our building!" She went on, "And so, I think that that's a barrier for them sometimes. Just like, if a service provider is going to be accepting, you know?"

In San Antonio, the larger homelessness campus—where the LGBTQ shelter was located—identified as spiritually integrated. The campus also had a chapel in the center of the campus. A few times during fieldwork, this chapel broadcast sermons over a loudspeaker across the entire campus.

Specifically, at the LGBTQ shelter, flyers at the front desk advertised churches in the area. Prada, a Hispanic heterosexual transgender youth staying at the shelter, said once that she didn't understand why the shelter had these flyers, as youth at the shelter only go to churches for free food. Jenelle, another Hispanic transgender youth staying at the shelter, told me that she hesitated to come to the LGBTQ shelter because she thought the larger campus sounded religious and would not accept transgender people.

The topic of religion and services for people experiencing homelessness came up in my interviews with the youth as well. Sitting together in the staff office at the LGBTQ shelter, Niguel, a twenty-four-year-old white Hispanic gay man, discussed with me the in-house recovery program (IHRP) he had recently finished. "Being in IHRP, it's more like faith-based. So, I'm in club praying and stuff like that," he explained. "It's all about drug rehabilitation—drug, alcohol, and substance abuse. You get like a counselor. You go to classes and AA [Alcoholics Anonymous] meet-ings all day, every day. And I think what they try to do is bore you out of doing drugs." Bringing the conversation back to religion, Niguel stated, "If you're not like heavily religious, it's kind of hard to get into." Explaining the twelve steps of recovery, he said, "It goes hand in hand with the Bible. And it's very—I mean God is like every other word."

Youth linked religion to recovery programs such as Alcoholics Anonymous. They also linked religion to accessing food. As Minnesota, a twenty-year-old white bisexual woman, detailed, "I just went to my first like little religious thing. Which, God damnit, if I have to go to another one, I'm going to kill myself. I didn't realize it was a religious thing. But they have food over there."

Trinity, who ran away from her gender-segregated CPS placement, refused to access some services on the streets that had religious affilia-tions. During the interview, she told me, that besides the drop-in center, she often got food at churches, but she stopped going to some churches. She explained, "Churches, for example, if you're like obviously homosex-ual, I feel like they look at you a certain way. They just disregard you. I find that that happens at a couple churches. And I haven't gone back since."

In *Pray the Gay Away*, sociologist Bernadette Barton introduces the con-cept of the "Bible Belt panopticon." In Bible Belt states, such as Texas, Christian symbols and Christianity are ubiquitous. And conservative

Christian establishments teach that LGBTQ people must self-discipline and self-police their gender and sexual identities and behaviors. The Bible Belt panopticon also warns LGBTQ people not to disclose their identities, because if they do, they risk losing their familial and community ties.[27] This belief works to produce LGBTQ youth as inferior and different, as sinners.

This Bible Belt panopticon also extends to services for people experiencing homelessness. Recovery programs often have a religious foundation or undertone. Churches also are a main source for accessing food. As Trinity noted, however, religious-based services, particularly if staff or volunteers display some form of prejudice, may repel LGBTQ youth or cause them to self-police any "obviously homosexual" behavior to avoid a disapproving gaze from religious volunteers or social service providers. In effect, LGBTQ youth experiencing homelessness may have more difficulties than other youth in accessing services that can help them.

Andres was a friend of Trinity. A twenty-three-year-old Hispanic gay youth, Andres wore aviator glasses, purple lipstick, and a tank top when we talked about his initial wariness regarding the Austin drop-in center where I met him. "I grew up in a really religious community. And so, I did a 'pray the gay away' for about six months." He recounted his experience with that program. "With this pray the gay away—at the end of it—I almost felt like I hurt [my family] even more. Because I was letting them to believe that there was a hope. I myself was convincing myself that there was a hope out of, like, wanting to satisfy other people and having their love still." In connecting these past experiences with religion to his initial hesitation of accessing services at the drop-in center, Andres explained, "'Cause it's a church, one. So, you think it's going to be weird. It's going to be what you always experienced at churches. But it wasn't at all, 'cause [the drop-in center] was not really affiliated with [the church in which the drop-in center was located]."

Religion and churches that serve communities of color often serve as a refuge from the racism experienced in the larger social world. But the church often upholds homophobic beliefs, creating conflicting experiences for many LGBTQ people of color.[28] In turn, the Bible Belt panopticon and the youth's responses to its gaze can take on particular and contradictory actions and feelings for LGBTQ youth of color. In his attempt to appease his religious family by going to a "pray the gay away" program,

Andre realized that he hurt them by giving them false hope. But he believed he needed to be Christian and heterosexual for his family to love him. Thus, religion interconnects with other institutions, such as the family. These institutions and institutional actors—through the queer control complex—come together to police and punish LGBTQ youth, and the result is to produce them as inferior. Furthermore, places such as the drop-in center—because of its location in a church or seeming affiliation with religion—drive away youth who may desperately need their services. Andres managed to overcome this hesitation, but some LGBTQ youth cannot perform the labor of reaching out to religious-affiliated services, especially if they experienced a great deal of pain and punishment from religious people and/or religious messages during their childhood.

Andres's good friend Jasper, a twenty-three-year-old mixed-race homosexual, discussed with me the policing of his gender and sexuality at a Christian-based recovery program that a judge sent him to instead of jail. "You have to go to like classes and groups with them—like Bible study, and church, and CR, which is 'Celebrate Recovery,'" Jasper explained. "It's like they took AA, and they were like how can we completely just ruin this program. And it's not about your addiction. It's about your hurts, habits, and hang-ups." Talking with me in the choir room at the drop-in center, Jasper mimicked the people who taught him at the recovery program. He imitated, "There's one true God! And what's his name? Jesus Christ! If you don't find him, you're not going to stay sober."

In a telling example of religious monitoring of behavior, Jasper detailed his conflict with this program. "One day, I went back to work. And they were like, 'What is this in [your] locker?' And it was a sweater and part of the sleeves were laced. And they were like, 'You can't have this. It's a woman's shirt.'" He continued,

> And I had some unisex cologne. And they were like, "This is a woman perfume." And that's what made me mad the most. I was like, how ignorant. It's a scent. The only thing that makes it for men or women is the label. . . . And two weeks down the road, it happened again. And it just made me mad. 'Cause I had a scarf. And they called me down. And they were like, "What's this?" And I was like, "It's a scarf." And this guy was like, "No, it's not." And I was like, "Yea, it's a scarf." He was like, "Jasper, this is what women wear to the beach." And I was like, "A sarong?" I was so angry.

Staff members punished Jasper for these gender transgressions. "They wrote me up. They put me on restriction," he recounted. "And I wasn't allowed to leave for a month unless I had an appointment. And those write-ups, you get four of them, and they can kick you out." Jasper linked part of this punishment to his sexuality. "They know I'm gay. And I feel like they purposely—whether or not it was on purpose or not—in their mind, that was something they were looking for." Service providers at the Austin drop-in center petitioned the court to get Jasper out of this program and into another program before staff suspended him, which would have violated his probation orders.

Although court-mandated recovery programs allow people to avoid imprisonment, these programs still penalize and involve supervising, controlling, and monitoring people.[29] As Black and Brown people get caught up more often in carceral systems—because of racial inequality and racial profiling (as discussed in the next chapter)—the policing of Jasper's Brown body could be what shaped his arrest, the judge sending him to this program, and the program's staff policing his gender and sexuality. This policing then led to the staff putting Jasper on restriction and almost expelling him. These policing processes, instead of helping Jasper, ended up labeling him a bad queer. Finally, a judge allowed Jasper to leave this program and go to a nonreligious halfway house.

Religion and its labeling of LGBTQ people as abominations and sinners make up part of the queer control complex. Negative religious messages work to produce LGBTQ people as different, as bad, as less than others. Some youth even internalize these negative messages and try to change their sexuality. Others may take them as just a necessary part of LGBTQ life experience. But the effect for LGBTQ youth experiencing homelessness is fewer services, as some cannot or will not access faith-based assistance programs, which are most of the services helping the poor today. Youth in this study have often already left their home, schools, and state child custody systems. Now, they also face barriers in accessing services for people living on the streets.

In this sense, religion, as part of the queer control complex, creates pathways into homelessness through negative messages about LGBTQ people in churches, families, and other social institutions. The queer control complex then continues to affect the lives of LGBTQ youth experiencing homelessness with further discipline and punishment from religious-affiliated services that raise barriers to youth getting their needs met. The youth thus keep living on the streets, as the queer control complex makes it difficult to find anywhere else to go.

WORKPLACE

Barriers also occur in relation to getting a formal-sector job, perpetuating homelessness for some people, including some youth in this study.[30] For starters, a job application asks for an address. Some people do not have an address or do not want to list a shelter as their address.[31] A potential employee also needs to present cleanly and neatly in proper clothes and have a telephone number, a social security number, a work history, work references, transportation to the job, and a clean criminal record.[32] As discussed in the next chapter, many youth in this study had criminal records. Youth also had to often rely on clothing closets to find clothes and shoes to wear to work or job interviews. At times, the center didn't have clothes that fit the youth. Or the clothes did not meet someone's work uniform requirements. For instance, during fieldwork, Minnesota worked at Papa John's and needed Khaki pants, but during the time I volunteered at the Austin drop-in clothing closet, the center often had no Khaki pants available.

Along with these general barriers, other obstacles existed related to policing and disciplining the youth's gender and sexuality. As Arthur—the twenty-five-year-old Black gay youth who fought back against his bully—explained to me, "I dress every now and then. Like when it's a day when I'm bored, and I just want to dress up and be pretty. Like, I'm a pretty boy, period. I like to wear makeup. But sometimes I gotta be a man 'cause jobs don't like it." Arthur, in turn, often self-policed his own gender expression when going to work.

Other youth experienced bullying from coworkers. Andres—the Hispanic gay youth who discussed his experiences in a "pray the gay away" program—talked with me about coworkers policing his sexuality and gender expression. "A lot of the guys at the places I worked at have been really mean to me," he stated. "The guys were saying, 'Did you need a glass of water—like a cold glass of water?' And I'd be like, 'Yea, that'd be awesome.' And they'd be like, "'Cause you're going to need that in hell.'" Sitting upstairs with me at the drop-in center in the director of street outreach's office, Andres continued, "And then they were like, 'You have HIV dude. If you don't have it now, you're going to have it.'" Andres saw part of this harassment as coworkers' negative reactions to his gender appearance. "Sometimes I do wear a skimpy shirt . . . but it makes them so uncomfortable," Andres exclaimed. "And it makes me uncomfortable if I'm like any other way. And I identify as a man. And I definitely like who I am. And feel like I was born this way for sure. Like there's nothing wrong now with me. It's just like society's problem with me."

During this study, no employment protections for sexual orientation, gender identity, and gender expression existed in the federal laws. These protections, though, would not end workplace discrimination, but they could provide some recourse to respond to workplace harassment. The structure of the workplace will need to change too, however. Arthur and Andres described the workplace as built on dominant notions of gender and sexuality. Arthur—who sometimes went by Isla Emerald when dressed in wigs, heels, and form-fitting clothing at the LGBTQ shelter—policed his appearance to fit into the workplace. Andres's coworkers tried to discipline Andres's gender and sexuality through their harassment. As a Brown gay man, who said he looks like a mixture of Bruno Mars and Napoleon Dynamite, Andres may experience heightened surveillance and harassment due to his being Brown. Indeed, racism and racial/ethnic bullying also prevalently occur in the workplace.[33] This racism in the workplace often consists of a type of gendered racism. For example, Black men say coworkers often see them as angry, threatening, and intimidating—stereotypes of Black masculinity.[34] But gay men of color with expansive expressions of gender such as Arthur and Andres may experience a greater degree of workplace surveillance. This workplace bullying and policing also produce LGBTQ people of color as deviant—as bad queers. The bullying also pushes LGBTQ people of color out of the workplace, making gaining economic security more difficult. This harassment, and need to act vigilant against the harassment, means that LGBTQ youth must do the labor of changing their work appearance as well.

Transgender youth also talked about workplace discrimination. Adelpha—the Black, Mexican, and white heterosexual transgender woman who discussed her experiences in child state custody systems—also experienced discrimination and barriers to employment in the formal economy. Sitting on the couch with me, she wore a black shawl and ate dinner, explaining why she thinks employers don't hire transgender people. "It's a whole bunch of bullshit, 'cause a lot of people just don't—especially fast food jobs—I don't think that they really want to hire somebody that's trans, 'cause you're in the public eye. I guess, they don't want customers to not come because of that trans person is working there." She went on to give an example of discrimination in hiring practices. "I went to the River Walk [a tourist part of San Antonio]. And I went into this one place all makeuped out, everything, dressed to the tee. And [an employer] was like, 'Okay sir. Your application is here, sir. Have a nice day, sir.' I'm just like so fuckin' pissed off cause like—if you don't know what to call me, leave it alone," she stated. "And then when it's public, everybody hears it. So, you're just like, 'Oh, awkward.' Just walked in here like a female, and then they just outed you to everybody."

Naomi—the eighteen-year-old bisexual transgender Latina whose mom pulled her out of school because of bullying—also experienced harassment at her job. She even said that she lost a job partly due to her manager discriminating against her. "When I first got there, [a manager] was already telling the other coworkers that I was a tranny," Naomi explained. "She said, 'I wish I was on her hormones, 'cause her boobs are growing bigger than mine.' I was like—it was so awkward." One day, the manager and Naomi got into a disagreement, and the manager fired Naomi from the job. "I was like, 'Okay, but next time you treat somebody doing this job, you need to make sure that you don't treat them mean. And you do it right, actually. And don't be so fucked up to them.'" Naomi continued, "I was like, 'You know what you did was illegal, right?' I said, 'You know what you did was discrimination, in every freakin' way?' I was willing to work. But the whole fucking being transgender thing. And I said I wish I was normal."

Transgender people often face harassment in the workplace.[35] Given racial discriminatory hiring practices and racism in the workplace, transgender women of color face a host of obstacles in hiring and in dealing with workplace discrimination. Adelpha felt employers did not want transgender employees, particularly if part of the job involved interacting with the public. Not hiring transgender people for jobs that require face-to-face interaction with customers erases transgender people, especially transgender people of color, from the public sphere. Adelpha, as well, experienced discrimination in the hiring process, while also having the person out her to everyone else in the room, generating feelings of awkwardness.

Adelpha faced discrimination in hiring practices, whereas Naomi discussed discrimination once hired. The harassment from Naomi's manager, including the manager outing Naomi to her coworkers, dehumanized her and reduced her to her body parts. Naomi felt that people see transgender people as not normal, and hence, treat them differently in the workplace—making the workplace hostile for transgender workers while also upholding dominant relations of gender. Naomi confronted the harasser, and the manager fired her. This process again pushes LGBTQ people of color, especially transgender people of color, into economic insecurity.

The workplace comprises part of the queer control complex. From self-policing one's gender expression to perceived discrimination in hiring practices to harassment and bullying from coworkers and bosses, youth in this study discussed how the workplace disciplines and punishes their gender and sexuality. These practices uphold the gender binary and structure the workplace as heteronormative. As racism also shapes the workplace, LGBTQ people of color face unique challenges in having their racial embodiment, gender expression, and sexuality all under antagonistic scrutiny in the workplace. These discriminatory processes constitute them as bad queers—pushing them out of the workplace and generating more economic insecurity in their lives.

As explored in the following chapters, probation requirements or shelter residence often stated that youth needed a job in the formal economy. Discrimination in the workplace, however, makes it difficult for youth to maintain a formal-sector job. Furthermore, lacking income means people experiencing homelessness cannot get off the streets. As LGBTQ youth experiencing homelessness are locked out of the formal economy, they often turn to the informal economy such as sex work and selling drugs. These discriminatory workplace experiences create further barriers to getting off the streets.

INSTITUTIONS, BAD QUEERS, AND LGBTQ YOUTH HOMELESSNESS

This chapter introduced the concept of the queer control complex to put forth an analysis on the punishment and disciplining of LGBTQ youth, especially of poor gender-expansive LGBTQ youth of color. The queer control complex shows how schools, state child custody systems, religion, and the workplace punish and discipline expansive expressions of gender and its association with homosexuality. This punishment often mainly targets Black and Brown people and produces poor transgender and gender-expansive Black and Brown youth as bad queers.

As I documented in the previous chapter, families engage in these disciplinary and punitive processes as well. Shelters, services for people experiencing homelessness, community centers, and other institutions can also make up part of the queer control complex. This concept even expands beyond youth to include how institutions and institutional actors police gender, sexuality, race, and LGBTQ adults. LGBTQ youth, however, experience the queer control complex in particular ways when navigating institutions such as families and schools that are meant to protect and nurture youth.

Notably, the queer control complex comes together through patterns of processes such as bullying and gender policing that happen within a variety of institutions. Youth experience bullying at home, but they find no respite in school, church, or the workplace. After being bullied all day at other institutions, they return home to more abuse. These institutions are connected in other ways as well, such as when school officials report abuse at home and the state then sends the youth to state child custody systems, where LGBTQ often again experience rejection and bullying.

Through this policing of expansive embodiments and enactments of gender and non-heterosexuality, institutional actors produce LGBTQ youth as unwanted and disposable, which pushes some LGBTQ youth to the streets and to jails. This production of disposability mutually constitutes the youth as bad queers through policing expansive expressions of gender and Black and Brown people and bodies. These intersecting processes constitute poor transgender and gender expansive Black and Brown youth as deviants, as criminals. The queer control complex sets the youth up to experience homelessness and perpetuates homelessness once on the streets.

In part, certain LGBTQ youth experience homelessness because dominant systems and institutions do not account for multiple marginalizations. Indeed, legal scholar Kimberlé Crenshaw coined the term *intersectionality* to show how an institution—the law—could not account for the multiply marginalized locations of women of color.[36] Dominant systems and institutions don't serve marginalized youth. Institutions and institutional actors instead serve to discipline and punish youth who deviate from the dominant modes of relation in society and to produce hierarchies of difference. In other words, if dominant institutions serve the purpose of punishment and discipline, then they are doing their job. Part of their job extends to carceral systems, through punishing and funneling certain youth to jails and into disposability. For some LGBTQ youth, the queer control complex pushes them to the streets and into contact with police. I now turn to the streets, police, and carceral systems and practices.

3 New Lavender Scare

POLICING AND THE CRIMINALIZATION
OF LGBTQ YOUTH HOMELESSNESS

"You can't really sit on a park bench. You'll get in trouble for that," stated Justice, an eighteen-year-old Black heterosexual transgender woman. With her face "beat for the gods"—meaning her makeup was flawless—she went on to describe her previous police encounters. "Since it's a high crime-rate area downtown, the cops can pretty much stop you whenever they want—for whatever they want—and search you and put you in cuffs until they are done." Justice said she got a "criminal trespass warning" for sitting at a bus stop in downtown San Antonio. "Being homeless, I'm just trying to have somewhere to sit. And so, one night, I was really tired, and I just happened to sit down. And the cops came by—whoop whoop—came and picked me up." She continued, "Then another time, I was just walking by some cops, and they stopped me. Saw that I had a warrant because I didn't go to court. So, I was in jail for a warrant for criminal trespassing." Explaining why she had come to the shelter for LGBTQ youth experiencing homelessness, Justice stated, "I got out of county, and I came over here. Just 'cause I knew it was going to be a cycle: sleeping on the streets, going to jail, coming out, sleeping on the streets, going to jail, coming out, sleeping on the streets."

Run-ins with police and cycling in and out of jail are common among many people living on the streets. Police encounters for people experiencing homelessness often occur due to "quality-of-life" ordinances in US cities. These ordinances make illegal many behaviors associated with homelessness, including sitting or lying down in public, sleeping in parks, camping in cities, aggressive panhandling, loitering, peeing outside, and other life-sustaining activities for people living on the streets.[1] Although technically these laws apply to everyone, in practice, police have the power to decide *where* to police and *whom* to police. For example, could we imagine a police officer ticketing a wealthy, elderly white woman sitting on a park bench or at a bus stop? But police charged Justice—who often lived and worked on the streets—with trespassing. As she could not or did not pay the fine or go to court, the charge escalated into a warrant for her arrest.

Significantly, these police encounters and the implementation of quality-of-life ordinances are tied to the policing of gender and sexuality. As we sat outside the LGBTQ shelter one early summer morning, Justice told me, "I mean, I always knew how to be good, ya know? Just try to avoid the police. But they had bothered me before. For example, one of the officers ticketed me for using the women's restroom downtown." Justice said that police frequently stopped and harassed her but did not protect her. After I met Justice, a date raped her.[2] "The police didn't do nothing," she stated. "When I got raped and almost killed, the police came, and they had that guy's license plate and face on camera. And the police officer told me, 'It's not that important.'"[3] Justice linked this police indifference to police profiling transgender people. She explained, "Because I'm transgender, they think I'm just out there trying to hook and stuff, and that's not even the case most times."

NEW LAVENDER SCARE

A 500 percent increase in the number of people incarcerated in the United States has taken place over the past forty years.[4] The United States incarcerates more people than any other country in the world, accounting for close to 25 percent of the world's prison population, despite the US population composing less than 5 percent of the world population.[5] As part of this "hyper-incarceration," police and other agents of the state target poor Black

and Brown neighborhoods, and thus, agents of the state have disproportionately imprisoned poor Black and Brown people, while also devastating
their communities and lives.[6] Legal scholar Michelle Alexander calls this
era of hyper-incarceration "the new Jim Crow," drawing attention to how
current incarceration practices perpetuate racial inequality through the discrimination and subjugation of Black and Brown people, despite laws no
longer explicitly discriminating against people of color.[7]

Hyper-incarceration and other carceral processes, though, do not relate
only to race and class. They also relate to gender and sexuality. I posit that
we live in an era of *the new Lavender Scare*—of current hyper-incarceration
practices extending to the punishment and criminalization of LGBTQ people. And these practices can be seen particularly in the criminalizing and
hypersexualizing of Black and Brown youth and their expansive expressions of gender.

For instance, although lawmakers in San Antonio passed an ordinance in
2013 decreeing that people can use the restroom that aligns with their gender identity, Justice said police ticketed her for using the women's restroom.
Police also ticketed her for trespassing. Police discretion in ticketing thus
enables them to target transgender women of color in the public sphere.
Police may have profiled Justice for violating quality-of-life ordinances
because she was seen as a sex worker. This trans profiling—police stopping
her for being a transgender woman of color—derives from police perceiving
certain Black or Brown people's expansive expressions of gender as sexually
deviant. Police respond discriminatorily.[8] This practice criminalizes people
of color, transgender and gender-expansive people, and poor people, furthering their marginalization and constructing poor transgender and gender-
expansive people of color as deviant criminals. In effect, Justice said that
when she appeared in the public sphere, police harassed, ticketed, and/or
arrested her. From these negative interactions, Justice viewed police officers
as indifferent toward, or even actively making worse, *her* quality of life.

Importantly, policing and punishing practices toward LGBTQ people
have historical roots. As historian David K. Johnson documents, the original Lavender Scare began in the late 1940s, during the Cold War, and
lasted nearly twenty-five years.[9] The federal government fired gay and lesbian people because of their sexuality.[10] Government officials saw gay and
lesbian people as "security risks" whom communist operatives might easily

blackmail. This apprehension—or moral panic, as no proof existed—that gay and lesbian people posed a threat to national security drove officials to remove people so designated from federal government positions. In 1953, President Eisenhower even signed Executive Order 10450, barring gay and lesbian people from federal employment, a ban that lasted until 1975.

In conjunction with the federal witch hunt to rid the federal government of gay and lesbian people, vice squads in Washington, D.C., and other cities began policing gay, lesbian, and gender expansive people. Through campaigns such as the Pervert Elimination Campaign, vice squads would "clean up" urban areas through raids on gay bars and bathhouses and by cracking down on same-sex liaisons in city parks. Police often stopped, questioned, and recorded the identity of any man in a known gay cruising area. These campaigns systematically harassed and intimidated gay men and charged them with disorderly conduct, loitering, indecency, or other violations.[11] Police also arrested people for cross-dressing, which lawmakers and cities codified as a type of fraud. Vice squad officers would sometimes share these arrest reports with government officials to assist with purging gay and lesbian people from the government. Significantly, the Stonewall riots of 1969, often credited as the birth of the LGBTQ movement in the United States, directly responded to these police raids and arrests. Even before Stonewall, the Lavender Scare compelled people to picket the White House against these acts of discrimination.[12]

The policing of LGBTQ people today, as well as the overrepresentation of LGBTQ people in jails and prisons, continues this history of punishing and criminalizing non-heterosexuality and expansive expressions of gender. Lesbian, gay, and bisexual people experience incarceration three times more than heterosexual people. Over 40 percent of incarcerated women identify as lesbian or bisexual.[13] One in six transgender people have experienced incarceration, with almost half of Black transgender people such as Justice experiencing incarceration at some point in their life.[14] Furthermore, LGBTQ youth make up around 15 percent of youth in juvenile legal systems, despite making up about 5 to 8 percent of the overall US youth population.[15] These numbers sound an alarm, but they do not allow us to see how carceral processes happen in LGBTQ people's daily lives and how certain LGBTQ people are affected by this era of hyper-incarceration.

In this chapter, I document how policing gender and sexuality—particularly policing expansive expressions of gender and expressions of sexuality that challenge heteronormativity—intertwine with processes of criminalization, urban policing, and incarceration. These carceral processes interconnect with policing poverty and Black and Brown people and bodies. These processes also try to create a sanitized urban public landscape. Sociologist Beth Richie has shown in her analysis of the "New Jersey Four"—a case about gender-expansive Black lesbians whom a judge sentenced to prison after they acted in self-defense against an attack in Greenwich Village—that during the trial people made constant references to the gender appearances of the accused as a threat to public safety. As Richie writes, "The convictions and the long sentences are important lessons about increased intolerance for perceived gender transgressions and open displays of nonhegemonic sexuality in the now much-less-tolerant Greenwich Village."[16] The criminalization of poor people and youth of color intersects with criminalizing expansive expressions of gender and perceived signs of homosexuality. Hence, poor Black and Brown LGBTQ youth bear the brunt of carceral practices, as they often do not have the economic, cultural, and racial capital to protect themselves.[17] Indeed, Justice voiced that police profiled her because she was a Black transgender woman living on the streets. As she lacked resources to challenge tickets and police harassment, these experiences kept Justice cycling between the streets and jails, furthering her experiences of instability and homelessness. I show in this chapter, then, that urban policing, incarceration, and other carceral practices contribute to homelessness and the subjugation of LGBTQ people, especially poor Black and Brown LGBTQ youth. These criminalizing processes also work to mutually co-constitute poor LGBTQ people of color in the public sphere as deviants and as criminals.

POLICING AND THE CRIMINALIZATION OF YOUTH HOMELESSNESS

Every week I saw police cars patrolling the neighborhood where the shelter in San Antonio was located. A few months into my fieldwork, I noticed blue-light emergency telephone boxes in the neighborhood. I had never seen blue-light boxes in a neighborhood before.[18] I had only seen them on college campuses, where students press a button on the blue-light system to contact police or campus security. These blue-light boxes meant that police could appear at the push of a button. On college campuses, the blue-light system gives some students a sense of safety. For marginalized people living on the streets, blue lights mean police surveillance, especially for the youth in this study who didn't see the blue lights or police as being there to protect them. Indeed, the constant police harassment in the lives of people experiencing homelessness causes them to not see police as a source of security at all.[19]

In Austin, I often saw police parked outside the drop-in center, and some days, police stood outside the entrance of the drop-in center. The police presence increased during freshman orientation at the University of Texas and during major Austin events such as the Austin City Limits and South by Southwest festivals. As Ciara, a twenty-two-year-old Black Hispanic bisexual woman, told me, "The state capital is taking over, and they're not—they're kicking more people out and arresting more people than anything. Homeless people are strictly bad for business. And they try to kick all of the homeless out of Austin is what I think."

Police interactions often increased feelings of vulnerability and instability for youth experiencing homelessness. The over-policing made the youth constantly move and subjected them to contact with carceral systems through ticketing. As Andres, a twenty-three-year-old Hispanic gay youth, explained, "I'll be sitting at a bus stop, bench, or something like that, and they will definitely come up and be like, 'You've got to move.'" Likewise, Winston, a twenty-four-year-old African American homosexual, stated, "Now even if you're not doing anything wrong, and you're homeless, and you're downtown, the police are going to try to get you for some stupid reason—whether you're just sitting down on a bench trying to cool off from the freakin' heat." Winston's best friend, Prada, a twenty-three-year-old Hispanic heterosexual transgender woman, told me about her park curfew violation. "The ticket I got—I was barely, fairly new here—I was like brand-new to Texas, so I didn't know the curfews to the parks or anything." Also, Jerico, a twenty-two-year-old Hispanic bisexual youth, said police gave him a ticket for camping. "They supposedly said we were camping. Like really? I told them, 'If we're camping, where's our tent? Where's our stuff?'"

People living on the streets inhabit the realm that police place under surveillance the most—the public sphere. Hence, police encounters frequently occur for people experiencing homelessness.[20] The police contact also increased with urban gentrification, zero-tolerance policing, and broken-windows theory. As middle-class people moved back to urban centers, gentrification in urban areas skyrocketed. Middle-class people wanted to "clean up" cities. These middle-class residents along with others, such as business owners, complained to police about the presence of people experiencing homelessness. Lawmakers and police responded to the public presence of people experiencing homelessness with zero-tolerance policies, as informed by broken-windows theory. This theory states that minor signs of disorder lead to more serious crimes. Something such as a broken window on a building theoretically encourages people to break into the building or vandalize it.[21] Out of this logic, police and lawmakers saw minor offenses such as loitering, littering, and panhandling as potentially leading to more serious crimes. Lawmakers passed quality-of-life ordinances, and police began applying broken-windows theory to people and their behaviors.[22] This zero-tolerance policing and harsh response to violations of quality-of-life ordinances detrimentally affects people experiencing homelessness, who engage in life-sustaining activities that lawmakers and police have criminalized. In criminalizing certain behaviors, police and lawmakers essentially criminalize people experiencing homelessness. And people living on the streets often don't have anywhere to go to escape police surveillance.

Policing and the criminalization of homelessness particularly affect youth living on the streets, especially Black and Brown youth. In *Youth in a Suspect Society*, cultural critic Henry Giroux explains that many people in society no longer see young people as an investment in the future. Rather, people now view Black and Brown youth as the cause of social problems—as lazy, dumb, spoiled, and a liability. Giroux states, "Poor minority youth have become especially targeted by modes of social regulation, crime control, and disposability that have become the major prisms that now define many of the public institutions and spheres that govern their lives."[23] Instead of addressing the insecure wage work and other social problems that young people face, lawmakers use policing and incarceration to punish poor Black and Brown youth.[24]

According to Andres, Winston, Prada, and Jerico—all youth of color—police harassed them, told them to keep moving, and ticketed some of them, even with no evidence for camping or breaking another ordinance. Likewise, police targeting of certain areas, such as downtown, and certain people, such as Black and Brown people, makes the crime statistics in those areas go up and skews the racial demographics of who supposedly commits crimes. These arrests and crime statistics then create the sense that people in certain areas engage in a lot of crime and need police intervention. These arrests and crime statistics also create the sense that Black and Brown people engage in more criminal activity, constructing them as deviants and criminals. Such police practices therefore end up punishing certain people for their young age, for their race, for their poverty, for experiencing homelessness, and for living in the public sphere.

STOPS, TICKETS, WARRANTS, ARRESTS, RECORDS

Julian, a twenty-two-year-old Hispanic gay youth, told me how he was harassed daily. Police made him move, ran his name, and checked his record for warrants. "We're looking for new places," he said, "'cause the cops just came through and told everyone to go other places and do other things. So now we're trying to look for another spot." While we were at the drop-in center in Austin, I asked Julian why he thought police hounded people living on the streets. He sarcastically replied, "Well, you know, 'cause we're the only things breaking the law 'cause we're sitting on the sidewalk. . . . So, every time I'm sitting down, they run my name. They run my name every chance they get. And they're trying—just waiting for one of my warrants to pop up. They're waiting 'cause they know I'm not trying to get in trouble. So, they're just trying to get me." When I asked Julian how often these police encounters occurred, he responded, "Every frickin' day."

With the erosion of welfare benefits and services, some people think that the state has abandoned the poor. Sociologist Victor Rios states, however, that "the state has not abandoned the poor but instead has punitively asserted itself into various institutions in the community."[25] Stops, tickets, warrants, arrests, and records create obstacles in people's lives, furthering their experiences of instability and criminalization. Tickets for violations of quality-of-life ordinances often turn into bench warrants if the person does not or cannot pay the ticket. This process allows police to jail people experiencing homelessness.[26] These arrests and criminal records then lead to disqualifications from jobs, housing, and social services. Each run-in with police generates fear of going to jail, creating more instability in the youth's lives.[27] Julian wanted to stay out of trouble, but he said police constantly harassed him, a common problem for Black and Brown youth, especially youth such as Julian who embody and enact expansive expressions of gender.[28]

Furthermore, police often hinder youth from accessing services. Kelsey, a twenty-two-year-old Black woman, who described her sexuality as "kind of everything," discussed her encounters with police. "If you stay in one spot every day, all day, the cops will come over, and they'll ask you, 'Hey, you've been hanging around here too long. You need to move around.' The cops don't like when you're just hanging out in one spot. With the homeless people, they think you're up to something bad."

We were sitting in a staff office at the Austin drop-in center. Kelsey, in gray leopard-print pants, boots, and a bright blue shirt, went on to describe an incident. "They came up to me before, and they gave me a ticket for no reason one day. They came up to me, and they were asking me what I was doing 'cause it was very early in the morning, and there was a church that serves breakfast in the morning. And I was going over there to the church to go hangout over there and go eat breakfast." The police did not believe her. "The cops said, 'There's no place open this early. You shouldn't be walking around.' And I said, 'I'm going to the church.' And I wasn't arguing with them or anything. And he stopped me. Tried to pull up my record." When nothing came up on Kelsey's record, they threatened to have her searched for drug paraphernalia but Kelsey said the police officers abandoned that prospect when they realized they would have to dispatch for a female police officer to come search her. "He gave me a ticket for jaywalking. He said I was jaywalking when I wasn't." Kelsey told me that she follows the law because she does not want to "get in trouble." "Being homeless, you can get problems. 'Cause some cops just like to harass just because you're homeless."

As Kelsey and other youth told me, police profiled people who "looked homeless" and forced them to move along. This displacement of people experiencing homelessness generates more instability for youth who have often already experienced instability in their homes, schools, and elsewhere in their lives. It also disrupts social networks and pushes people into more dangerous parts of town. Furthermore, policing of areas where homelessness services are located moves people experiencing homelessness away from needed services and hinders social workers from reaching the populations they serve.[29] Trying to access a morning meal, Kelsey instead got a citation for jaywalking.

Moreover, police disproportionately stop and frisk Black and Brown people.[30] Their treatment of Kelsey stemmed from larger racial profiling processes. Black and Brown youth experiencing homelessness disproportionately contend with racial biases in policing, since they often live outside, and hence, are constantly under the scrutiny of police. Police also run Black and Brown youth's names more often to check for warrants, resulting in a greater possibility of them going to jail.

Indeed, another major barrier exacerbating homelessness that arises out of these entanglements with police and carceral systems involves the mark of a criminal record. Rosario, a twenty-one-year-old Black bisexual youth, explained, "My felonies—it's probably going to be the hardest 'cause it's hard to find a job now with a felony. And recently being off parole makes it even harder 'cause they want people that have been off parole or been not incarcerated for at least six to twelve months." A twenty-two-year-old Black lesbian, Sade, linked her criminal record with difficulties in finding a place to live. "My background—getting my own place—people look at you have assaults, and they really don't care if its aggravated or not," she stated. "Some people don't even want to hear the story. So, it does make it a little more difficult."

In discussing the stigma of a criminal record and the challenges youth experiencing homelessness face, one service provider detailed to me, "Criminal record—it depends on what they have. So, they can have a felony—that might not be a big deal—just depends on what the felony was for. . . . Assault or drug charges, or like, sex offenders are gonna have a hard time—a harder time finding [a place to live] than someone who like stole something. And then, how long ago was it? All those things come into play." As another service provider also discussed with me, "You can't be at supportive housing if you have a felony. And most of our kids do. And most housing places you can't, if you have a felony. So even if they do have a job or are making—do have income—they can't get into an apartment because they have a record."

A criminal record perpetuates homelessness. Employers are one-half to one-third less likely to consider an ex-offender for a job. Moreover, racial inequality collides with the stigma of a criminal record. Black and Brown people disproportionately have criminal records due to over-policing and racial profiling in their communities. Employers also discriminate against a Black or Brown person in hiring, especially if they have a criminal record.[31] Likewise, criminal background checks make up part of rental housing applications, furthering the "institutional exclusion" that people with a criminal record face.[32] Laws also exclude people with a criminal record from other government benefits, including housing assistance, food stamps, and Pell grants to help with education.[33] Thus, the barriers in place against young Black women with a record such as Rosario and Sade make life difficult in terms of gaining employment and in getting housing—two things often needed to avoid experiencing homelessness.

In all these cases, police use of stops, tickets, warrants, arrests, and records against youth experiencing homelessness, especially against Black and Brown youth, furthered their experiences of instability and marginalization. Criminalizing the youth creates barriers to accessing services and gaining housing stability, which further marginalizes them and constructs them as deviant. In turn, the youth keep cycling between jails and the streets. The policing of expansive expressions of gender and sexuality that challenge the gender binary and heteronormativity brings about further barriers.

GENDER, SEXUALITY, AND CARCERAL PROCESSES

Trans Profiling: "Walking While Trans"

Like over-policing Black and Brown people, over-policing expansive expressions of gender and signs of non-heterosexuality directly relates to contact with carceral systems. Jenelle, a twenty-one-year-old Hispanic heterosexual transgender woman, discussed with me her experiences of trans profiling. "I would walk from maybe twelve at night to two in the morning and just walk around," she began. "And 'cause there was a known transgender prostitute that was known by everybody and was arrested multiple times, [police] assumed that I was a prostitute too. Because people think once you're transgender, obviously you're a prostitute." Jenelle attributed some of the police profiling to her attire. "Since, you know how when you are young and want to show as much skin as you can, I guess that's what got me in trouble." Jenelle said police have never arrested her but have stopped her "a couple times." She added, "And they check my ID, and I have nothing on my background, so they can't say anything." Jenelle felt, though, that police judged her when they checked her ID card. "They're always confused. And then when I have to give them my legal ID, that's when they're like, 'Oh, okay.' They take second looks at me. I'm just like, 'I'm sorry am I supposed to change into a guy now?' 'Cause it's weird. It's gross how they look at you."

People use the phrase "driving while Black" to capture how racial biases and racial profiling lead police to disproportionately pull over Black motorists. As a consequence, police disproportionately ticket, check the warrants of, and/or arrest Black people. Similarly, people use "walking while trans" to capture how biases around gender, sexuality, and race also shape policing practices. Police engage in trans profiling when they selectively decide to implement solicitation laws and other quality-of-life ordinances against transgender and gender-expansive people of color. For example, police often hypersexualize transgender and gender-expansive Black and Brown people. Part of this hypersexualization stems from police seeing transgender and gender-expansive people as always engaging in sex work. As police often view sex workers negatively as well, these stereotypes—along with the illegality of prostitution in most of the United States—influence police to stop and potentially ticket, check the warrants of, and/or arrest transgender and gender-expansive Black and Brown youth living on the streets. Some police view expansive expressions of gender as the intention to engage in prostitution. This profiling relates to policing sexuality and race, as police profile transgender and gender-expansive Black and Brown people as hypersexual—as sex workers. This profiling attempts to marginalize and erase transgender and gender-expansive people of color from the public sphere through arrests or trying to make them afraid of going into public spaces for fear of getting arrested.[34]

Jenelle attributed part of this profiling to her attire, that police attempted to regulate her sexuality through profiling her for dressing in ways they deemed too sexual for the public sphere. Or, again, police link showing skin on a Brown transgender body with sex work and thus profile Jenelle as a sex worker. Jenelle continued to dress how she wanted, but she experienced police stops and encounters. Jenelle also noted how not having the proper gender marker on her legal identification made these negative interactions with police more painful. Not having the proper gender marker could "out" someone to police as transgender—if police didn't already profile them as transgender—potentially causing further discrimination in the encounter. These experiences tell transgender people of color that police watch and profile them when they enter the public sphere. Policing practices that aim to uphold the heteronormativity of the public sphere and protect the privileged class, meaning mainly white, middle-class men, simultaneously criminalize poor Black and Brown transgender and gender-expansive people as hypersexual and deviant.

Police Discrimination and Mistrust

A twenty-two-year-old Hispanic heterosexual transgender woman, Camila, whom, along with Jenelle, I also met at the LGBTQ shelter, talked about her negative experiences with police. "I was assaulted about a month ago. And I made a report. And it's like—I let them know it was a hate crime. And—it's like they put me to the back. San Antonio PD [police department]—they don't really—they're really obvious about their bias toward the LGBT community. . . . And so, I got to a point where I don't even try to bother with the SAPD anymore—don't really help much." Camila elaborated, "And so, just being [at the LGBTQ shelter] just makes me feel somebody is really looking out for us. Somebody really cares about us."

Police also arrested Adelpha, an eighteen-year-old Black, Mexican, and white heterosexual transgender woman, when she went to report an assault. During my fieldwork in San Antonio, Adelpha had gotten into a fight with Arthur and Kareem—a Black gay couple, who, along with Adelpha, also stayed at the LGBTQ shelter. "Went to make an assault charge, got arrested," Adelpha told me. Instead of investigating the assault,

Adelpha said that police ran her name and a warrant in another county came up for her arrest. Police arrested her on site.

Sociologist Victor Rios calls this process the "overpolicing-underpolicing paradox." Police exist everywhere in the lives of marginalized youth, but police and laws do not protect the youth when they need help.[35] Criminologist Laura Huey documents a similar process among people experiencing homelessness—a process she calls the "security gap." People experiencing homelessness disproportionately experience other people committing crimes against them, but the state and police do not protect them. Police don't protect the security of people living on the streets.[36]

This paradox or gap also relates to upholding heteronormativity and the gender binary. As research has shown, police mishandle and often ignore crimes committed against transgender people such as Camila and Adelpha. This police indifference furthers negative interactions between transgender people and police.[37] Justice—who opened this chapter—even said that the police indifference toward a man raping her came from police viewing her as a sex worker. Police often do not take sex workers' allegations of violence seriously and may even arrest the sex worker when they report the crime if the sex worker has a warrant on their record.[38] Police, indeed, arrested Adelpha when she reported an assault. Warrant checking thus dissuades people experiencing homelessness and other marginalized groups from reporting crimes to police.[39]

This overpolicing-underpolicing paradox tells transgender and gender expansive Black and Brown youth that they deserve punishment but not protection and that their quality of life does not matter to the state. The state protects middle-class, white, heterosexual people and maintains dominant power structures. In turn, these practices produce poor people, people of color, and/or LGBTQ people as not worthy of the state's protection. Hence, some poor LGBTQ youth of color resist turning to police for help.

Discriminatory experiences continued after police arrested youth that I spoke to. "I was hanging out with a forty-year-old transgender girl that I met when I was seventeen," began Naomi, an eighteen-year-old bisexual transgender Latina, whom I also met at the LGBTQ shelter. "She had got a big pile of fucking jeans—five hundred dollars' worth—and stuffed it in the bag. And I was freaking out in the mall. She was like, 'Let's go.' ... "I was, like, 'Bitch, if I'm going to hold this shit and almost have it this far from my freaking hand, I'm going to take something for me.' 'Cause it wouldn't have even been worth it, if I get caught with this shit." Police caught her.

In talking about her subsequent experience at the police station, Naomi detailed, "[A police officer] was shoving me to the back. And . . . the fucking police officer in the back treated me so fucked up. . . . They took off my wig and said look at the camera. And they put the wig back on, they put it all the way back here [motioning to the back of her head]. I was like, this is so fucked up. This is discrimination."

For youth experiencing homelessness, peer support on the streets is sometimes the first social support they have ever received. But this social connection and peer support can sometimes influence youth experiencing homelessness to engage in criminalized behaviors.[40] Stealing with another transgender woman, Naomi got caught up in carceral systems. Once in contact with police, Naomi faced police harassment. Removing Naomi's wig and not putting the wig back on her properly constitute a form of defacement—a tactic to humiliate transgender women.[41] These negative experiences with police further erode any trust with police among transgender and gender-expansive people. And harassment creates another form of punishment on top of the punishment of the arrest, going to jail, and potentially getting a criminal record. These criminalizing practices further label transgender women of color as deviants and as deserving of punishment for challenging the gender binary and heteronormativity.

Gender Segregation of Jails and Prisons

Youth also discussed the issue of gender-segregated jail cells and prisons as another form of punishment after getting arrested. A nineteen-year-old white Hispanic lesbian, Alaina, said that police treated her "like a man." She explained, "[Police] say the same thing, 'Want to dress like a man? Going to beat you like a man.'" Alaina stated that police placed her "in the men's cell." She detailed, "He knew I was a girl. But he put me in there for about two hours. I said, 'You better move me to that girl cell. I'm a girl.' And then he was like, 'You want to be like a man, then I'll put you in a man's cell.'"

Cookie, a twenty-five-year-old Black heterosexual transgender woman, was sent to a men's prison for credit card fraud. We spoke in her room at the

LGBTQ shelter. "At first, it was horrible because I'm gay, and I'm in an all-male facility," Cookie explained. "And I fought and I earned my respect. . . . I beat up gang members to gangsters, you name it, because I refused to get pushed over. And actually, being there, that's where I got 'Cookie' from."

In a national study, researchers found that non-heterosexual youth do not engage in greater illegal behaviors than heterosexual youth, but non-heterosexual youth experience more criminal punishment.[42] The same study also showed that gender-expansive youth, particularly gender-expansive women of color such as Alaina, suffer a disproportionate amount of punishment within carceral systems. Furthermore, the gender segregation of jails and prisons, as a defining feature of carceral environments, affirms the gender binary.[43] Agents of the state use this gender segregation to punish transgender and gender-expansive people by placing them in cells that do not affirm their gender identity.

Gender segregation also leads to experiencing a great deal of hostility and violence for transgender and gender-expansive incarcerated people. For instance, agents of the state putting a transgender woman into a men's jail or prison automatically outs her as transgender. These spaces create unsafe environments for gender-expansive men as well. Cookie, who identified as a heterosexual transgender woman, often also called herself gay. The interchangeability of these terms captures how Cookie viewed herself, but also perhaps, how others viewed and treated her in jail. Often, people perceive transgender women as effeminate gay men, denying and erasing the possibility of transgender people. Police and other people in prison often harass transgender people and effeminate men, which means jails and prisons can be violent, unsafe spaces for LGBTQ people, and which further punishes them for their gender expression. Cookie said she resisted and had to constantly fight to gain respect. Transgender women in prison often struggle to find ways to garner respect and gain protection while still trying to affirm their gender identity in this masculine prison space.[44]

Solitary Confinement and Strategic Segregation

To keep transgender and gender-expansive people from experiencing violence from other inmates, some authorities at jails and prisons put transgender and gender-expansive people in solitary confinement. But

Camila—the twenty-two-year-old Hispanic heterosexual transgender woman who talked about police not helping LGBTQ people—saw solitary confinement as "horrible." "The guards definitely mistreated me," Camila stated. "I was put in lock down, 'cause they didn't want me in the same pod with my ex-boyfriend, which was what they considered the gay pod. So, I was put in lockdown. I was stuck in a cell all day by myself. It was pretty horrible."

People experience solitary confinement as another form of punishment. Through forced idleness, solitary confinement seeks to contain and manage people and their bodies.[45] This confinement also isolates people from human contact and generates stress, often taking a psychological toll on the confined person.[46] These conditions create compounding experiences of punishment beyond the punishment of being locked up.[47] Prison guards and administrative prison authorities punish and sentence people again—after their sentence to prison—through the discretion to use solitary, needing no judge or jury to review this decision.[48] Likewise, solitary confinement marks transgender and gender-expansive people as different—as supposedly needing their own separate space. Hence, transgender and gender-expansive people experience solitary confinement as differentially punitive.[49]

Historically, prison authorities have often tried to segregate incarcerated gay people to prevent sex in prisons.[50] This practice upheld the stereotype of all gay men as hypersexual. These continued practices of segregation and solitary confinement work to normalize placing transgender, gender-expansive, and/or non-heterosexual people in this inhumane, isolated space. As the documentary *Cruel and Unusual* shows, the use of solitary confinement to supposedly protect transgender people violates the Eighth Amendment against cruel punishment, as isolation and its mental health effects constitute cruel punishment.[51] Solitary confinement also works to further the marginalization and criminalization of transgender and gender-expansive youth, especially Black and Brown youth.

Notably, to avoid putting some LGBTQ people in solitary confinement, a specific gay and transgender cell block existed at the Bexar county jail in San Antonio. Adelpha—the eighteen-year-old Black, Mexican, and white heterosexual transgender woman whom police arrested when she reported an assault against her—described this cell block to me. "So then, I was in the sixth floor [of the jail]—with all the gay, trans, all that," she detailed. "That was fun, 'cause all we did was dance and sing. It was a cliché. But it was so fuckin' fun. We had group. We shared our feelings—how we felt."

Lawyer Sharon Dolovich, who studied a gay and transgender cell block in Los Angeles county, calls this type of cell block "strategic segregation." It helps protect non-heterosexual men and transgender women from physical and sexual assault within the general jail population. And as Dolovich argues, within the current carceral conditions, this state-sponsored, identity-based segregation serves as a best option in creating a safer carceral space for non-heterosexual men and transgender women.[52]

This cell block not only protected Adelpha from potential violence in the general population area but also allowed her to meet and bond with other non-heterosexual and transgender people. But the fact that jails and prisons serve as a main space for certain poor Black and Brown LGBTQ people to meet each other and find community should set off alarm bells. Although this cell block seems more humane than other jail conditions, it still confines LGBTQ people and effectively normalizes the punishment and criminalization of poor LGBTQ people of color by serving as a designated space to warehouse them. The fact that this cell block exists, in fact, reveals that poor transgender and gender-expansive Black and Brown youth face a great deal of criminalization in this era of hyper-incarceration.

Urban Policing and the Perpetuation of LGBTQ Youth Homelessness

The policing and punishing of expansive expressions of gender and non-heterosexuality also perpetuates experiences of homelessness. Zoe, a nineteen-year-old Hispanic heterosexual transgender woman recounted to me her experience leaving an LGBTQ bar in San Antonio one night. "I got harassed by a police saying I was prostituting. Just came out the club to sit down on the corner, 'cause, you know, that's the spot where the hookers go, where drags go, queens go. He threatened me that I better get off the fucking block or he was going to take me to jail." Another time, Zoe said, "[Police] thought I was working with Justice [a Black transgender woman] over here on Colorado Street. They harassed me. Yes, that's another thing—they harassed me. And I'm all the way over here on fucking Roosevelt Street, right?" Zoe told me that police treat LGBTQ people differently. "I know they do," she exclaimed. "I better give them head. I better suck their dick or else—or they will let me go. No baby, I respect my body too much to put your—to put you in me."

In a study on Black youth's experiences of urban policing, young Black men said police routinely treated them as suspects. The Black men also reported a great deal of police violence toward them. In the same study, young Black women said police often stopped them for curfew violations and expressed concern about police sexual misconduct.[53] Transgender women of color experience both processes. Police profile them as suspect, and some police sexually harass and assault them. As a study in Los Angeles County documented, police often verbally harass and physically and sexually assault transgender Latinas.[54] Police also sometimes bribe transgender Black and Brown youth for sexual favors, sexually objectifying and dehumanizing them.

Furthermore, police may assume all transgender women of color on the streets together are sex workers. In profiling Black and Brown transgender youth living on the streets, police also run their names to check for records. Hence, this trans profiling constantly brings transgender and gender expansive youth of color in contact with police and carceral systems. For instance, Zoe got into a fight one day with another transgender woman. Police saw the fight and handcuffed Zoe and the person she fought. Experiencing homelessness and living in the public sphere where police often patrol, Zoe—as a transgender woman of color—came under police scrutiny. When a warrant for Zoe came up for prostitution, police took her to jail.

To get Zoe out of jail, the director of the LGBTQ shelter submitted a letter to a judge on her behalf. The letter told the judge that Zoe had a place to live and that Zoe had done well living at the shelter. According to the director, a lawyer told her that county officials keep people experiencing homelessness in jail because county officials do not want people experiencing homelessness on the streets. "But by us being able to simply write a letter with a letterhead," the director explained, "saying that we have a program and that [Zoe] has a place to come back to—the fact that she had a place to come back to—she was able to get probation and not be sent to prison." The director detailed what an attorney told her about how police and county officials treat people experiencing homelessness in San Antonio. "Because if you're homeless, and you're convicted of something, you're gonna sit in jail," the director stated. "And the attorney told me that. I mean, I didn't know that. But he said the fact that you're able to say that [Zoe] has some place to return, they will give her probation and not send her to prison."

After getting out of jail, Zoe needed a job to meet her probation requirements. Having a criminal record and facing workplace discrimination as a transgender woman of color made finding a job difficult. Zoe often worried that if she did not find a job, she would go back to jail for violating probation. A contradiction occurs: youth with a criminal record find it difficult to get a reliable job, but one needs a job to fulfill probation requirements and prove that one has "rehabilitated" from their criminal past through this labor participation in the formal economy.[55] The probation requirement also ignores other structural barriers to employment, such as discrimination against transgender women of color in the workforce. These barriers make getting a job and compliance with post-release supervision requirements a form a discipline that poor transgender and gender-expansive Black and Brown youth struggle to achieve. The policing of gender and sexuality kept Zoe in constant contact with police— getting harassed, ticketed, and arrested—cycling between the jails, streets, and shelters. Each arrest record made getting a job and finding stable housing more difficult.

Zoe told me that all she wanted for Christmas was for her felony to get off her record. The last I heard, police had Zoe back in jail for another prostitution charge. The director of the shelter planned to go to court to testify on her behalf.

THE NEW LAVENDER SCARE AND LGBTQ YOUTH HOMELESSNESS

The new Lavender Scare shapes which people and bodies police and other agents of the state criminalize, arrest, and attempt to erase from the public sphere. The original Lavender Scare targeted white gay men and lesbians who worked in the federal government during a time when US society codified homosexuality and gender expansiveness as illegal through legislation such as anti-sodomy and anti-crossdressing laws. Now, agents of the state use their discretion in this era of hyper-incarceration to police LGBTQ people. This new Lavender Scare also intertwines with the new Jim Crow—targeting mainly poor Black and Brown transgender and gender-expansive youth in the public sphere. Racial processes shape the new Lavender Scare specifically through police targeting Black and Brown people and bodies that publicly challenge the gender binary and heteronormativity.

Police have targeted Black and Brown gender-expansive people in the past, of course, and many of these policing practices continue the discriminatory practices of the original Lavender Scare. The *new*, then, in the new Lavender Scare is how these policing practices do not remain static but adapt and change with the times—currently a time of gentrification, hyper-incarceration, quality-of-life ordinances, and other carceral processes. Jim Crow entailed de jure segregation, while hyper-incarceration (or the new Jim Crow) continues the de facto marginalization and subordination of poor Black and Brown people.[56] Relatedly, the original Lavender Scare entailed de jure discrimination against LGBTQ people, but now, in these times of advancing LGBTQ rights, the new Lavender Scare operates as de facto discrimination. Significantly, the new Jim Crow is harder to challenge than earlier forms of racism because many people do not see hyper-incarceration as explicitly about racial discrimination.[57] Challenging the new Lavender Scare may be harder as well. As I have written elsewhere, with the dominant societal notion that legal LGBTQ discrimination does not exist anymore, people tend to see these policing practices as targeting people engaging in criminalized behaviors—not about specifically targeting and criminalizing poor LGBTQ people of color.[58]

Furthermore, white, middle-class LGBTQ people also contribute to the new Lavender Scare. Many white, middle-class LGBTQ people partake in gentrification practices that push poor Black and Brown LGBTQ people out of their neighborhoods. Some support quality-of-life ordinances, upholding criminalizing processes that harm poor Black and Brown LGBTQ youth and perpetuate homelessness for some of them. For example, previous research has shown that in the Castro—a gay neighborhood in San

Francisco—and in Boystown—a gay neighborhood in Chicago—LGBTQ youth of color have reported feeling invisible, as these gay neighborhoods now mainly accommodate middle-class, white gay men. Community members in gay neighborhoods have even called police on LGBTQ youth of color. As gay neighborhoods transform into commercial spaces, often commodified for white gay men and straight women, community members and business owners see people experiencing homelessness and/or LGBTQ youth of color as not significantly contributing to businesses and as bringing crime to these neighborhoods. Hence, community members and business owners work to exclude LGBTQ youth experiencing homelessness from belonging in these LGBTQ spaces.[59] While the original Lavender Scare impacted the criminalization of middle-class, white LGBTQ people, now, many middle-class, white LGBTQ people invest in gentrification practices and carceral processes—processes that push further to the margins poor LGBTQ people of color.

Lawmakers and other authority figures reason that these arrests and other carceral practices are a way to "clean up" cities—now through quality-of-life ordinances. This policing of race, gender, sexuality, and class mutually co-constitute the youth as deviant, furthering the criminalization of poor Black and Brown non-heterosexual, gender-expansive, and transgender people. In turn, Black and Brown transgender and gender-expansive youth see that *their* quality of life does not matter to the state. Justice—who opened this chapter—and most other youth in this study not only experienced quality-of-life ordinances as making their quality of life worse but as the state threatening their lives—attempting to erase them from public spaces. Their erasure from the public sphere stems from lawmakers and agents of the state seeing them as "bad for business," as the youth Ciara stated in this chapter. Quality-of-life ordinances make middle-class, white people's lives better at the expense of marginalized people—people that some see as not contributing to capitalism, and hence, as not belonging to the nation-state.

Lawmakers and police not only use zero-tolerance policing as a primary way for the state to govern and deal with poverty and Black and Brown people but also for the state to govern expressions of gender and sexuality that challenge the gender binary and heteronormativity. Thus, the state grants police the power and legitimacy to uphold white heteronormativity in the public sphere. Youth experience, then, the policing of their gender, sexuality, and race as simultaneous, not as separate, analytical categories or experiences. For instance, police see Black and Brown gender-expansive people as a problem, often through hypersexualizing their bodies and seeing them as sex workers. Police see sex work also as a problem—the wrong way to make money under capitalism—and work to control LGBTQ people and uphold heteronormativity, the gender binary, and their intersections with other dominant structures.[60] These processes also contribute to the perpetuation of LGBTQ youth homelessness, as tickets, arrests, and criminal records make accessing services and getting employment and housing harder. The new Lavender Scare continues the policing, criminalizing, and erasing of LGBTQ people in US society, with the perpetuation of homelessness being one of the most punitive consequences of these carceral practices.

The youth, however, developed strategies to navigate the streets and to resist these forms of oppressions. I turn, in the next chapter, to the youth's queer street smarts.

4 Queer Street Smarts

Kelsey had her hair in a mohawk and wore a yellow tube top and purple shorts. "What makes it hard to get by is if you just don't know anything. If you don't utilize services—that's what makes it hard," she said. Kelsey is the twenty-two-year-old Black woman we met in the previous chapter who described her sexuality as "kind of everything." She went on to explain to me that people living on the streets need to find out "where you can go eat, where you can go take a shower, where you can go do your laundry, and everything."

A remarkable amount of knowledge and work goes into living on the streets. Imagine: You have nowhere to stay, no knowledge of a city's social services, no job, no ID card, no one to trust, no access to transportation, nowhere to clean yourself, and no sense of the weather forecast. What do you do? To obtain a job in the formal economy, you need an ID card and a social security card. To procure an ID card, you need an address, often money, and other forms of identification such as a birth certificate and school records. Many youth experiencing homelessness do not have these documents. If they do possess them, they often have no secure place to keep them. Minor barriers turn into major obstacles that make experiencing homelessness ever more frustrating and difficult.

But before worrying about an ID card and a job, the youth in this study faced two foundational necessities: finding a safe place to sleep and getting something to eat. As Trinity, a twenty-year-old white lesbian, explained, "I prefer to sleep in the woods. But if I need to, I'll sleep in like an alleyway or behind a dumpster or something. I know it's a dirty place. But it's the safest place, where no one's going to see me." Youth also slept in parks, by churches, in cars, at libraries, on friends' couches, and on rooftops. Andres—Trinity's friend from the Austin drop-in center—described to me how he accessed some rooftops. "I'd just climb the electric meters on the sides of the buildings because they're like little ladders that go up the wall." A twenty-three-year-old Hispanic gay youth, Andres also had creative strategies for finding food. "I'll just go to fine-dining restaurants. Or I'll go to like Red Lobster. And I'll just stand outside. And there always be like a skinny bitch that has leftovers and will want to not eat them," he detailed. "And so, I will definitely be like, 'Hey'—we call it whiteboxing— and so, I'll whitebox. And that's how I eat like a king now."

QUEER STREET SMARTS

Marginalized people develop street smarts to help them navigate their social worlds while coping with the insecurities of poverty and violence. Street smarts include forms of lower-class and working-class knowledge and forms of racialized knowledge, mainly used to navigate social structures while having limited resources. Marginalized youth of color even see street smarts as a vital body of knowledge in navigating racism and the public sphere, while book smarts represent white, middle-class ways of knowing.[1]

Youth experiencing homelessness also gain street smarts. As Melissa, a twenty-one-year-old white pansexual gender-fluid youth, told me, "You have all this shit to do to get your life straight. But you can't do any of it 'cause you don't have a car. You don't have money. You don't have clothes to wear to an interview." For youth experiencing homelessness, street smarts entail knowing how to navigate service systems, find ways to make money, deal with weather conditions, figure out public transportation routes and schedules, get and keep an ID card, meet daily needs, have a shower, look for laundry services or clean clothes, and trust someone to guard one's pets and/or belongings when going to job interviews or court-rooms or other places.[2]

Street smarts pertain not only to navigating the streets in relation to class and race, however, but also to how gender and sexuality operate within the public sphere. I call this knowledge *queer street smarts*—knowing how gender and sexuality shape the public sphere and finding strategies to navigate the heteronormative public landscape. For LGBTQ youth experiencing homelessness, developing queer street smarts helps in getting something to eat and finding a safe place to sleep. Importantly, class-based knowledge and race-based knowledge intersect with gender and sexuality knowledge to shape how the youth in this study develop queer street smarts.

For instance, Andres applied queer street smarts to gendered stereo-types about skinny women not wanting leftovers in order to find food for the day through whiteboxing. Queer street smarts also allowed Andres to understand that some people at campsites would spurn him because of peers' negative reactions to his sexuality. As we sat together in a staff office at the Austin drop-in center, he explained to me, "[Men at a campsite] wouldn't want to help me, or they wouldn't want to include me in some-times because of that reason—my sexuality. Like I would sometimes need a camp to stay at. And I'd be friends with one of the girls. But the boy-friend and all his friends at the campsite would want to be like, 'Ugh, no.'" Andres, instead, often slept alone on rooftops. These strategies, or queer street smarts, in response to heteronormative barriers often had unin-tended consequences. For example, sleeping alone could keep Andres iso-lated and without social support.

In this chapter, I show how the streets, shelters, and services for people experiencing homelessness uphold heteronormativity and the gender binary. Heteronormativity creates barriers for LGBTQ youth experiencing homelessness, especially for poor Black and Brown LGBTQ youth. Thus, the youth develop queer street smarts to navigate their public worlds. In describing these queer streets smarts, I capture the daily knowledge and strategies around gender and sexuality—along with race and class—that LGBTQ youth experiencing homelessness use to navigate the streets and service systems. I also document that many of these strategies often have

unintended consequences that leave the youth vulnerable and marginalized as they try to overcome the obstacles created by heteronormative and
other dominant social structures.

SEEKING SHELTER

"It is a cesspool of shit. Literally, the worst humanity has to offer congeals
there," stated Jonah, a twenty-three-year-old white bisexual man. Jonah
went on to describe a men's shelter in Austin that he refused to go to. "You
got kleptomaniacs who steal your dirty underwear if they can get a chance
to. You got people who get into fights every day. I saw a guy smoke crack
out of a TV antenna." We sat together in the choir room at the church
where the Austin drop-in was located. Jonah wore a button-up white shirt
and khakis, and his socks were full of holes. He told me that he preferred
sleeping in a parking garage to going to this shelter, saying, "It's bad when
you would rather sleep in a parking garage by yourself rather than be with
other people and at least have a soft little mat to sleep on."

Scholars who study homelessness have documented why some people
experiencing homelessness prefer living on the streets instead of staying
in a shelter. Like Jonah, many people living on the streets see shelters as
dirty and crime ridden. In addition, shelters are often located in dangerous parts of town and, as explored in more detail in the next chapter,
enforce strict rules and curfews and lack privacy. Some people prefer to
avoid shelter staff interfering in their lives. As shelter policies often frame
people experiencing homelessness as addicts who need rehabilitation,
some choose life on the streets, resisting service institutions that treat
them as a problem.[3]

Notably, for many LGBTQ youth in this study, harassment and discrimination based on gender and sexuality explicitly informed their resistance to
staying at shelters. Trinity, for example—the twenty-year-old white lesbian
who said in the opening of this chapter that she preferred sleeping in the
woods—linked her avoidance of the main shelter in Austin to the drugs
there and men sexually harassing her. "Have you walked outside that place?
Have you even gone within like a two-block vicinity?" she rhetorically
asked me. "That shit's insane. Drugs out of the ass. Crazy people out of the

ass. So many men out there that are so degrading to women as they're walking by down the street. It's disgusting." Jasper, a twenty-three-year-old mixed-race homosexual—whom I also met at the Austin drop-in center—told me why he does not go to the Austin shelter. "Being gay, I just sort of keep to myself, 'cause I don't want to deal with [being treated differently]. I think that's one thing for a lot of gay people who are homeless—from what I've seen—they just keep to themselves."

No shelter specifically for youth over the age of seventeen existed in Austin, Texas. Although some transitional living programs existed, the director of street outreach at my Austin field site told me that street youth often had a hard time following the rules in those programs. The youth often did not go to those programs and/or the drop-in center staff did not refer the street youth to them. Many youth also resisted going to adult shelters.

For women experiencing homelessness, the harassment and violence that comes from living outside in the masculine-dominated public sphere is a continuous ordeal. For this reason, women access shelters more than men, seeing them as safer than the streets.[4] But sexual harassment keeps certain women, such as Trinity, from accessing services and shelters. And Jasper believed that most gay people experiencing homelessness—including himself—refused shelter living so they could avoid people who treat gay people differently. This strategy, however, makes accessing services and social support difficult, potentially making the youth easier to exploit and abuse.

This resistance to shelters and services in avoidance of harassment and discrimination based on gender and sexuality prominently came up in San Antonio. There, the main place for people experiencing homelessness to access services was a large courtyard at the city's homelessness campus. At the courtyard, people got an identification badge—a blue badge for men and a pink badge for women—which corresponded with the gender-segregated sleeping arrangements and bathrooms. During most of my fieldwork, staff at the courtyard assigned badges based on a person's assigned birth gender. Justice, an eighteen-year-old Black heterosexual transgender woman, described to me how these formal policies and practices around gender segregation affected her. "They said I couldn't shower with the women," she detailed. "I couldn't sleep with the women because I wasn't a woman. I had an [officer at the courtyard] tell me I was not a woman. That was kind of hard for me."

The dominant notions of femininity, being based on whiteness, position Black women already outside of the dominant gender relations in US society. Poor Black transgender women such as Justice must contend with the surveillance of service providers and other authority figures, both for being transgender and for being Black. These policing processes—as tied to race, class, and gender—denied Justice her identity and kept her from meeting her needs.

During my fieldwork, however, the US Department of Housing and Urban Development (HUD), under Secretary Julián Castro, passed an Equal Access Rule stating that any organization funded under programs administered by HUD's Office of Community Planning and Development had to allow people to identify their own gender when accessing shelters and other services. By the end of my fieldwork, youth reported that staff at the courtyard were allowing transgender and gender-expansive people to decide which badge they wanted.

The changes in these formal policies had no effect on the culture, however, and the informal interactions in which LGBTQ people felt disrespected and unwelcome. The youth in this study still saw the courtyard as a dangerous place, and staff at the LGBTQ shelter echoed the common refrain that dogs in kennels are treated better than the people staying in the courtyard.

As Dante, a twenty-two-year-old Black bisexual youth, explained to me at the LGBTQ shelter, "First day I was in [the courtyard], I got picked on for hanging out with Justice [the Black transgender youth whom courtyard staff had barred from showering and sleeping on the women's side of campus]." He stated. "I beat somebody up. I beat them bad because they pissed on my shoes. They peed on my shoes because I was hanging out with Justice." Camila, a twenty-two-year-old Hispanic heterosexual transgender woman, also talked with me about her experiences of discrimination at the courtyard. "With [the courtyard], they really mistreat you if you're gay. It's not outright, so you can't just point it out." She went on to give an example. "Being on the streets, women have sexual assaults all the time. I mean, I was assaulted twice. And I tried getting help. I tried talking to people in [the courtyard]. And it's just like, they put you to the back—to the side—you know?"

LGBTQ youth experiencing homelessness often do not access services because of fear of stigmatization and unfair treatment.[5] They also encounter violence and harassment at shelters.[6] Formal policies such as gender segregation together with informal discriminatory interactions are thus both at the root of why LGBTQ youth often feel safer living on the streets.[7] Some youth in this study, including Justice, saw the courtyard as an important place to shower and get food. But experiences of discrimination at the courtyard made accessing services difficult. Transgender and gender-expansive youth had to deal with staff and other people misgendering them, as well as unsafe gender-segregated spaces.

Dante said he experienced violence because of his friendship with Justice. LGBTQ people need to form relationships and networks of social support. These friendships take on important meanings for LGBTQ people of color such as Dante and Justice, in dealing not only with anti-LGBTQ discrimination but also racism and other forms of oppression. Dante resisted this violence. He fought back. Still, he preferred living on the streets to dealing with these violent encounters. As he told me, "Because the only thing I had to worry about under a bridge was a car running me over. When I was at [the courtyard], I had to worry about diseases. I had to worry about scabies. I had to worry about somebody stabbing me in my sleep, somebody trying to beat me in my sleep, somebody trying to rape me. There was a lot to worry about over at [the courtyard]."

Camila, as well, did not like going to the courtyard, and she found no help there for her experience of sexual assault. This was not uncommon. Transgender women of color experience a great deal of assault and harassment on the streets, but they often cannot find services to assist them. Moreover, the youth in this study said they experienced more discrimination when reporting an assault. These experiences tell transgender women of color that their lives do not matter, furthering their marginalization and constructing them as less than others—as unworthy of the rights and benefits of society.

Thus, youth had to gain the knowledge of which services and shelters discriminated against them based on their gender and sexuality. As the youth could not safely access certain services, they resisted. They slept in parking garages, the woods, under bridges, at parks, and other outdoor spaces. Some youth also hung out alone. They avoided going to shelters and did not trust certain service providers. Some youth also fought back against the discrimination and violence that they encountered. These strategies mean that some LGBTQ youth experiencing homelessness have little to no access to services, leaving them alone and without support. Their queer street smarts have taught them that the streets might provide more safety than shelters and other service-providing spaces. But the streets did not provide a safe place to live.

SURVEYING THE STREETS

Audrey, a twenty-three-year-old Hispanic lesbian in a relationship with Trinity, told me about a time she overdosed in a parking garage. She said that paramedics woke her up with Narcan. Later, she "fell back into the drug stupor." While she was in this condition, a man raped her. "He ended up taking me off somewhere and having sex with me. And I didn't consent to it. I wasn't—I wasn't in the right mind enough to consent to it. So, I was taken advantage of," she explained. Audrey continued, "I've had sex with guys already. But not taken advantage of or raped. It's a fucking miracle it happened to me so late in my life, 'cause most women go through that shit unfortunately way earlier."

As brought to national attention by the #MeToo movement, sexual violence is too common all over the United States. Audrey even saw experiencing rape so late in life—in her early twenties—as a "miracle." Her comment indicates how sexual violence—from street harassment to rape—exists as a normalized aspect of US culture. More specifically, sexual violence against women maintains gender inequality and the gender binary of the dominating man and submissive woman. Whether consciously or not, men who enact sexual violence objectify women, which functions as a way to control women through fear. This fear makes women feel vulnerable and limits women's life choices, such as making them wary about walking alone in public places or at night. Men's violence maintains the public sphere as a masculine-dominated space and inhibits women from enjoying basic pleasures in life.[8] Sexual violence builds a barrier for women to navigate their lives freely.

Some men enact sexual violence against non-heterosexual women, such as Audrey, out of a sense of their masculinity being threatened by women's non-heterosexual desires. Some men even rape non-heterosexual women to try to "make" women heterosexual and to punish women for not exclusively desiring men.[9] Hence, many non-heterosexual women experiencing homelessness constantly stay on guard in navigating the streets.

In addition to staying on guard, some non-heterosexual and/or gender-expansive youth also carry a weapon to ward off the violence of the streets. Sitting in a staff office with me at the Austin drop-in center, Julian, a twenty-two-year-old Hispanic gay youth, kept shifting in his chair while telling me why he always kept a knife on him. He said he held on to it for protection and that he started carrying it after a person raped him on the streets. "It was in an alleyway. I was tweaked out on ice. And I was coming down," stated Julian. "And somebody fuckin' had a knife to my throat in an alleyway in between Sixth and Brazos. It was really difficult." Julian stated matter-of-factly that he no longer cared about the rape. But the rape altered his sense of safety in the public sphere.

Both Audrey and Julian mentioned drug use in relation to their experiences of sexual violence. Using drugs is a common way of coping with the stresses of experiencing homelessness. Non-heterosexual youth experiencing homelessness often use drugs more than others because of their extra burden of stress in dealing with anti-LGBTQ discrimination.[10] This strategy, though, like most strategies, comes with unintended consequences. For instance, another person on the streets may perceive someone on drugs as vulnerable. Hence, experiencing homelessness and using drugs often correlates with experiencing sexual victimization.[11] This potential of drug use to render people vulnerable to assault may be a particularly challenging aspect of the lives of LGBTQ youth experiencing homelessness.

Moreover, the public sphere upholds heteronormativity. Public signs of non-heterosexuality such as a same-gender couple holding hands in the public sphere challenge underlying heteronormative assumptions of sexuality. Some people respond to these public challenges against heteronormativity by enacting harassment or violence toward LGBTQ people.[12] Julian—who sometimes went by Bree when wearing dresses, makeup, and heels—also challenged the heteronormativity of the streets through his expansive expressions of gender. Most violence against non-heterosexual people involves genderbashing—policing their expansive expressions of gender.[13] Perpetrators of violence often focus on gender-expansive people of color in the public sphere. Hence, LGBTQ people of color experience more violence in public spaces than other groups.[14]

This violence also punishes Julian for disrupting dominant assumptions about what kind of bodies dominant society wants and allows in public. This violence tries to construct Julian and other gender-expansive people of color as deviant. Julian responded by carrying a knife, but he had to hide it and hope that no one would catch him so that he could access services for people experiencing homelessness, since shelters and other service sites ban weapons.

Talking together in the room where the youth at the LGBTQ shelter slept, Adelpha, an eighteen-year-old heterosexual Black, Mexican, and white transgender woman, discussed with me how gay and transgender people on the streets alter their gender appearance to navigate street harassment. "They already treat gay people like shit—you know, homeless [gay people]," she began, "but gay people can disguise it better. 'Cause they're not changing their appearance. All they had to do was maybe talk a little different, and they can be accepted better." Transgender women, Adelpha said, are subject to men hypersexualizing them. "Guys just think trans—if you're walking around trans, you're like a prostitute. We could literally be walking down the street, and we're labeled already." Linking this hypersexualization to physical and sexual violence, Adelpha continued, "They're gonna either treat you like a prostitute, want to fuck you, or treat you like shit or whatever. I mean we're getting like raped, killed, all this stuff."

As documented in the previous chapter, police often profile transgender women of color as sex workers. Other people also hypersexualize and treat transgender women of color as sex workers and sexual objects. These dehumanizing processes expose transgender women of color to physical and sexual violence. Likewise, Adelpha's comment that gay people experiencing homelessness may experience less harassment and violence on the streets than transgender people shows how certain people's reactions to gender-expansive embodiments and enactments determine whom perpetrators of violence target. Some people may try to alter their gender appearance or behaviors to avoid some harassment and violence on the streets. But this strategy puts the labor of altering one's gender embodiments and enactments on the individual instead of challenging the larger social structures causing and shaping the violence.

Indeed, physical and sexual violence is often connected to gender-based violence aimed at upholding the gender binary and heteronormativity.[15] This violence aims to scare anyone who publicly challenges dominant relations of gender and sexuality in US society.[16] Because people of color face more surveillance of their bodies and behaviors, including their gendered embodiments and expressions, perpetrators particularly target transgender and gender-expansive people of color. Transgender and gender expansive people of color who are experiencing homelessness are more likely live and work in the public sphere; therefore, they contend with people policing them and enacting violence against them to a greater degree.

Through these harrowing experiences, youth have developed queer street smarts for navigating the public sphere and the harassment and violence that come from living on the streets. Youth sometimes carried a weapon, some changed their voice or appearance or engaged in other strategies to try to avoid sexual and gender-based violence. Often youth used drugs to relieve stress, but this could make them more vulnerable. Likewise, if caught with a weapon, youth could be barred from accessing services. These strategies, however, are what youth had to rely on to deal with the harassment and violence that comes with living on the streets.

BRAVING BATHROOMS

"Texans should feel safe and secure when they enter any intimate facility," stated Texas Attorney General Ken Paxton in relation to the "Privacy Protection Act," or what became known as a "bathroom bill," which would prohibit transgender and gender-expansive people from using public bathrooms in line with their gender identity. In trying to justify the legislation, Paxton said that the state wanted to fight "to protect women and children from those who might use access to such facilities for nefarious purposes."[17]

During this study, bathroom bills began popping up across the country. Part of the discourse around bathroom bills generated a moral panic about transgender people being pedophiles and rapists. This moral panic—a fear that a dominant group utilizes to construct a marginalized group as a threat to society—further pathologizes and marginalizes transgender people. Relying on this moral panic, certain conservative politicians attempted to ban transgender and gender-expansive people from public bathrooms. Youth experiencing homelessness often struggle to find a restroom, as many businesses only allow paying customers to use theirs. Bathroom bills and the accompanying moral panic have dire consequences for LGBTQ youth experiencing homelessness, since they often do not have access to private bathrooms and showers.

LGBTQ youth experiencing homelessness also struggle with accessing restrooms because they fear harassment and discrimination in these public facilities. Jasper—the twenty-three-year-old mixed-race homosexual who discussed not going to shelters and preferred living alone on the streets—talked with me about the harassment he experienced in the bathroom at his court-ordered recovery program. "I'd go to use the restroom at the same time as someone else. And they'd be like, 'Oh, hell no.' And like walk away." Jessie, an eighteen-year-old white gay gender-fluid youth, commented on his fears of using the showers at the courtyard on the homelessness campus in San Antonio. "I didn't look anyone in their eyes," he exclaimed to me while we sat in a private therapy-style interview room. "I just went in there and showered and got the fuck out. Plus, I was scared they were going to rape me." Kareem, a twenty-one-year-old Black gay youth, also discussed the courtyard showers. He stated, "People looked at [me and my boyfriend] funny. I hated it there. Because the showers—like ugh, ew! I'm not about to shower where anybody can see me. So, we was dirty for a couple days."

Some LGBTQ people experience public bathrooms as dangerous spaces and sites of surveillance. Jasper said men walked out of the bathroom when he went to use it—marking him as an object of disgust. These actions highlight the fear that some men have of using a bathroom with a Brown gay man, whom people stereotype as hypersexual. As youth experiencing homelessness often do not have access to private bathrooms, they can face these types of discriminatory encounters daily. Such acts mark LGBTQ people of color as deviant.

Moreover, Jessie and Kareem—whom I both met at the LGBTQ shelter in San Antonio—discussed their feelings of being watched in the courtyard bathroom. Indeed, the structure of public bathrooms, with mirrors, reflecting surfaces, and stall doors that rarely reach the floor, generates a feeling of fear and uncertainty that people watch and observe each other in public restrooms.[18] This feeling of surveillance was heightened at the courtyard, where the bathroom stalls had no doors and the shower walls only went up to the waist. Transgender and gender-expansive people face a whole host of harassment and violence issues in communal bathrooms, at shelters, and at other service places for people experiencing homelessness.[19] Bathroom bills and the gender segregation of these facilities only make LGBTQ people's vulnerability in these spaces worse.

This strategy of avoiding restrooms and showers because of harassment could lead to a host of other barriers in the youth's lives, as youth need to present a clean look to go to job interviews or court or, indeed, to get dates if one engages in sex work. Adelpha—the eighteen-year-old Black, Mexican, and white heterosexual transgender woman who discussed her experiences of sexual violence on the streets—also saw accessing a shower as a way to feel the battles of the street a little less. "It's the little stuff. Take a shower. Use your scrubs. Put on your clothes. Do your makeup. And you feel less—you feel the struggle less." Moreover, for transgender and gender-expansive people, getting clean and dressing in clothes that affirm their gender identity enhances their well-being and potentially helps them avoid violence on the streets.[20]

Notably, the gender segregation of public bathrooms presented challenges for transgender women of color experiencing homelessness. Dante—the twenty-two-year-old Black bisexual youth who experienced violence at the courtyard for his friendship with Justice—discussed with me how his friend Prada—a twenty-three-year-old Hispanic heterosexual transgender woman—faced discrimination at shelter bathrooms. "Let's say I walk into—I'm homeless, so I go to [a homeless shelter]. And, say, Prada—homeless—she walks into [the same homeless shelter]. We both have to go to the bathroom," Dante explained. "I go to the men's room. She goes to the men's room. She gets kicked out. She goes to the women's bathroom. She gets kicked out. No matter where she goes—men or women—she gets kicked out of the bathroom because of her appearance, one, and two, because of what is hanging between her legs. And I don't think that should matter. She is a she. So, she should be able to use the women's restroom."

The discriminatory treatment of transgender and gender-expansive people in bathrooms involves a type of "gender panic" about challenges to the gender binary. People respond in ways that reassert the supposed naturalness of the gender binary. The result is legislators passing bathroom bills. These bathroom bills and the gender segregation of bathrooms limit transgender and gender-expansive people's ability to move freely in the public sphere. Moreover, gender panics often directly link to a fear of someone with a penis in women's spaces. As Dante's comment emphasized, gender panics often relate to penis panics. Gender panics detrimentally affect transgender women and create a moral panic of transgender women as a danger to other women and children. This penis panic upholds the idea of genitals as the primary determiner of gender.[21]

Likewise, as dominant gender stereotypes cast people of color as hypersexual, such as the myth of the Black male rapist, these gender panics have a potentially more detrimental effect on transgender and gender-expansive people of color, who must navigate sexual stereotypes as well as racial stereotypes. Racialized gender panics also continue the legacy of racially segregated public restrooms. Racial stereotypes about sexuality and the fear of interracial contact, particularly in spaces deemed intimate, such as a restroom, thus serve to keep transgender and gender expansive people of color out of public restrooms.

Moreover, focusing on body parts, especially genitalia, dehumanizes and objectifies transgender people's bodies and erases their lived realities. These gender panics have dire consequences for transgender and gender-expansive people experiencing homelessness, who often have no access to restrooms except public ones. The gender segregation of restrooms and shelters also keeps LGBTQ youth from staying together in the same place. As Dante said, shelter staff would kick Prada out. These institutional arrangements divide the youth up, keeping some of them isolated, which limits their ability to stay together to keep each other safe.

Prada—Dante's friend and fellow resident at the LGBTQ shelter—talked with me about her confusion in using public restrooms. "I don't have the surgery yet," she said. "But legally, by the state of Texas, I'm a female. But you know how a lot of females here in Texas are, 'That's still a guy.' But not by the state!" Prada paused and rummaged through her backpack to pull out the legal paperwork to show me that the state of

Texas recognizes her as a woman. She then went on, "And if I go into the guy's restroom, would I get in trouble? 'Do you guys have a family restroom?' That's the first thing I'll look for anytime I go somewhere, and I know there are only two bathrooms. The first thing I'll—where is the restroom for like the family or disabled?"

Likewise, Zoe, a nineteen-year-old Hispanic heterosexual transgender woman, had a creative way to find restrooms to clean herself. As detailed in the introduction of this book, Zoe faced harassment in the men's bathroom at the courtyard. She also experienced harassment in the women's bathroom there. "I have a problem with the girls talking shit. So, I'm just tired—I'm just tired of this shit talking," Zoe stated. "It's like, mind your damn business. I'm not looking at you. I'm just trying to clean my body and get the fuck out." In response, Zoe avoided communal showers, and she cleaned herself in sinks. "I don't smell rough like most people do due to the streets. I'd find a way to keep clean. I'd sneak into restrooms and do a quick rinse, so they don't know nothing. It's just like I'm in and out."

Public bathrooms exist as one of the last gender-segregated public spaces in the United States. This segregation works to uphold the gender binary.[22] Historically, public bathrooms also upheld racial segregation through having "white only" restrooms and restrooms for people of color. This history of racial segregation sometimes places people of color under heightened surveillance when they enter public restrooms, as this fear of interracial mingling in a space deemed intimate still carries on today. Transgender and gender-expansive people of color such as Jasper, Prada, and Zoe thus face especially heightened gender policing in public bathrooms. Stereotypes about people of color and LGBTQ people mutually co-constitute LGBTQ youth of color as deviant in the public sphere. Given these experiences, transgender and gender-expansive people of color may try to retreat from public life, but if they are experiencing homelessness, the option to retreat from public life is not available.[23]

Instead, the youth in this study learned strategies to navigate the violence and harassment they encountered in gender-segregated public bathrooms. They had to learn which bathrooms to avoid. Another strategy in response to the institutional arrangements of gender-segregated restrooms involved a queer mapping of the city to locate single-use restrooms, such as family restrooms. In these ways, their queer street smarts in relation to public bathrooms took on a classed-based knowledge, as people with access to private restrooms do not need to acquire this knowledge. As youth of color experience more surveillance in public spaces, including public bathrooms, they particularly needed to learn how to navigate the tendency of people to watch and judge their presence.

Prada used her queer street smarts to look for family and handicap-accessible restrooms that felt safer and more private. Zoe did quick rinses in restrooms to avoid using the showers at the courtyard. Other youth chose not to shower or showered quickly in order to escape the bathroom surveillance. Not cleaning properly, of course, could lead to health concerns and make it difficult to get dates or look presentable in court or for a job interview. Thus, some strategies still left the youth vulnerable and marginalized in navigating other parts of their lives. Bathroom barriers were a main challenge for LGBTQ youth experiencing homelessness.

THE PRACTICALITY OF GENDER AND SEXUALITY

Because of the heteronormativity of the public sphere, the LGBTQ youth faced a great deal of oppression, harassment, and discrimination on the streets. Youth also learned various ways to use their gender and sexuality to build relationships and obtain resources when the formal economy and society failed them. I turn now to these strategies.

Connecting with Children

During my fieldwork, I helped to conduct a youth point-in-time count.[24] While engaged in this count I ran into Kelsey—the twenty-two-year-old Black woman who opened this chapter—outside of the downtown Austin library. Answering the point-in-time count survey, Kelsey reaffirmed her pregnancy—something I had already known from my interactions with her at the drop-in center. In filling out the rest of the survey, Kelsey told me that she had stayed at her parents' house the night before. She marked on the survey, however, that she did not have a stable housing situation. She said that her pregnancy had reconnected her with her parents and helped her get off the streets at night. But how long she could stay with them was uncertain.

For many of the young parents in this study (especially the women), having a child played a role in reconnecting with family members and in accessing services. For example, Lola, a twenty-year-old Hispanic bisexual woman pregnant with her third child when I interviewed her, talked about her plans after the pregnancy. She told me, "I'm planning to have my own place here in Austin. If not, I'm moving down to Corpus Christi and have my aunts help me. 'Cause right now, I'm not financially stable. And I told my aunts that I need to be financially stable." Lola already had her other two children with other family members. I learned later during fieldwork, that after she had her third child, Lola got into a youth parenting program, which included housing, in Austin.

Some youth also saw their child as inspiration for their lives. "I have my daughter with my family right now. They are taking care of her," stated Silvia, a twenty-two-year-old Hispanic bisexual woman. "And now I'm just trying to look for my job. Trying to get to where I need to be." Talking with me at the Austin drop-in center, Silvia said she needed to get an apartment and food, and then she will work on living independently with her daughter. Likewise, Ciara, a twenty-two-year-old Black Hispanic bisexual youth whom I also met at the Austin drop-in center, told me, "Now that I have a son, I have to take care of myself now. So, I'm trying to get my life straight."

Emmett, a twenty-three-year-old white Hispanic bisexual youth, was the only man in this study who discussed having a child. Like Silvia and Ciara, I also met Emmett at the drop-in center, where he told me that having a child "changed my life." He went on, "I want to be in the kid's life 'cause I know that life sucks at some points, and I know the corrections early." Emmett said he wanted to teach his child "what's right from wrong, wrong from right." During the study, Emmett's child lived with the mother in Ohio. Emmett hoped to reunite with his child soon. He explained, "I'm going to move [the mother and child] back down here once I have a steady job."

Queer street smarts include knowledge and strategies that on the surface may not seem so queer. Young parents with children—who in this study all identified as bisexual and who all conceived their children through heterosexual relations—learned how having a child can grant access to certain services, and it helped some of them reconnect with family members. For instance, women with children, such as Lola, can access youth parenting programs and shelters that specifically take in mothers. For many young women, having a baby provided an important pathway off the streets, as they were able to access more housing and medical resources and/or reunite with family members.[25] Dominant US society constructs mothers with children—at least on the surface—as a more deserving sector of the poor population compared to other poor groups. Hence, lawmakers have instituted policies and services to help them. Notably, the fact that women, especially women with children, often access shelters more easily than men reifies the notion that society wants to keep women in the private sphere.[26] Nonetheless, in one study, having children best predicted receiving public assistance among people experiencing homelessness. At the same time, women with children remained the poorest population of people experiencing homelessness.[27] Although more government programs and benefits exist for young poor mothers, these resources do not suffice for most women and their children to get by. Having a child helps some women with children get off the streets, but often—like Kelsey—they still experience housing instability.

Furthermore, wanting to provide a better life for one's child inspires certain youth experiencing homelessness to try to make up for the childhood that they feel that they never really had. Poor parents of color also want to work to combat the stereotypes and controlling images of poor parents—especially of young poor mothers of color—as inadequate, absent, and careless parents.[28] The young mothers of color in this study, such as Silvia and Ciara, and the young father, Emmett, saw their child as a reason to want to get off the streets.

Perhaps, as well, having a child through heterosexual relations helped to downplay the stigma of their non-heterosexuality, whereby family members come to accept or ignore the youth's bisexuality. Indeed, the child allowed some of the youth to stay with—or at least reconnect with—family, even if these familial ties stayed tenuous. The youth may also have had their child stay with family members because public assistance did not provide enough for the youth to support themselves and their child or to live stably with their child. The youth also experienced disappointment, as the burden of addressing homelessness gets placed on the individual, and structurally, for young poor parents of color, getting out of poverty often does not happen. However, for mainly non-heterosexual women, who often have fewer resources to access while living on the streets, learning about these resources for mothers experiencing homelessness and the reconnections with family members have an impact on their lives.

Providing for Partners

"People out here are looking for people that are useful to them," stated Minnesota, a twenty-year-old white bisexual woman, whom I met at the Austin drop-in center. "They can sell drugs for them. They can buy drugs from them. They can be their partner. They can be their pet toy."

For youth experiencing homelessness, peer and romantic relationships can be sources of emotional and instrumental support. Through these relationships, young people integrate into street life, learn the "code of the street," and counteract loneliness.[29] Although all relationships on some level involve utility, relationships built on the streets are important in helping youth find social support and temporary housing and in learning to navigate street life.

For example, during fieldwork, Trinity—the twenty-year-old white lesbian who avoided shelters and often slept in the woods, alleys, or behind dumpsters—temporarily lived in housing because her partner, Audrey— the twenty-three-year-old Hispanic lesbian who discussed sexual violence on the streets—had a place for them to stay. "Currently, I'm residing with my partner. But we're about to be homeless again," Trinity stated. "And I've been staying there for a few months to have a relationship with her and also a place to put my head." For Audrey, Trinity's presence has been a source of social support. Audrey explained, "I've had drug problems. I've had heroin—problems with heroin—struggles with that. And she's been there through it all. Even when it probably looked pretty hopeless."

The other couple in this study—Kareem and Arthur—also talked about the social support they provided one another. In talking about Kareem, Arthur, a twenty-five-year-old Black gay man, told me, "Kareem—he helps me get through the stress. And he helps me just, like, he just be there for me. And be there to be my comfort. Talk to me. Be like, 'Look babe, we gonna do this. We gonna do that. We gonna get out of here.'" Lucas, a twenty-year-old white heterosexual transgender man, also discussed how his girlfriend supported him while living on the streets. "We slept outside," he stated. "And it was raining. We were soaked and cold. And we ended up finding this building right here by the McDonald's downtown. And we slept under it. We just cuddled. And she helps me through every day—cope. And she's my motivation."

People experiencing homelessness depend on relationships and friends for resources and support because they often have little money and are estranged from or have tenuous ties with their families of origin.[30] Many youth experiencing homelessness have not found such support elsewhere.[31] These relationships establish a type of kinship. Marginalized groups, such as people experiencing homelessness need love, social support, companionship, and economic resources just like anyone else. While such ties on the street often do not last long, they can assist in navigating homelessness.[32]

The youth in this study also built street families, or "families of choice," to support one another. Experiencing similar circumstances around discrimination in relation to gender and sexuality can bring people together to form friendships and families. These street families in some cases provide a youth with a sense of belonging and acceptance for their gender and sexuality for the first time.[33] Moreover, these families carry significant meaning for poor LGBTQ people of color who experience not only discrimination around gender and sexuality but also racism and poverty.

Intimate relationships also inspired youth to want to get off the streets. Like having a child, a partner can motivate youth to try to get into housing. This motivation might turn into disappointment, as youth discover that getting into housing involves difficulties and often remains unstable, as Trinity and Audrey discovered. But relationships, at times, provided the youth in this study emotional and instrumental support, a place to stay, intimacy and connection, a buffer against the impact of stressors, and other resources.

While a partner can offer support, a partner also might bring about tension, conflict, and violence. This situation occurred most prominently with the transgender women of color. "There was one night I actually ended up in the hospital 'cause of an ex-boyfriend of mine," explained Prada—the twenty-three-year-old Hispanic heterosexual transgender woman who discussed her experiences navigating public restrooms. She told me, "That day—I didn't want to hear him. I didn't want to talk to him. I just wanted to walk off and go to the library and chill and just calm down. And he said, 'Why are you ignoring me?' Bow! Face started bleeding."

Camila—the twenty-two-year-old Hispanic heterosexual transgender woman who did not like sleeping at the courtyard—often slept in her ex-boyfriend's car. This ex-boyfriend tried to rape her. "I'd be like in my ex-boyfriend's car—smoking—and then I'd go out with my friends. And go and get drunk," Camila stated. "Come back stumbling. Pass out in the car. Wake up to him trying to have sex with me. And be like, 'What the fuck are you doing, dude?' Without permission, you know, trying to take things. And I'm like no, no, no baby. He's trash."

Studies have shown that women experiencing homelessness attach themselves to a man to find protection on the streets—a masculine-dominated space that is often dangerous for women.[34] Moreover, some women experiencing homelessness stay in their relationship when their partner victimizes them, assessing such victimization as an exchange for protection and support on the streets.[35] Some transgender women of color on the streets also may suffer abuse. Prada faced physical violence from her partner. Camila had a temporary respite in her ex-boyfriend's car but experienced sexual violence from him. This violence signifies transgender women of color as deserving of punishment, furthering their positioning outside of the dominant structures of race, class, gender, and sexuality. As poor women of color, many of the transgender women in this study often had to rely on men for resources, and hence, had to navigate or even accept this violence as part of living on the streets. Marginalized groups often navigate the margins in complex ways.

For LGBTQ youth experiencing homelessness, queer street smarts include, then, building relationships as sources of support, inspiration, and resources such as temporary housing. Friendships and relationships with other LGBTQ people also help youth feel more accepted and afford them social support in combating the discrimination they face on the streets. Importantly, poor LGBTQ youth of color rely on these networks for support to face and combat discrimination around gender and sexuality as well as racism and poverty. Because of their intersecting racial, classed, and gendered social locations, transgender women of color notably experience

vulnerability and violence, including sexual violence, in navigating relationships on the street. Thus, the transgender women of color in this study
experienced greater marginalization, and some relationships generated
more instability in their lives.

Selling Sex

"So, the day the rent is due, I want to keep my apartment," said Samara, a
twenty-year-old Hispanic bisexual youth. "So, I started prostituting myself
around in the same apartment complex. I was doing it for the rent. That's
all that was on my mind. I had a job too. I had a job—a day job and a night
job." When I asked Jessie—the eighteen-year-old white gay gender-fluid
youth who discussed avoiding public showers because of discrimination—
how he got by on the streets, he replied, "Well, I was prostituting. So, I'd
either sleep at their house, or I'd sleep downtown on a bench."

Economic reasons primarily influence the reason people engage in sex
work.[36] And the youth in this study often engaged in sex work for these
practical, economic reasons. Samara needed to pay the rent. Her day job—
at a fast-food place—did not pay a living wage. She supplemented this
income with sex work—a job in which she could set her own hours and
work around her day job hours. For many people, getting a second job in
the formal economy proves difficult, as service job hours often change
weekly. Samara did not have this problem with her night job. Jessie
obtained shelter some nights by staying at a date's place—often a safer
option than the streets and shelters. Thus, sex work helped youth to keep
an apartment or to access temporary shelter when the shelter and streets
were not safe.

The transgender women of color in this study engaged in sex work the
most. Jenelle, a twenty-one-year-old Hispanic heterosexual transgender
woman, explained to me why she engaged in sex work. "This sounds con-
ceited, but I have a really pretty face. And I'm a pretty girl," she began. "So,
men would constantly be like, 'Why are you on the streets? Talk to me. Are
you hungry? Do you need any food?'" She went on, "And they'd be like,
'Oh, I have this apartment. And you can stay there. Or you can go shower
and stuff like that.' That's how I get by." Jenelle linked sex work to meeting
her basic needs. "I hadn't eaten in, say, like three days. And I desperately

needed a shower. I can't sleep outside. Like, it's hard. It was hot. So, I basically just did it for that." As she reflected, "'Cause when you're homeless
and starving, and you know that five dollars at McDonald's can buy you a
whole meal, so you wouldn't be hungry, it's hard to deny someone telling
you, 'Hey, I'll give you four hundred dollars.'"

Because of employment discrimination, rejection, and other structural
and social barriers that transgender people face, sex work becomes a via-
ble way for some transgender people, especially transgender women of
color, to make money.[37] Notably, Jenelle believed that her pretty appearance helped her. As research has shown, women experiencing homelessness sometimes use femininity to gain protection and support from men
on the streets.[38] Some transgender women also rely on expressing femininity to find dates, and hence, make money, get a place to shower, have
food, and access other things they want or need. However, the sex work
industry often privileges and upholds feminine white women as the most
desirable.[39] Women of color, including transgender women of color, have
to do more labor in performing this fantasy of femininity to gets dates
when engaging in sex work. When society does not meet people's basic
needs, such as food, shower, and shelter, sex work operates as a means to
obtain these necessities.

Like the situation with intimate partners, some transgender women of
color also experienced sexual violence in sex work. Indeed, because of how
racial, classed, and gendered discrimination and stereotypes shape practices of sex work, poor transgender women of color are more likely to engage
in street-based sex work, which often has more unsafe conditions than
other types of sex work such as escort services.[40] Justice—the eighteen-
year-old Black heterosexual transgender woman who experienced harassment in the courtyard—discussed this situation. "Transgender girls can also
have it easier because of the whole prostituting thing. But at the same time,
it is very dangerous. And I just had a situation this past week where I went
with this guy. And I mean—I wasn't even trying to prostitute with him. And
he went, took me out to Corpus, raped me, put a gun to my head, and said
get the fuck out of my car."

Zoe—the nineteen-year-old Hispanic heterosexual transgender woman
who experienced harassment at the courtyard, notably in the showers—
talked about sex work, violence, and fighting back against a date. "If I can

get a quick hustle on for a motel, then, hey, thank you Lord," she exclaimed. "'Cause you never know, I could not be here talking to you. Maybe I needed that motel room for that night." Zoe said men desired her "'cause they thought I was a female with no boobs." She went on, "They were just titillated by me. Some of them would just want to talk to me or tell me their freaky stories for just forty bucks, fifty bucks." In discussing her choice to engage in sex work she also described encountering violence. "Whenever I did have sex, it was because I wanted to. Because I was hungry. And I only got raped one time. And that guy will remember me, because I bet you his door is not on his apartment. And he had to go get that wire back in his jaw."

Queer street smarts entail learning the practical value of sex. Indeed, on the streets, people experiencing homelessness can find sex work banal. It is just a way to exchange sex for money, drugs, food, shelter, and other resources.[41] Justice felt that transgender women could potentially make money more easily than other young people on the streets. Gender and femininity and the gendered knowledge of presenting as feminine helps some youth—such as the transgender women of color—find more dates.

For Zoe, sex work was done to get temporary shelter at a motel, which she saw as potentially keeping her alive. She also asserted that it was her choice to engage in sex work. Her hunger though—a basic need not met by society—constrained this choice. Moreover, those who engage in sex work more often experience sexual victimization and other assaults and crimes.[42] A man raped Justice and the police did nothing about it. And although Zoe resisted and fought back against the man who raped her, the quotidian nature of violence that transgender women of color experience continues their marginalization and works to mutually co-constitute transgender women of color as less than, as other. While sex work helps to access some resources, it could make some youth, particularly transgender women of color, vulnerable to other violence and instabilities.

NAOMI'S STORY

As I have shown through weaving the same individuals throughout various sections of this chapter, the youth in this study simultaneously experienced many obstacles in dealing with homelessness. The youth had to develop queer street smarts over these issues as they daily navigated the streets. To drive home this point of the youth facing multiple barriers at the same time, I turn to Naomi's story.

Naomi was an eighteen-year-old bisexual transgender Latina whom I met at the LGBTQ shelter in San Antonio. During our interview, we sat together outside at a picnic table on the larger homelessness campus where the LGBTQ shelter was located. Before getting into the shelter, Naomi had lived on the streets. In describing to me life on the streets for transgender women of color, Naomi stated, "It's so scary for us, 'cause we don't know what the fuck is going to happen to us. We turn a corner. We don't know how these people are going to react. We don't know if we are gonna be raped, killed, beaten. We don't know. We have to live with that uncertainty every freakin' day."

To get off the streets, Naomi stayed briefly at the courtyard. She faced sexual harassment there from other people experiencing homelessness. Wearing a purple wig with a big red bow—making me think of Minnie Mouse—Naomi detailed to me her experience at the courtyard. "A lot of sexual encounters," she stated. "Like they tried. But I never wanted to give. They just—I knew they were looking for someone just to take advantage of. So, I just didn't follow up with it. I was just always kept to myself. Going to work. Coming back."

Naomi had to learn queer street smarts to stay on guard and avoid violence. As Naomi noted, this fear that comes with living on the streets entails the "every freakin' day" psychological stressors of uncertainty. This uncertainty of encountering violence on the streets and the targeting of transgender women of color furthers experiences of instability and marginalization. The whiteness and heteronormativity of the public sphere also can keep transgender women of color afraid to appear in public. She also found no respite at the courtyard—a main place for people experiencing homelessness to access services in San Antonio. There, people sexually harassed her. People often hypersexualize and dehumanize transgender women of color. Naomi resisted and kept to herself to avoid the sexual harassment, but staying isolated and without social support potentially made her easier to exploit and abuse. She eventually returned to the streets.

In discussing with me other challenges of living on the streets, Naomi talked about sex work and making money. She stated, "I don't click with doing it—sex for money. 'Cause I'm not—been there, done that, learned my lesson. And I had picked up something because of that. And I learned my lesson to not do it again." Naomi continued, "And I don't want to lower my value or how much self-confidence I have for an asshole that just wants to get a quickie. Yeah, the money's okay. The money may be okay. But once that money's gone—was it really worth it—catching something over this fucking asshole? No!"

Naomi learned through queer street smarts that sex work provides a means to make money, but contracting a sexually transmitted infection made her reject it as an option. In certain cities, police often profile and target transgender women of color; they will assume prostitution and confiscate their condoms or arrest them.[43] Power dynamics also influence the use of condoms and other sexual practices between a date and a sex worker. These structural and interpersonal processes make transgender women of color vulnerable to contracting a sexually transmitted infection—another form of sexual violence that transgender women of color face when experiencing homelessness. Sexual violence demonstrates the vulnerabilities that transgender women of color face, often because white supremacy, the gender binary, and heteronormativity push some of them to engage in street-based prostitution to meet their needs. The devaluation of sex workers, including the stigmatization of street-based prostitution, also influences the self-worth of people engaging in sex work. After moving into the LGBTQ shelter, Naomi stopped prostituting. She got a job in the formal economy at a food court in a mall. As documented in chapter 2, however, a manager soon fired her, discriminating against her for being transgender.

Lastly, and perhaps most harrowingly, Naomi also had to deal with relationship violence from Obadiah—a twenty-year-old white man who dates transgender women and who also stayed at the LGBTQ shelter. At one point during fieldwork, Naomi and Obadiah left the LGBTQ shelter to live together in hotels and on the streets. Naomi eventually returned to the shelter. She disclosed to me Obadiah's abusive behavior. "That was my first abusive relationship that I ever got into—ever—in my life," she stated. "We were at a hotel. And he—I had this feeling every time I went to the restroom that there was something going on behind my back. He made me delete my Facebook with all of my high school friends—like everything—I didn't have nobody." After their money ran out, they went from living in hotels to the streets, and during my interview with Naomi, authorities had Obadiah in jail for raping and assaulting her. "He had raped me when we were staying on the streets," explained Naomi. She woke up from sleeping to Obadiah raping her. "I was pissed. I was crying," she exclaimed. "I started getting shit and hitting him with it. I got this glass thing, and I just fucking threw it at him. And it shattered at him, girl." In reflecting on why she thought she dated Obadiah, Naomi said, "I miss that warmth of a person. And I feel like that's what I had got with Obadiah. I wanted some warmth next to me. I wanted someone holding me or being there by my side."

After leaving the shelter together, Obadiah began isolating Naomi from her friends. Isolation makes a person vulnerable to exploitation and abuse. And intimate partner violence, domination, and control are particularly prevalent for transgender women of color. In a review of the scant research on the topic, about one-third to one-half of transgender people experience intimate partner violence in their lifetime.[44] Naomi resisted and fought back, but she also realized that her isolation and aloneness—that she often experienced while living on the streets—shaped her decision to date Obadiah and endure sexual violence.

The last I heard of Naomi, she had gotten housing assistance to pay her rent for a year. She lived on her own in an apartment.

QUEERING STREET STRATEGIES

People experiencing homelessness engage in a variety of strategies—such as recycling cans, sex work, drug dealing, and panhandling—to get by on the streets.[45] These strategies and the street smarts needed to implement them help people experiencing homelessness to meet basic needs, when structural conditions make fulfilling these needs difficult. But not all people experiencing homelessness engage in the same strategies. Larger social forces such as the gender binary and heteronormativity shape which strategies people access, how people implement those strategies, and how people develop new strategies.

For instance, gender inequality and the masculine-dominated public sphere shape street strategies, whereby women experiencing homelessness often navigate the streets differently than men experiencing homelessness. As studies have documented, women experiencing homelessness perform femininity such as passivity and tenderness to form relationships with men and to have men serve as their protectors on the streets.[46] On the other hand, some women experiencing homelessness dress in masculine attire, act tough and aggressive, and/or present as a "bag lady" to try to avoid street harassment.[47] Some heterosexual women experiencing homelessness also try to pass as lesbians to try to avoid unwanted male attention and harassment. However, since the streets maintain heteronormativity, women trying to pass as lesbians experience victimization because of their perceived non-heterosexuality.[48] Women experiencing homelessness thus use a variety of gender-related and sexuality-related strategies to navigate their street lives.

Building on this work, this chapter explicitly shows how heteronormativity and the gender binary impact LGBTQ people's lives in the public sphere and how LGBTQ youth experiencing homelessness learn queer street smarts to navigate this landscape. From gender-segregated shelters and bathrooms to the sexual violence of the streets, youth learned to stay on guard, to resist certain service places, to change their appearance, and to find other places and ways to meet their needs. As documented in previous chapters, youth learned similar strategies such as staying on guard, changing their appearance, and carrying a weapon in navigating families, schools, and other institutions. They now built on these strategies to navigate the streets and services for people experiencing homelessness.

Importantly, institutional arrangements such as the gender-segregation of shelters and bathrooms uphold heteronormativity and the gender binary—two intertwined systems of oppression. Queer street smarts entailed understanding how gender and sexuality simultaneously shape experiences on the streets and other public spaces and how to avoid unwanted discriminatory interactions. The youth also faced unintended consequences in implementing their queer street smarts such as not getting the services they needed, experiencing isolation, and facing violence from an intimate partner or date. These heteronormative processes make experiencing homelessness for LGBTQ youth often more violent and getting off the streets even more difficult.

Nonetheless, youth continued to resist and adapt. They made lives for themselves, took care of themselves and each other, built new families and systems of social support, and found creative ways to get resources and temporary shelter. These queer strategies expose the heteronormative institutional and public sphere logics of gender and sexuality and high-light the queer street smarts people utilize to adapt. To fully understand homelessness and the public sphere, we need to take seriously how heter-onormativity and the gender binary impact people's public lives in various ways. Any analysis of the streets, homelessness, and the public sphere needs to consider how gender and sexuality shape these spaces and peo-ple's experiences.

This chapter also pushes us to think through an intersectional lens in understanding street strategies broadly and queer street smarts specifi-cally. Race and class intersected with gender and sexuality to shape what queer street smarts the youth needed to gain and how they implemented their strategies. The youth in this study needed a class-based knowledge of finding safe public places to shower and sleep that other LGBTQ peo-ple, who have more access to private spaces, do not need to gain. Likewise, the Black and Brown youth in this study had to learn how to navigate racial discrimination and people violently targeting them on the streets and in public bathrooms. The transgender women of color particularly had to learn to deal with intimate partner violence in their lives. White LGBTQ people do not have to gain this type of racialized knowledge. The youth in this study not only had to learn gender-based and sexuality-based strategies for navigating homelessness, but also how poverty and racial discrimination shaped these strategies. An intersectional analysis illumi-nates which street strategies people can access and how people implement those strategies.

Notably, although the youth faced a great deal of oppression, harass-ment, and discrimination against their gender and sexuality, they also used their gender and sexuality as a resource to navigate the heteronorma-tive streets. As a study on lesbian, gay, and bisexual youth experiencing homelessness documented, the youth experienced rejection from families of origin and other institutions such as schools because of their sexuality.

But being lesbian, gay, or bisexual was not always a disadvantage. The youth found inclusion and community with other lesbian, gay, and bisexual people experiencing homelessness. Their sexuality allowed them to find friends.[49] For the youth in this study, having children, getting into an intimate relationship, and engaging in sex work allowed some youth to access resources including money, food, and temporary shelter. The youth learned the practical values of sex and sexuality. They also learned how to use their gender expression to help in getting dates and building relationships. The youth also found friendships and other relationships through experiencing similar discrimination based on their gender and sexuality. At times, these experiences created fraught and dangerous experiences. Youth learned, though, how to use their gender and sexuality in ways to help them navigate and get by on the heteronormative streets and to obtain resources that they often could not get from heteronormative service systems or from society in general.

The youth in San Antonio also had the LGBTQ shelter to obtain resources and to serve as a respite from the streets. This shelter challenged some heteronormative aspects of service systems. But staff at the shelter often regulated the youth's behaviors, including behaviors related to their gender and sexuality. Hence, the LGBTQ shelter upheld dominant notions of gender and sexuality and contributed to the youth's experiences of homelessness as well, a problem to which we now turn.

5 Respite, Resources, Rules, and Regulations

HOMONORMATIVE GOVERNMENTALITY AND LGBTQ SHELTER LIFE

"They offer so much help," stated Camila, referring to the staff and resources at the LGBTQ youth shelter. A twenty-two-year-old Hispanic heterosexual transgender woman, Camila went on to detail some of the support that staff and volunteers at the shelter provided. "So much therapy—so much therapists have come in and offered their services. Certain nurse practitioners—they offer their services free of charge. So, they get us prescriptions. They see us." In seeing the youth, staff also worked to provide LGBTQ-specific services. As Camila explained, "I definitely been able to get all of my hormones, since I've come to [the LGBTQ shelter], which I've been wanting to do for years. But now, I have the support—the resources." Additionally, Camila lived among other transgender people. "I feel comfortable because there are other people around you who share my experiences. Share my—they can relate to me being transgender."

Along with the resources and support that Camila accessed at the LGBTQ shelter, she also had to comply with the shelter rules. As discussed in the introduction of this book, shelter staff suspended Camila—along with Zoe—for doing drugs and missing curfews. After this thirty-day suspension, Camila eventually moved back into the LGBTQ shelter. Staff then caught Obadiah—another youth staying at the shelter—and Camila having sex together. Staff suspended them for three days, as the shelter rules prohibited sexual contact and relationships between people residing there. According to the shelter handbook, this ban on relationships and sex at the shelter sought "to maintain a safe space and inclusive community." Both suspensions sent Camila back to the streets. Once on the streets, she would often start doing drugs again to cope. The drug use exacerbated her health conditions, as she often had seizures. It also made getting off the streets difficult, as she needed to pass a drug test to get back into the LGBTQ shelter. On my last day of fieldwork, I ran into Camila at the main intake center in San Antonio for people experiencing homelessness. She had not stayed at the LGBTQ shelter for quite a while. With dark brown hair to her shoulders and wearing new glasses, Camila looked well. While waiting in line at intake, she told me that she hoped to get into a detox program.

HOMONORMATIVE GOVERNMENTALITY

In this chapter, I explore the tension of the LGBTQ shelter functioning as a refuge while also serving as a site of gender and sexual regulation. I document how the shelter provided LGBTQ-specific resources for youth who often could not access these resources elsewhere. The shelter also provided a place for LGBTQ youth experiencing homelessness to build friendships, families, and social support with other LGBTQ people. But the rules of the shelter regulated the young people's lives and behaviors, including their gender and sexual behaviors. Staff suspended many youth for violating the shelter rules, which often sent them back to the streets for the duration of the expulsion. The youth thus kept cycling from streets to shelters to jails, and the shelter often contributed to, rather than solved, their homelessness.

I introduce the concept of homonormative governmentality to capture these contradictory supportive and regulatory processes around gender and sexuality at the LGBTQ shelter. Governmentality involves the processes of control and management of people's conduct. Governmentality tries to make people's conduct align with the dominant relations in society.[1] Most shelters and social services are sites of governmentality—of controlling and managing poor people, including people experiencing homelessness.

Notably, shelters often receive funding, including from the US government. This funding shapes the programming and structures of shelters and influences how they use regimented schedules of activities, goals, and rules to enforce dominant middle-class, capitalistic values. Life-skill programs and employment-readiness training, which many social services receive funding for, work toward molding a self-managed, self-disciplined person. The logic goes: if people experiencing homelessness could engage in self-governing middle-class, capitalistic behaviors, they would gain housing stability.[2]

At the LGBTQ shelter, this governmentality came with a homonormative twist. Homonormativity entails LGBTQ people assimilating into and upholding heteronormative institutions and relations in society such as monogamy, marriage, domesticity, and reproduction. The "good gays" are LGBTQ people who productively contribute to middle-class, capitalistic society and who uphold notions of personal responsibility.[3] Homonormativity partly seeks to dismantle the welfare state. For instance, same-sex marriage privatizes social issues, whereby LGBTQ people rely on the family—their spouse—and not the state to attain what they need.[4] Middle-class whiteness and homonormativity also go together. Nuclear family structure, monogamy, and middle-class assimilation rely on notions of normative whiteness. This middle-class whiteness helps to normalize certain gay people who also conform to dominant gender relations in US society, while further pushing to the margins poor gender-expansive LGBTQ people of color.[5]

I define *homonormative governmentality* as the structures and processes within LGBTQ institutions and spaces that discipline LGBTQ people who do not or cannot uphold the white, middle-class, capitalistic relations within society. This homonormative governmentality at the LGBTQ shelter simultaneously affirmed and regulated the youth's gender and sexuality. A main point of this chapter showcases that the shelter produced an important communal space for LGBTQ youth experiencing homelessness, but the institutional logics of the space—as needing to meet the requirements of funders to get youth to "self-sufficiency"—constrained the staff in their mission of getting the youth into stable housing. If the goal is stable housing for LGBTQ youth experiencing homelessness, we need to examine and challenge how the social organization of shelter life regulates and punishes certain behaviors, especially behaviors related to gender and sexuality and behaviors that do not harm others.

AN LGBTQ REFUGE

"Do do doop dum, Do do doop do doop da dum. Do do doop dum, Do do doop do doop da dum." Prada's phone was playing "Always Be My Baby" by singer Mariah Carey. A twenty-three-year-old Hispanic heterosexual transgender woman, Prada was dying her hair in the bathroom at the LGBTQ shelter. I could often expect a music party happening in the bathroom, as youth tried on wigs, got ready, and tested out various makeup and clothing styles. The youth always found ways to entertain themselves at the shelter.

One night, Cookie, a twenty-five-year-old Black heterosexual transgender woman, lip synced a performance of Whitney Houston's "I Will Always Love You" for some of the youth and me, a rainbow US flag and transgender flag hanging behind her. Another night, some youth and I tried on Cookie's wigs. We took selfies with the different hairstyles while joking and making funny faces. Throughout the year, as well, the staff—all of whom except one identified as LGBTQ—would organize to take the youth to LGBTQ events, including Transgender Day of Remembrance, Family Pride Fair, and the San Antonio Pride parade, in which they marched. The youth found joy in their queerness and expansive expressions of gender at the shelter. As Justice, an eighteen-year-old Black heterosexual transgender woman, put it one night when someone knocked on the door to "the pod," where all the youth slept—"Come in, we're all queer!"

Listening to pop divas, engaging with LGBTQ pop culture, and sharing space together brought joy that helped the youth endure the experiences of living in a shelter. Joy, particularly collective joy, can also open new worlds for marginalized groups facing adversity. As performance studies scholar Javon Johnson shows, Black joy has allowed Black people to persevere amid structural racism and white supremacy. Moving beyond seeing Black joy as only a way to endure, Johnson theorizes that Black joy also allows the expansion of other possibilities outside of white supremacy. Black joy provides new ways to think about freedom and ending racism.[6] We can expand this theorizing to think about how Black and Brown queer and transgender joy enables LGBTQ youth experiencing homelessness not only to endure but also to imagine new possibilities. The joy in these collective moments at the shelter challenged heteronormativity, the gender binary, and their intersections with other structures of oppression, as the youth reveled in their queerness, transness, gender expansiveness, and Black and Brownness. Systemic inequalities have pushed the youth to the streets and into a shelter. They still resisted and endured. They found joy.

Bathrooms and Showers

Most of the youth also appreciated the resources that the shelter provided, including things some people take for granted, such as a shower. "Oh, let me tell you! Girl, I thank God as soon as I hop in that damn shower. Oh Lord, it felt so good to be clean. This water feels so good to be clean. That's what I say every morning when I hop in that shower," stated Zoe, a nineteen-year-old Hispanic heterosexual transgender woman. As documented in the previous chapter, most shelter bathrooms segregate by gender and create violent spaces for the youth in this study. At the LGBTQ shelter, the communal bathroom was "all gender." The bathroom had three stalls with doors, three showers with curtains, and two sinks. The stall doors and shower curtains gave the youth more privacy than most other shelter bathrooms. The director of the shelter told me that one person, when moving to the LGBTQ shelter, hugged the shower curtain. This person had not seen a shower curtain in over four years. Feeling safe in the bathroom at the LGBTQ shelter, Zoe could get clean in a shower—instead of in a sink, as she did on the streets—and she could do so without having to stay vigilant against violence, harassment, and discrimination.

LGBTQ people, especially transgender and gender-expansive people, need safe bathrooms. Gender-inclusive showering and sleeping arrangements at shelters show LGBTQ young people that the design of the space—and ideally, the staff working there—respects LGBTQ youth.[7] This gender inclusivity may hold significant meaning and consequences for poor LGBTQ youth of color, who have to deal with racism and its link to poverty and who thus can lack access to private spaces. The privacy provided by the stall doors and shower curtains furthers this notion of respecting the youth. Services such as bathrooms and showers that the youth could safely access did not exist in San Antonio before the shelter opened.[8]

Changing Gender Marker and Name

During my eighteen months of fieldwork, I constantly heard about young people trying to get an identification card. A person needs an ID card to obtain a job in the formal economy, to vote, to open a bank account, to fly on an airplane, to get a library membership, to access some forms of health care, to enroll in education and government benefits programs, and so many other things in life. In 2005, Congress passed the Real ID Act requiring that to obtain an ID card a person needs their social security number, date of birth, address of residency, and proof of legal status in the United States. With these requirements, getting an ID card can be a bureaucratic nightmare.[9]

Many youth in this study constantly worked to get their ID card. The drop-in center in Austin or the LGBTQ shelter in San Antonio could serve as proof of residency. Both organizations also paid for the services to help the youth acquire their supporting identification documents and their ID card. Obtaining a birth certificate, school records, social security card, and other supporting identification documents often took at least a month. This disconnect—the lengthy time bureaucracies take to process documents versus the urgency of the need for an ID card—creates more barriers for youth in accessing services and in getting a formal-sector job.[10] Indeed, as one service provider told me, "It's a nightmare. It really is. And just an additional barrier, I think, because we have to work so hard on getting IDs and supporting documents to get that ID that we can't focus on things that really need help."

Moreover, getting an ID card with the proper gender marker and name change generated another burden for some transgender and gender-expansive youth. Jenelle, a twenty-one-year-old Hispanic heterosexual transgender woman with fiery red hair, lip piercings, and a bridge piercing, discussed this issue with me. "Honestly, legally changing your name and gender marker does help. Because to me, I fill out my resume online sometimes, and it says Jenelle. And they call me. And they hear my voice. And they're like, 'Okay, ma'am, you can come down,'" she explained. "And then they see me. And they're like, 'Okay, you look like you're okay for this job. Would you mind taking your piercings out or color your hair?'" When they get to the legal documentation, the interactions change. "And I have to put my legal name down. That's when they're like, 'Oh okay, we'll call you back.'" They never called back. Jenelle concluded, "I'd prefer to have my gender marker changed, so I wouldn't have to be like, 'Yeah, my legal name is so and so.' It just hurts to say it out loud."

Administrative systems often exclude transgender and gender-expansive people. The gender binary of M or F on most administrative forms is part of what lawyer and trans activist Dean Spade calls "administrative violence."[11] For example, an ID card includes the gender marker—often male or female—and one's first name. This classification of M or F on the ID card assumes that gender remains a permanent feature of the body that cannot or does not change. If a person's presentation does not match this marker, such as Jenelle's gender presentation, the person experiences heightened scrutiny.[12] The use of only M or F on an ID card makes the identity of transgender itself or any other nonbinary gender identity impossible.[13] Transgender and gender-expansive youth need proper identification that does not misgender them, as in Jenelle's case when she noted the pain of saying her legal name out loud. She also perceived that people did not hire her because of this mismatch between her ID card and her gender presentation. Transgender and gender-expansive people need a proper ID to lessen the discrimination that they face in such situations.[14]

Notably, transgender and gender-expansive people of color are particularly vulnerable to gender surveillance in relation to ID cards. Congress passed the REAL ID Act in 2005 in response to a moral panic around terrorism and undocumented immigration. This act granted the government more surveillance over US citizens and people trying to immigrate to the country. Part of this surveillance included a new national database of identification cards. The act sought to regulate and place under surveillance people of color for the sake of "national security." Officials often check people of color's ID cards more often to scrutinize their appearances. When a person of color's ID gender marker does not match their identity and/or appearance, such as in Jenelle's case, surveillance practices heighten.[15]

Understanding these barriers, the shelter prioritized helping the youth to not only get their ID but also to get their gender marker and name changed. For instance, Prada—the 23-year-old Hispanic heterosexual transgender woman who was listening to Mariah Carey in the bathroom—moved into the LGBTQ shelter on the day the shelter opened. She was the first youth at the shelter to get her gender marker and name changed on her ID card. Prada told me, "It was actually a quick process because [the director of the shelter and I] got together with [the shelter director's] sister, who runs her own law firm. . . . The [shelter director] helped pay for it. And it was about two seventy-something to change it legally. And about three to four days later, I already had a meeting with the judge for the name change and the gender marker change."

Another night, when I arrived at the shelter, Jenelle—the Hispanic heterosexual transgender woman who had problems getting hired because of her ID card—ran up to me excited because she had a court date set to get her gender marker and name changed. The director of the shelter paid the court fees out of her own pocket until the grant money came through to help pay for this service. As Jenelle explained, "I was originally going to do it, but I don't have four hundred dollars. So, I can't do it myself. And I can't hire an attorney." A month later, Jenelle met with the judge. She got her name and gender marker changed.

To change one's gender marker and name takes financial resources and knowledge of navigating bureaucracies. In Texas, one had to get a letter from a doctor. According to information at the shelter, counseling services to change your name and gender marker cost about $100. The doctor's letter must verify that the person has pursued undergoing gender change.[16] Importantly, having the social capital of knowing a medical professional willing to provide this documentation speeds up the process. The staff at the shelter had access to supportive health professionals who would provide the needed documentation.

After getting this medical letter, the youth had to fill out two forms: (1) the Petition to Change the Sex and Gender Identifier of an Adult and (2) the Final Order to Change the Gender and Sex Identifier of an Adult.

A person also had to fill out other forms to change their name. The legal services for the paperwork and court appearance cost up to $500. For the name change, a person also had to get fingerprinted and could not have a felony conviction within the past two years. Once the doctor's letter, petition forms, and fingerprinting are in order, the person files their petition to change their gender marker and name. A court date gets set. The judge exercises discretion in granting these changes. For Prada and Jenelle, the LGBTQ shelter director's sister was a lawyer who knew a judge who granted these changes. After getting a certified copy of a court order granting the changes, the person goes to the Texas Department of Public Safety to get their ID card changed.

The shelter's recognition of the problems for LGBTQ youth surrounding ID cards made putting financial resources toward gender marker and name changes a priority, which was a great help for the LGBTQ youth. It is important to remember, however, that requiring a gender marker on an ID card upholds the gender binary. Youth who do not identify as either male or female do not have any other options to pick in Texas. Gender-expansive and non-binary youth also still face discriminatory encounters if they do not embody and enact the M or F on their ID card.

Moreover, as documented in chapter 3, poor Black and Brown transgender and gender-expansive youth disproportionately have felony records because of police profiling. Hence, the fingerprinting to change one's name erects another barrier. Not changing one's name creates more obstacles to securing employment in the formal economy, such that if a youth's name on their ID card does not match their gender appearance *and* the youth has a criminal record, they can face multiple employment barriers. By the end of my fieldwork, staff members were working to get legal services at the shelter to help get youth's criminal records expunged.

Hormone Replacement Therapy

Staff also worked to provide hormone replacement therapy (HRT) for the youth who wanted it. Adelpha, an eighteen-year-old Black, Mexican, and white heterosexual transgender woman, discussed the importance of accessing hormones and how social workers at her previous Child Protective Services group home did not understand the need. "I was talking about getting on hormones and doing all that kind of stuff. And then [staff at the group home] were like, 'What do you mean hormones? What's wrong?' And I'm like—they didn't know what that was or anything about it." After she turned eighteen, Adelpha found out about the LGBTQ shelter. "I was just like, okay, hormones. There's going to be transgender, gay, all that. And I've never been around all those. And that's all that I ever wanted. And so, I was excited. But I didn't know what all it entailed." At the LGBTQ shelter, Adelpha said, "Now, I'm on hormones. Now, I'm a lot happier and stable."

Hormones help some young people feel their body coming in line with their identity.[17] Some youth in this study would get their hormones on the streets before they could access HRT through the LGBTQ shelter. As studies have shown, low-income transgender people and transgender people of color are more likely to access hormones on the streets because they experience more transgender-related discrimination in health care settings and face barriers in accessing transition-related care compared to other groups.[18] Improperly taking street hormones, however, leads to serious health problems.[19] Seeing HRT as an important resource for LGBTQ youth experiencing homelessness, the staff at the LGBTQ shelter used resources to pay for HRT. Staff, as well, utilized some youth's health insurance—if the youth formerly resided in Child Protective Services and had Medicaid—to help pay for HRT as well. The staff also knew LGBTQ-competent medical professionals who would assist in helping the youth get on hormones. Having an appearance more in line with how one identifies helps in navigating the formal economy, sex work, the streets, encounters with police, and other daily interactions, as people may not misrecognize the youth's gender as much. HRT helps some youth navigate their social worlds more easily within the current dominant gender relations of U.S. society.

Social Support

Along with safe showers, ID cards, and HRT, the shelter provided a supportive environment. In talking about other shelter resources, Adelpha listed "hormone replacement therapy, job search or job things, obviously shelter, and like an environment where you feel accepted and comfortable."

Adelpha also discussed the importance of living around other LGBTQ people at the shelter. "I think it's important 'cause it's like we have to come together. We have to come together—be supportive of each other." Notably, Adelpha saw this support as combating isolation and as building confidence. "I know there's a lot of LGBT people out there. But we're so, like, disconnected. So, we feel like we going through the struggle alone. So, having a place like this—just I feel like it builds confidence, reassurance, a lot of stuff just within yourself." The shelter also served as a respite from violence and discrimination. As Adelpha explained, "Plus, you don't need to be harassed and tooken advantage of and bullied and treated like shit. You're already going through it. So, you need a place."

Cookie—the twenty-five-year-old Black heterosexual transgender woman who lip synced Whitney Houston—also saw the support that the shelter offered as a main benefit. She stated, "It is always good to have a group behind you—some support behind you—to help you continue going on. Because if you don't have any support, how can you make it?" Cookie, as well, saw the shelter as a respite from harassment and discrimination. "For the simple fact because the people here are like me. Number two, because I don't have to worry about what anybody think or say," Cookie explained. "I don't have to worry about, 'Oh my gosh, he's gay. She's gay. That's a faggot or whatever.' Because everyone shows you the same respect." She concluded, "It's great. I mean you can be yourself, ya know? You can be a crossdresser, transgender, transsexual. If you wanted to be a freakin' gay boy, it is your prerogative to do what you want. And you don't have to worry about what anyone thinks because we are here."

In both Austin and San Antonio, many youth in this study lived isolated lives on the streets. With the LGBTQ shelter opening in San Antonio, some LGBTQ youth experiencing homelessness found a space to help them feel less alone. As Adelpha noted, this lessening of feelings of isolation builds confidence. Social support also serves as a buffer against the stressors on one's mental health, ameliorating some mental health challenges that youth experiencing homelessness often face.[20] LGBTQ spaces have served as havens from the hostile heteronormative world and as places to find similar others and build community.[21] At the LGBTQ shelter, youth did not have to stay vigilant against harassment and discrimination, as they often had to do on the streets, at other shelters, and in other spaces and places in their lives.

Furthermore, this LGBTQ space particularly benefitted the youth in this study. Poor LGBTQ people often lack the economic resources to live in gay neighborhoods and to access LGBTQ events, and LGBTQ people of color experience racism in these spaces.[22] The LGBTQ shelter served as a place they could interact with other people like themselves. But we need other and more LGBTQ spaces for poor LGBTQ youth of color. A shelter for people experiencing homelessness should not have to function as the only space to build community and find support.

Likewise, living with other LGBTQ people helped in building friendships and families. Dante, a twenty-two-year-old Black bisexual youth, detailed, "I get to experience a lot of different things, because before I wasn't in an LGBTQ environment. I was just bi by myself. I learned a lot from a lot of the people here. I feel for a lot of the people here. Even though I have my own personal circle, I feel for a lot of people here. And I can count them all as friends." Niguel, a twenty-four-year-old white Hispanic gay man, described a similar experience. "I wanted to be with people that I'm a bit more comfortable with. Like I've never really—like all the people I've hung out with like my whole life, I always hang around straight people. I never go to like the gay bars or anything like that," he explained. Now around other LGBTQ people, Niguel stated, "I'm building a new support system. A new group of friends that will eventually be more like family, you know?" Dante's close friend Tori, a nineteen-year-old white lesbian, also saw the support as relating to being "like a family." She told me, "I'm around people that are actually supporting me and everything else. We're like a family. Because we have the same, you know, we are LGBT."

Most other marginalized groups in society such as people of color, working-class and poor people, immigrants, and religious minorities often grow up around people like them, including their immediate family members. LGBTQ people often do not have that experience growing up. Friendships thus help them learn about LGBTQ life and build support against the judgments of society. LGBTQ people of color have historically formed "ballroom communities" that have been supportive and caring through the HIV/AIDS crisis, experiences of homelessness, racism and poverty, and other hard times. Today, LGBTQ friendships and families still provide social support.[23] Poor LGBTQ youth of color experiencing homelessness often have few, if any, safety nets, social networks, or institutions to help and protect them. As discussed in the previous chapter, they therefore form kinships to draw on others like them to help fulfill needs that society and families of origin do not fulfill for them.[24]

Living with similar others also helped the youth I interviewed, particularly the transgender women of color, feel "normal." Jenelle—the twenty-one-year-old Hispanic heterosexual transgender woman who got her gender marker and name changed—explained, "It's more like where you can be yourself 'cause other trans women understand. Other trans women get the struggles. How you hate yourself. How you don't understand why you feel like a freak. So, in all honesty, they can help with that." Naomi, an eighteen-year-old bisexual transgender Latina, detailed a similar sentiment. "I wake up in the morning. And I see these other girls that are going through the same shit—as far as being trans—I don't feel so like trapped as much. I feel like I'm normal." She continued, "It normalizes me as far as feeling like a female. Because I feel like we're just a bunch of females in the dorm. At the same time, we can relate 'cause we're going through it. We understand the mental, physical, emotional struggle. And no other person's going to understand that unless you're going through it. And I love it. I love it."

Many negative stereotypes about transgender women of color circulate in the US imaginary. Some transgender women of color themselves internalize these stereotypes and "feel like a freak." We can challenge and change these stereotypes. As sociologist Salvador Vidal-Ortiz asks, in pushing us to question our ideas and stereotypes about transgender women of color, "Does she inhabit the streets? Is she a sex worker? Can you imagine her being your co-worker at the local university? Can you hear her theorizing from her own experience—and accept it? Or see her working on something completely unrelated to her identity and experience?"[25] Jenelle and Naomi saw living with other transgender women as expanding how they thought about transgender women, and hence, how they viewed themselves. Transgender friendship provides acceptance and belonging, especially for transgender women of color. The shelter supplied a space to forge friendships that broke down stereotypes, provided support, and made these young people not feel so alone in a hostile world that had cast them to the streets.

At the end of the day, though, the shelter remained a shelter. To access these resources and support, the youth had to follow the rules and regulations of shelter life. I turn, now, to examine what the youth had to give up to stay at the LGBTQ shelter.

THE SOCIAL ORGANIZATION OF SHELTER LIFE

I walked across some train tracks and through a parking lot, heading to the twenty-plus-acre homelessness campus in San Antonio. To my left was a clothing warehouse on which someone had painted a body lying down with a Purple Heart medal over it and the inscription: "i thought i would never have to sleep on the outside." I veered to the right to go through the guard shack, the point of entry for the campus. Inside, people who lived on the campus had badges slung around their necks. They waited in line to go through a metal detector, have their bags searched, and blow into a breathalyzer. I flashed my red volunteer badge to a guard and walked past the line and around the metal detector to enter.

I headed toward the men's side of campus, where the LGBTQ shelter was located. A sermon was blasting over the loudspeaker. Bright red signs exclaimed that the men's side forbade women and children. I pondered how I never visited the women's and children side, which the LGBTQ youth were not permitted to access. Getting out of my head, I put my badge up to a card reader and entered the LGBTQ shelter.

To my left was a teal hallway leading to dorm-style rooms, where ten LGBTQ adults experiencing homelessness resided. To my right, the front desk had flyers advertising city events and resources scattered about. Behind the desk, I peeked into the office to say hello to the director. I then continued down the hallway to pop into "the pod"—where eight LGBTQ youth experiencing homelessness lived. There were four bunk beds and lockers for each youth. Crumbs speckled the couch, and the library DVDs stood in a stack next to the television. Since no one was around, I went and looked in the "all-gender" bathroom. No one around again. I headed back to the office to chat with the director until the youth started coming in around the 10:00 p.m. curfew. The following morning—when my nine-hour volunteer shift ended—I used my badge on a card reader to get through the exit turnstiles. I would be back next week.

Shelter Rules

The goal of both organizations where I conducted my fieldwork involved getting the youth to "self-sufficiency." Self-sufficiency often meant stable housing. As the director of the LGBTQ shelter told me, "Well, the mission is to help these young adults become self-sufficient, so they can attain and sustain housing on their own." To achieve this goal, staff implemented rules. For instance, the handbook given to the youth residing at the LGBTQ shelter stated that they must "participate in at least one service or activity per day" and "be productive." From the organizational perspective, the youth should take GED classes or another type of educational class and/or should get a job in the formal economy. The rules stated that the youth had to leave the shelter from 8:30 a.m. to 4:30 p.m. every weekday. The rules set the curfew at the campus at 10:00 p.m. on weekdays and 11:00 p.m. on Friday and Saturday.[26] The youth also needed to wake up and go to breakfast by 7:30 a.m. The youth often had to plan their days around when the cafeteria on campus served meals. The staff also kept a logbook in their office where they would record shelter incidents, the comings and goings of the youth, missed curfews, prescriptions that needed to be refilled, and other documentations of the young people's behaviors.

To enter the shelter, the youth had to be completely sober, as they had to blow a .00 on the breathalyzer to get into the campus. Since a guard searched their bags and made them go through a metal detector, the youth also could not bring drugs or weapons to the shelter. The staff could also drug test the youth at any time and go through the youth's belongings. I—with my volunteer badge—never had to go through the metal detector, never had my bag searched, and never blew into a breathalyzer. Only the people experiencing homelessness had to give up certain rights and privacy to be on the campus.

In describing to me life at the LGBTQ shelter, Jenelle—the twenty-one-year-old Hispanic heterosexual transgender woman who got her gender marker and named changed through the shelter—said, "It's not that it's hard to make friends here. It's just—feels like it's a prison." She went on to give more detail about the rules of the shelter and how that to live there she had to give up certain rights and privileges. Jenelle explained, "And then I don't understand why we all have to be in our beds by ten. It's just stupid to me. I'm not a child." Jenelle asserted that she knows how to take care of herself. "I have an alarm on my phone that wakes me up," she stated. "I know how much sleep I need to function the next day. I know what I do in the morning to get ready."

These rules at the LGBTQ shelter correspond with the social organization of most homeless shelters, which is often shaped by funding. Many US shelters, especially those that receive government funding, input data into the homeless management information system. This system tracks how organizations serve people experiencing homelessness and monitors the outcomes of those services. The federal, state, county, and city governments partially use these outcomes to determine which programs should receive funding. These outcomes entail many different measures. For instance, the "Client-Level Outcome Measures for Homeless Programs," according to the US Department of Housing and Urban Development (HUD), includes linking people experiencing homelessness to employment programs to help them get to a place of financial self-reliance. The outcome measure of this goal at the client level equaled the percentage of people who have earned income at program exit. The outcome measure at the system level for the same goal equaled the reduction in average length of stay at the shelter. Other similar measures include linking people experiencing homelessness to mental health and substance use services and seeing how that also reduces the average length of stay at the shelter.[27] According to government officials, the answers to solving homelessness lie in these statistical numbers, measures, and outcomes.[28]

As part of this government-funded system of outcome goals, organizations and shelters implement rules and requirements for people using their services. Some of these rules—such as no physical violence—help to ensure safety at the shelter. Many rules also relate to organizations' effectively managing resources and operating efficiently, with the aim of reaching the outcomes that their funders gave them money for.[29] As the director of the LGBTQ shelter explained, "And the catch-22 is if you're writing for grants, they want to know, what have you done. You have to show some successes, or what is your plan, or what does your program look like and what are you doing in order to get funding." This system and the service providers operating within the shelter system see and define success by these measures. As a service provider at the LGBTQ shelter told me, "It's really great to see someone succeed in whatever way they need to be succeeding at the time. Somebody getting a good score on one of their GED tests. Somebody getting a job. Somebody having a resume for the first time, when they've never had one before. Just all those. Somebody getting housing." Education and getting a job register as successes on the way to housing. These successes, though, work in line with governmentality—the upholding of white, middle-class, capitalistic values and behaviors and of putting the burden to solve homelessness on the individual.

Dante—the twenty-two-year-old Black bisexual youth who discussed making friends with other LGBTQ people at the shelter—often discussed his problems with how staff members treated the youth at the shelter. He did not like how the staff monitored his medication. Upset that the staff would not believe him when he had physical pain and couldn't get to appointments and job interviews, Dante told me, "I can see a power-hungry struggle going on here as far as the staff goes. They want to tell us to do stuff and won't let us discover it on our own. They don't treat the eighteen-to-twenty-five [year-old] members like adults, when we really are adults." He went on, "My biggest issue was: I'm taking medicine for a whole bunch of different things. I take a lot of different medicines. And you have me switching up every couple months— every couple weeks—because you don't like the medicine I'm on." He continued, "I switched up to something that made me sick, so I switched back. So why would you want me to take something that is making me sick? And I'm already stable on some medicine. It doesn't make sense to me. It's just you want me to take what you want me to take."

People experiencing homelessness often feel as if service providers treat them as children, a process that scholars studying homelessness have seen as "infantilization." Infantilization involves a pattern of behavior whereby someone often in a position of authority interacts and treats a subordinate adult as a child.[30] Infantilization has a history tied to subordinating people of color, women, and LGBTQ people. Historically, white men constructed women and Black people as not fully adults, and white men used this logic to warrant not giving women and Black people equal rights.[31]

We can think of calling Black men "boys" or calling women "girls" as emblematic of the infantilization of Black men and women. Likewise, dominant society has stereotyped gay men as promiscuous and obsessed with their bodies, drugs, and looking and acting youthful. This construction upholds the idea of gay men as not fully formed adults.[32] Such stereotypes can also apply to other non-heterosexual and transgender people, as reaching full adulthood is often tied to heterosexuality, the nuclear family, and upholding the dominant relations of gender in society. These processes of infantilization constitute people of color, women, and LGBTQ people as subordinate within US society, with LGBTQ people of color affected the most.

People residing at homeless shelters experience some rules as a form of paternalism and may see service providers as believing they know the best course of action for people experiencing homelessness.[33] Within this framing, shelter rules construct people experiencing homelessness as not fully adults and as incapable of making their own decisions.[34] LGBTQ youth experiencing homelessness experience this infantilization as simultaneously about subordinating them for their age, race, gender, sexuality, and class. Infantilization works to mutually co-constitute poor LGBTQ youth of color as subordinates. Infantilization also works alongside governmentality in subordinating and surveilling the youth for not living up to white, middle-class, capitalistic values and behaviors—values and behaviors that people often see as constituting an independent adult in US society.

Some staff see the rules, such as the drug prohibition, as not only helping the youth get to self-sufficiency but also part of maintaining a "safe" campus, particularly for the children. Notably, however, the LGBTQ youth could not even access the women's and children side of campus. Some transgender women residing at the LGBTQ shelter would often discuss among themselves during my fieldwork that they should live on the women's side of campus. They stated that the segregation of the transgender women to the LGBTQ shelter on the men's side of campus showed that campus staff did not fully acknowledge the transgender women's gender identification. This segregation and notion of "safety" entails a type of gender panic and penis panic, as discussed in chapter 4 in relation to the fear of transgender women entering women-only spaces. The segregation thus marginalized and dehumanized transgender women by reducing them to their genitals. Importantly, not every LGBTQ youth experiencing homelessness wants the segregation that comes with an LGBTQ-specific shelter. Some see this segregation as denying them their identity by not integrating them into other spaces.

Furthermore, some staff utilized punishment to try to get the youth to comply with the shelter rules. As one service provider told me, "We need to become more strict [at the LGBTQ shelter]. And let [the youth] know, you can't do this, you can't do that. If you want to call your own shots, and do this, and do that, then, you know what, move out. Get your own place. And become the king of your own castle." Arthur, a twenty-five-year-old Black gay youth, also saw living alone as the only way to escape rules. He told me, "I feel like they shouldn't have the rules that's here. . . . Live on your own. Make sure that you have your own place. And live by your own rules. 'Cause you have to listen to everybody else's rules when you live with them. I've learned that. And it's like, no, I don't want to live with nobody."

Certain staff and youth saw getting to independence and making one's own decisions as a privilege that only people who have their own place can experience. Living in a shelter means giving up certain aspects of independence. This way of thinking, though, erases the independence that comes with living on the streets, as people do not see having street skills as valuable, since they do not uphold middle-class, capitalistic values and behaviors. Likewise, during fieldwork, another service provider said to me that the youth deserve chances, but if a certain youth did not comply with the program, other youth who will comply are on the waitlist. Only people who will follow the rules of the shelter are seen as people worthy of receiving services and residing there. Another service provider even talked about acting as a counselor, mother, advisor, nurse, and babysitter for the youth. She went on to explain why she punishes them. She stated, "The rewarding moments are when they, after you ground them—you punish them for something they do wrong. They analyze it. They come, and they thank you. They thank you, 'cause they—without the punishment, without the lesson, they wouldn't have succeeded."

These punishments, such as grounding the youth, imposing an earlier curfew, or even suspending them, show that a person experiencing homelessness often only obtains services if they succumb to governmentality.

Addressing homelessness connects with *changing* people experiencing homelessness to fit the outcomes of organizations and their funders' goals, rather than *serving* people experiencing homelessness.[35] Staff worked to get the youth to find a job in the formal economy, to get an education, and to act personally responsible for their housing. Once again, these strategies and their relation to governmentality put the burden of solving homelessness on the LGBTQ youth.

Regulating Gender and Sexuality

Shelter surveillance at the LGBTQ shelter also involved the regulation of the youth's gender and sexuality. According to the shelter handbook that the youth received, rules forbade the youth from dating, getting into a relationship, or having sex with another youth residing at the shelter. As mentioned in the opening of this chapter, these prohibitions were to maintain "a safe space and inclusive community." My own volunteer handbook said to not have intimate relationships with the youth, to not stay in a room alone with any youth, to avoid all contact that someone might see as inappropriate, to not discuss my sex life with the youth, to allow the youth to initiate all physical contact, and to not shame the youth for their sexual exploration. Some of the shelter rules, however, contradicted this last rule.

For instance, the temperature in the shelter remained cold. I almost never took my jacket off when there. Why the cold? I never found out. But the youth often commented that the shelter felt like an ice box because staff wanted the youth to keep their clothes on. This perception that the staff tried to regulate them to not show their skin perhaps stemmed from some staff trying to regulate the youth's attire, including their gender attire. One evening, Naomi, an eighteen-year-old bisexual transgender Latina, had on a shirt with slashes through it on the back to show some skin. That night, though, she had the shirt on backwards, revealing her bra and chest through the cut-out part of the shirt. A staff member told Naomi to turn her shirt back around. This staff worker said that the LGBTQ shelter would be reviewed for renewal soon. Staff worried that the youth dressing provocatively might harm the shelter's chance of getting renewed to stay on the homelessness campus. They wanted the youth to dress "appropriately."

Within US society, adults often view youth as not sexually autonomous—often because they do not have economic independence. But adults also see youth sexuality as unrestrained. In response, adults—especially parents—try to control young people's sexuality.[36] Adults tell young people that dressing provocatively means that the young person lacks self-respect. Poor and working-class Black and Brown women already deal with a stereotype of being "sluts" and/or as sexually promiscuous. Dress codes and their messages often target them to control their assumed hypersexuality.[37]

As service providers see people experiencing homelessness as not economically independent, they try to control their sexuality as well. Within the framework of governmentality at shelters, sexual autonomy is for those who have a private place to live. Youth in this study also faced stereotypes about LGBTQ people, especially about transgender or gender-expansive people as being hypersexual. As poor transgender women of color, whom many people stereotype as sex workers, Naomi and other youth in this study experience heightened surveillance from staff at the shelter regarding their clothing and presentation. Staff did not want the transgender women to dress "provocatively." This surveillance of the youth's gender and sexuality is a form of homonormative governmentality. Some staff see Black and Brown LGBTQ youth as needing to restrain their sexuality, appearance, and clothing styles to achieve the outcomes of independence that the staff and funders want for the youth. The shelter rules reproduce the racial, classed, gendered, and sexual stereotypes about poor LGBTQ youth of color. Homonormative governmentality works to constitute the youth as outside the dominant gender and sexuality relations of US society.

Despite the handbook rule on relationships, the director of the shelter did admit a Black gay couple—Kareem and Arthur—into the shelter. However, they had to always prop the door open if they lounged in a room together. The rules forbade any intimate touching. Youth could hug and do each other's hair, but they could not hold hands, cuddle, or have sex. As twenty-five-year-old Arthur explained, "It's kind of stressful because I can't chill with my man the way I want to. I can't cuddle up with him or anything. So, it's like ugh! It gets on my nerves. I don't like it sometimes."

Tori, a nineteen-year-old white lesbian, even got in trouble for affectionately touching her partner on the homelessness campus.[38] Tori said they had been sitting close to one another in the cafeteria and a staff person—not at the LGBTQ shelter, but on the larger campus—cited them for public display of affection. Tori went on to say that she felt like staff on the homelessness campus targeted LGBTQ people. She often saw mixed-gender couples engaging in public displays of affection, who did not get in trouble.

In a 2007 review of the scientific literature on homeless shelters, the authors note that most research on shelters do not mention sexual orientation.[39] Most scholarship on shelters does not even discuss sexuality. An exception, anthropologist Elliot Liebow's study on women experiencing homelessness in Washington, D.C., documented that the main problem with sex at shelters was the lack of it. The lack of privacy and gender segregation at shelters (which assume people's heterosexuality and/or that people only engage in sexual conduct with someone of another gender) contribute to this lack of sex. People residing at shelters often cannot have people in their rooms or visitors from outside of the shelter, and they must leave their doors open. Hence, having sexual relations is difficult.[40]

Partly, this regulation of sex at shelters stems from societal stereotypes surrounding poor people and/or people of color and their sexuality. For example, the 1990s welfare reform laws partially targeted the presumed promiscuity of poor women, especially poor Black and Brown women. Conservative responses to the issue of poverty entailed promoting traditional heterosexual marriage and abstinence-only sex education. The logic went that if poor women stopped having children out of wedlock, they would not experience poverty anymore. In effect, their solution was to cut social safety nets and ignore structural racism, telling poor people of color their sexuality was keeping them in poverty.[41] Staff at the LGBTQ shelter did not see intimate contact as helping the youth get to self-sufficiency. Instead, staff wanted the youth to focus on getting their GED and/or a job in the formal economy—not on relationships and sex.

Importantly, while most, if not all, shelters have rules that regulate people's sexuality, these rules have a discriminatory impact on LGBTQ youth experiencing homelessness, as they uphold stereotypes about LGBTQ people's hypersexuality and contribute to their marginalization through furthering their experiences of homelessness. To enforce rules around sexuality, staff suspended certain youth. During my fieldwork, staff suspended Camila, Naomi, and Obadiah for having sex at the shelter. Some staff said banning sex at the shelter came from a public health concern (and the handbook said the sex ban sought to maintain a "safe space" and "inclusive community"). But the youth did not really have other options to have sex with each other. If caught having sex in a public place, police could arrest them.

Furthermore, the curfew at the shelter made hanging out with a significant other at night or engaging in sex work difficult. As Lucas, a twenty-year-old white heterosexual transgender man, explained, "I was actually ended up kicked out [of the LGBTQ shelter] because I was staying too many nights with my girlfriend." Youth could only miss curfew five days a month; after that, staff suspended them. Likewise, staff did not see sex work as a legitimate night job. Justice, an eighteen-year-old Black heterosexual transgender woman, told me one evening that she wanted to go out to work the streets but she had already used up all her nights out for the month. She was upset because she said it was easier to pick up men downtown at night.

Staff at many shelters enforce rules by suspending people. This practice heightens the insecurities that people experiencing homelessness already feel and face.[42] For instance, staff suspended Lucas for missing curfew too many times because he kept staying with his girlfriend. To get back into the shelter, Lucas had to sign a contract with stricter rules, such as a 5:30 p.m. curfew, going to GED class every day, and attending all his case management meetings. If he broke the contract, staff would suspend him again. Lucas already seemed stressed from staff suspending him once before, and he feared that he would break these even stricter rules. Indeed, he did miss the stricter curfew on his second day. Staff suspended him again, cycling him back to the streets.

Essentially, suspensions—or the threat of them—generated more instability for the LGBTQ youth in this study. Likewise, these regulations regarding gender and sexuality upheld and furthered the stereotypes of poor people, young people, LGBTQ people, and people of color as hypersexual. Homonormative governmentality thus marked the poor LGBTQ youth of color as deviant.

Suspensions also perpetuated homelessness. Suspended youth sometimes turned to drugs to cope with living on the streets. Taking drugs made it difficult to pass a drug test to get back into the shelter post-suspension, as Camila's story showed at the beginning of this chapter. More importantly, many rules did not let the youth act young and did not respect their sexual exploration. If they violated the rules, they could end up back on the streets.

HOMONORMATIVE GOVERNMENTALITY
AS QUEER NECROPOLITICS

The LGBTQ shelter served as a site of homonormative governmentality— a site supporting LGBTQ people while simultaneously regulating their gender and sexuality. This homonormative governmentality contributed to perpetuating LGBTQ youth homelessness. Violating rules brought about suspensions that kept the youth cycling among the streets, shelters, and jails. Although shelter staff often saw anti-LGBTQ discrimination as the cause of their homelessness, the focus remained on changing the LGBTQ youth—not society—as the way to address the problem. Some staff saw the youth's failure to accept the shelter's rules as the reason they still experienced homelessness. Youth cycled back to the streets, where they faced discrimination, and would often come back to the shelter after their suspension, because the shelter served as an LGBTQ refuge. But the shelter regulations sent some of them back to the streets again. The cycle kept repeating.

Shelters and homelessness make up part of the necropolitical power structure—defining who matters and who deserves social or literal death.[43] The LGBTQ shelter, as a site of homonormative governmentality, also contributed to a "queer necropolitics"—accepting certain LGBTQ people and marking other LGBTQ people for social or literal death.[44] The LGBTQ shelter saw molding LGBTQ youth into white, middle-class, capitalistic behavior as the ideal way to help the youth get into stable housing. The staff and funders of the organizations did not see the skills and networks that youth often needed on the streets—such as sex work and building relationships—as valuable or as helping the youth to get to self-sufficiency. Instead, staff regulated these same skills that proved to be assets for the youth when on the streets. This homonormative governmentality put the burden of solving homelessness on the individual, eclipsing the systemic and interpersonal causes.

Staff punished youth who challenged these regulations, including regulation of their gender and sexuality. Homonormative governmentality places poor LGBTQ youth of color under further surveillance and regulation. This surveillance and punishment contributed to youth going back to the streets, furthering their experiences of instability and homelessness. Hence, homonormative governmentality maintains a queer necropolitics of only accepting LGBTQ youth who maintain dominant relations of power and pushes further into social or literal death LGBTQ youth who do not conform to shelter rules. In other words, this queer necropolitics pushes to the margins youth who do not uphold white, middle-class, capitalistic values. Homonormative governmentality and queer necropolitics maintain dominant structures of capitalism, white supremacy, heteronormativity, and the gender binary. These processes relegate poor LGBTQ youth of color into social or literal death.

The youth enacted pleasures to find solidarity and, perhaps, imagine better futures. Queer necropolitics, however, works insidiously. The homonormative governmentality enacted by the shelter gave the youth some LGBTQ resources and space, even to meet each other. But staff punished them for any behaviors that challenged the dominant notions of success as established by funders. This insidiousness continued as well in the form of staff caring about the youth. Queer necropolitics is not always intentional. Staff thought they did the best thing for the youth. Staff even felt hurt and upset when the youth did not measure up to their definition of success and/or ended up back on the streets.[45] Nonetheless, the shelter and its implementation of homonormative governmentality did not really address LGBTQ youth homelessness. Rather, it often contributed to perpetuating homelessness.

Conclusion

THERE'S NO PLACE LIKE HOME

November 30, 2016, I received a text message. "Do you know anyone that can help me with my rent?" Fieldwork ended in June. I had not seen any of the youth in this study in months. The last time I saw Jenelle—a twenty-one-year-old Hispanic heterosexual transgender woman—she had taken a job as a hostess and had moved out of the LGBTQ shelter and into a single-room occupancy on the larger homelessness campus. Through social media, I later learned that she had moved off the homelessness campus and into an apartment. However, she now was having trouble paying her rent. "It's not okay, but what can I do, I don't know many people that can help even if they wanted to," she texted. I replied with resources and words of support. She responded that because she makes over $12,000 a year, she did not qualify for assistance. Instead, as her last text to me stated, "The only option I have is to break my lease, but that just leaves me in debt and homeless."

When I present and discuss this research project, people often ask me if any success stories happened. People want to know, do any youth get into stable housing? In those moments, I think of Jenelle. Or I think of Emmanuel, whom I wrote about in the introduction of this book, as constantly cycling between housing, the streets, and the LGBTQ shelter. I also think of Audrey and Trinity, the couple who got housing for a few months but who went back to living on the streets by the end of this study. Yes, some youth got into housing. But this housing remained unstable. The youth often ended up back on the streets.

What can we expect when the dominant solutions to addressing homelessness put the burden of addressing homelessness on the individual? Get a job. Most youth in this study worked. Work harder. Hard work does not bring about a living wage and affordable housing. One even gets penalized, like Jenelle, who did work and then no longer qualified for assistance, even when she still needed some help. And what about other difficulties, such as facing discrimination in trying to get a formal-sector job as a transgender woman of color and/or as a person with a criminal record? Dominant solutions to addressing homelessness often ignore structural conditions and interpersonal interactions that produce and perpetuate homelessness.

In this conclusion, I shift the focus to addressing homelessness away from the individual, because putting the burden of solving a complex social issue on marginalized people just creates an additional burden for them. Instead, I turn to the insights provided by the youth in this study to think through collective and structural ways of addressing homelessness—specifically, LGBTQ youth homelessness. I outline queer approaches to thinking through new ways of supporting LGBTQ youth by redesigning systems for them, approaching justice without punishment, providing essential services, and housing all who want housing. The goal is freedom and liberation for all LGBTQ youth, including the most marginalized, such as the youth in this study.

QUEERING FEMINISM, QUEERING HOMELESSNESS

I ground the contributions of this study in the youth's voices but also in queer politics and analyses as articulated by political scientist Cathy Cohen. Queer politics and analyses move away from identity to understanding people's relations to power and to examining through an intersectional framework how exploitation, violence, material realities, and economic configurations shape people's lives.[1] I build on a queer of color analysis to push the fields of feminist and queer studies to a different analytical level. I contend that separating gender and sexuality as analytically distinct fails to document embodied and relational processes of gender and sexuality and their intersections with race and class. Anthropologist Gayle Rubin saw this separation of gender and sexuality as important in trying to center sexuality as its own analytical frame.[2] However, this analytical strategy does not capture the lived experiences of LGBTQ people, particularly poor, gender-expansive, and/or LGBTQ people of color. Indeed, non-heterosexual women of color feminists have always pushed for a more complex intersectional framework.[3]

By turning to the youth in this study and how their embodiments shape their lives, I build on women of color feminism and a queer of color analysis to contend that an analytical separation of gender from sexuality or even from race or class will fail to capture people's lived experiences. Hence, this separation produces dull analyses. A queer analysis needs to focus on embodiment and how embodiment locates and shapes a person's relation to power, often more so than identity. The words we use to try to describe gender and sexuality fail to capture lived experiences, such as those of the youth in this study, who often used words around gender and sexuality interchangeably and who experienced regulation of their lives through policing their gender, sexuality, race, and class. The concepts I explore in this study—heteronormative compliance, the queer control complex, the new Lavender Scare, queer street smarts, and homonormative governmentality—all capture the deeply intertwined relationship of gender and sexuality, as well as how gender and sexuality always intersect with race and class. As I have noted, processes like racial profiling, gender policing, and sexual regulation happen simultaneously, such that using separate terms fails to capture these intertwined processes. We need new ways of thinking and describing these processes, grounded in people's lived experiences and realities.

Likewise, we need to grapple with the unevenness of LGBTQ social change. We need to parse through how relations of gender and sexuality and their intersections with race and class within US society affect these processes of change. For instance, certain sexuality-based rights such as same-sex marriage chip away at heteronormativity. As a response to these challenges to the heteronormative order, a reinvestment in the gender binary occurs to try to restabilize the dominant relations of gender and sexuality. Bathroom bills, the Trump administration wanting to define gender as biological and immutable, and the disproportionate murder rate of transgender women of color exemplify this backlash. Poor LGBTQ youth of color—such as most of the youth in this study—often fare the worst in this gender binary re-entrenchment. In effect, the success of gay rights does not fully help LGBTQ people who experience marginalization for more than just their sexuality. Expansive expressions of gender, along with race, class, and sexuality—often more so than an LGBTQ identity—shape the lives of many LGBTQ people in significant ways. We need to move away from a focus on rights and identity to understand and challenge the ways in which certain LGBTQ people—often poor transgender and gender-expansive and/ or non-heterosexual youth of color—face criminalization, poverty, homelessness, violence, and other forms of marginalization.[4]

Another main finding of this study entails queering the work on homelessness and urban poverty. Experiencing homelessness does not happen because of poverty alone. Structural racism disproportionately pushes people of color to experience homelessness, despite white people experiencing deep poverty more than people of color.[5] In the same vein, I insist that we cannot understand the pathways into and experiences of homelessness without examining how heteronormativity and the gender binary shape processes of poverty and housing instability. Documenting these processes begins to get at how and why LGBTQ youth of color are disproportionately represented in the youth homelessness population in the United States. For example, in upholding the dominant relations of gender and sexuality, employers exclude LGBTQ people from economic mobility through making employment in the formal economy difficult, especially for transgender and gender-expansive people of color. The gender segregation of shelters and services also marginalizes transgender and gender-expansive people seeking assistance to get off the streets. These processes could theoretically affect not only LGBTQ people. Heterosexual single mothers of color also disproportionately experience poverty and housing instability, and they too fall outside of the dominant gender and sexuality relations within US society—relations based on middle-class whiteness, marriage, and the myth of the nuclear family. Queer politics and analyses examine how heteronormativity, the gender binary, and other structures marginalize heterosexual people as well as LGBTQ people.[6] This queer and intersectional analysis of poverty and homelessness helps to specifically address LGBTQ youth homelessness, but also helps to address poverty and homelessness within US society more broadly. Targeted policies that address relations of domination and processes around gender, sexuality, class, and race make for effective interventions.

QUEERING SOLUTIONS

"Basically, to end homelessness, help the homeless," stated Ciara, a twenty-two-year-old Black Hispanic bisexual youth. In this conclusion, I center the youth's voices to address homelessness. Youth experiencing homelessness need to partake in all conversations around supporting them. I learned so much from the forty LGBTQ youth in this study. My hope remains that the findings from this study and the young people's calls for social change will guide how we address LGBTQ youth homelessness moving forward.

Queering Support

"Parents need to be more supportive of their kids," stated Audrey, a twenty-three-year-old Hispanic lesbian. "That's like the root of the problem." Audrey's girlfriend, Trinity, a twenty-year-old white lesbian, gave a similar reply to my question about addressing LGBTQ youth homelessness. "For parents to get the sticks out of their asses," Trinity exclaimed. "And to love their children despite what they might have grown up thinking—to love their children despite their sexuality, despite their differences, and to keep their children in their home. So many of the LGBT, like they're kicked out because of the fact that their gay, and it's messed up." A nineteen-year-old Hispanic heterosexual transgender woman, Zoe, recommended that people, including parents, stop acting hateful. "For parents to love their child for who they are," Zoe said. "And for people to stop being so hateful—stop being so hateful. Parents, stop being so hateful toward your children for them liking who they like. I mean stop!"

Support, love, and care are essentials according to LGBTQ youth experiencing homelessness. Like the dominant discourse on LGBTQ youth homelessness, some youth—such as Audrey, Trinity, and Zoe—saw a main cause of LGBTQ youth homelessness as parents rejecting their LGBTQ child. This narrative does capture part of the youth's familial experiences. But as documented in chapter 1, this narrative does not provide the full picture. The youth in this study came from backgrounds of poverty and instability that often intersected with structural racism as well. This background shapes how some LGBTQ youth navigate and negotiate their gender and sexuality within their marginalized families of origin. Solutions need to avoid pathologizing poor families of color and need to avoid putting the burden of solving homelessness on already marginalized families.[7]

One solution involves rethinking family reunification as a strategy to addressing youth homelessness. Family reunification—in its current form—often does not account for families of origin that are marginalized and impoverished. People experiencing homelessness come from fragile social networks that lack financial capital and emotional support. This "network impoverishment" showcases how the entire social world of people experiencing homelessness is itself experiencing poverty and other inequalities, such as structural racism. Someone in the network who tries to help a person experiencing homelessness may fall into more instability and potentially homelessness as well.[8] As Jenelle's text to me mentioned in the opening of this chapter, even if the people she knew wanted to help, they would not be able to. We need, then, to invest in marginalized families and communities if we want to reunite young people with their communities and families of origin. Through this investment, reunification would cause less strain and poverty within social and familial networks.

In addition, LGBTQ organizations could help by assessing how to make programs more accessible for marginalized families who have an LGBTQ child. For example, in both cities where I conducted this study, Parents, Family and Friends of Lesbians and Gays (PFLAG) held their meetings in the evening. Many people work in the evening, cannot find childcare arrangements, need adequate transportation, and face other structural constraints to accessing these meetings.[9] LGBTQ organizations need to make services more accessible for marginalized families.

Notably, some middle-class parents reject their LGBTQ children. But it seems that rejected LGBTQ youth from the middle class often do not experience homelessness.[10] We need to continue to figure out what networks and resources LGBTQ youth from the middle class have access to when their families reject them. This information can help in implementing safety nets and social support systems for all LGBTQ youth. Also, not all poor and marginalized parents reject their LGBTQ children. We need a better understanding of accepting families to grasp how some poor LGBTQ youth stay united with their families.

We also need more expansive notions of families, communities, and support. Many LGBTQ youth experiencing homelessness do not want to reunite with their communities and families of origin. We need to recognize that some LGBTQ youth, like many youth in this study, build families with other people—including other LGBTQ people.[11] Hence, we need to invest in all forms of families. Families need safety nets, resources, and stability. Through gaining these resources, families can focus on accepting, nurturing, and supporting their LGBTQ child. We also need to consider abandoning the notion of the traditional family altogether, especially the notion of the nuclear family that is linked to middle-class, white society, and hence, marginalizes other family formations. The institution of the family can enact oppression toward certain family members, so challenging and rethinking notions of the family and its institutional purposes can provide an alternative way in helping LGBTQ youth.

To not put all the burden and labor of supporting LGBTQ youth on families, we need a *queer and trans support complex*. In his study on the policing of Black and Brown young men, sociologist Victor Rios calls for a "youth support complex" to nurture marginalized young people. This complex includes access to resources and mentors who see Black and Brown young people as an investment in the future and who help young people to reach their full human potential.[12] LGBTQ young people often do not grow up with and around other LGBTQ people. This queer and trans support complex can help fix the isolation and loneliness that comes with growing up as an LGBTQ child. Moreover, a queer and trans support complex fosters gender and sexual diversity through supporting young people's gender and sexual explorations.

Recently, sociological studies have documented how some parents support their transgender and gender-expansive children. These families often do a great deal of labor to support and raise their child. For example, the parents access conferences, lectures, and other resources, as well as research topics on their own. The parents often advocate for their transgender and gender-expansive children in many spaces, such as educational and sport settings. Families do not always have these options, lacking the time and economic resources to engage in such advocacy.[13] We need a queer and trans support complex to advocate for all LGBTQ youth so that LGBTQ youth feel respected in enacting and exploring their gender and sexual selves and other aspects of their lives.

Queering Systems

"I feel like there needs to be more awareness," stated Xander, a nineteen-year-old Black gay youth. "Educating staff is a huge issue. I need them to educate them as much as possible." Gwen, a seventeen-year-old Hispanic lesbian who resided at the same Child Protective Services shelter as Xander, told me, "There's not much stability when you're in care. There's no stability actually, which is what we need." She went on, "When you're our age, you're trying to graduate high school. You're trying to do all this and be able to like settle down somewhere. 'Cause, I mean, we don't really know how to settle down in one place. And so, that's probably a pretty big struggle with not just me but the majority of us."

As Gwen stated, we need systems to provide stability for LGBTQ youth. As documented in chapter 2, the organizational institutions—schools, state child custody systems, religion, the workplace—and the actors within these institutions often punish and discipline poor gender-expansive LGBTQ youth of color. These institutions also contribute to the youth's experiences of instability and experiences of marginalization. Institutions also interconnect, so experiencing instabilities in state child custody systems also means experiencing instabilities through switching schools. These punishing practices and experiences of instability and marginalization push some youth into jails and to the streets and create more barriers in the youth's lives. We need to overhaul institutions.

Dominant institutions do not accommodate and support people who experience intersecting marginalized social locations.[14] This failure generates systemic problems for marginalized people like poor LGBTQ youth of color. For example, the gender binary and heteronormativity shape institutional practices of segregating youth based on their assigned birth gender. These practices therefore misgender youth, try to suppress their expansive expressions of gender, label and stereotype LGBTQ youth, and police the youth's gender and sexuality. LGBTQ youth of color disproportionately face these marginalizing practices, as racism and racial profiling often shape how institutional actors relate to and police Black and Brown youth.[15] And because of structural racism and its interconnection with poverty and state surveillance, youth of color can end up in state child custody systems, in under-resourced schools, and in other institutions that generate more instability in their lives. We need to redesign institutions and systems to undo these punishing practices and to provide support and stability for marginalized youth.

To begin this work, we need LGBTQ-affirming policies along with policies that address racial equity. As Xander mentioned, we also need to train and educate teachers, service providers, and governmental staff about racial inequality, gender and sexuality, and LGBTQ people. For instance, anti-homophobia education needs to focus on how policing people's gender expression is tied to policing expressions of non-heterosexuality and how policing Black and Brown youth's gender expression makes up part of these racialized gender-policing practices. Education needs to also include how certain ideas about poor people and people of color also influence how institutional actors punish and police Black and Brown youth's expressions of gender and sexuality.

Congress needs to pass federal protections for sexual orientation, gender identity, and gender expression. We need to change the workplace to accommodate and support LGBTQ people, including finding ways to end discrimination in hiring practices and to end bullying in the workplace. As labor remains precarious and most service-sector work does not pay a living wage, getting a job in the formal economy is not the solution for addressing homelessness. Indeed, most work that people experiencing homelessness get does not bring about housing stability. Hence, we need a living wage, labor protections, and good jobs. More importantly, we need to work with LGBTQ youth to help them get into careers where they can develop and advance in their work. These careers need to feel meaningful and need to lead to financial stability and independence.[16] We need to change the larger structures of the formal economy as well as the culture of the workplace.

Again, these problems stem systemically from the dominant society. Policies need to tackle common ideas—the beliefs and attitudes that circulate within institutions—*and* institutional experiences—how institutions uphold certain beliefs and attitudes.[17] A step organizations need to take involves hiring LGBTQ staff, especially LGBTQ people of color. We can also change institutions by eliminating gender-segregation practices, respecting the self-identity of young people, having inclusive signs, posters, and intake forms, teaching about a loving and not a punitive higher power(s), tackling how schools uphold cultures of bullying, eliminating zero-tolerance policies, and a host of other strategies that challenge heteronormativity, the gender binary, and other structures of domination that currently shape how many institutions operate. We need to redesign institutions through validating the lived experiences of marginalized people. Youth-driven approaches can help us to imagine and design institutions and systems that help them.

Queering Justice

Jerico, a twenty-two-year-old Hispanic bisexual youth, told me that rehab and housing provide better solutions than incarcerating people. "What they do in Amsterdam, which is pretty much put people in rehab," he began. "And eventually work with them. Get them a house. Pay for them for about a year. That's what they do over there." He went on, "They always help people. Like, they see some drug addict, they'll go out there and just inject him with fluids to revive him again. And put him back in the streets or putting him in jail—they don't do that. They rather put him in rehab."[18]

As documented in chapter 3, the criminalization of homelessness perpetuates homelessness. Tickets, arrests, and criminal records made accessing services and jobs in the formal economy more difficult. Moreover, transgender and gender-expansive people of color disproportionately experience these criminalizing processes. Some also engage in criminalized behaviors such as stealing and prostitution because dominant institutions and institutional actors have discriminated against them and locked them out from resources such as a formal-sector job and a living wage. Police also target transgender and gender-expansive people of color through acts such as trans profiling. For these reasons and more, the criminalization of homelessness needs to end.

Housing Not Handcuffs calls for rescinding policies that criminalize homelessness. Instead of criminalization, we need to protect people experiencing homelessness from discrimination and violence, as many of the youth in this study experienced harassment and violence on the streets. A main protection would ensure housing for everyone. People would also move freely in public space without facing discrimination and harassment—including from police. I am also skeptical of service organizations that work with police. I do not see this strategy as effective. This strategy alienates people who would rather not interact with police and leads to "therapeutic policing," whereby police try to force people experiencing homelessness into shelters and service programs.[19] Police do not need to get involved in addressing homelessness.

Instead, we need direct action and advocacy against police and state violence. We need to help and care for people caught up in carceral systems. We can divert funds from wars, police, and prisons into housing, health care, jobs, education, and other social goods to starve carceral systems and nurture approaches to safety that do not rely upon carceral apparatuses. For instance, we can respond to a person who overdoses with care and with service providers, not with punishment and police. We also need alternative, community-based responses to violence. This work happens through transforming and healing relationships and communities, whereby collective accountability practices focus on transformative justice.

Importantly, criminalization and carceral processes work to uphold the gender binary, heteronormativity, white supremacy, and other structures of domination. Policing gender and sexuality and Black and Brown people and bodies centrally constitute crime and punishment—not a flaw in the system. Police exist to uphold hierarchies of domination.[20] Moreover, agents of the state perpetuate violence against marginalized people such as LGBTQ youth of color. Prisons do not make us safer and do not protect us from violence. Instead, carceral systems generate more violence. Ultimately, we need to abolish prisons, policing, and carceral systems. We need to continue to imagine a world without prisons and work toward a world where we do not put people in cages. Organizations such as TGI

Justice Project, Critical Resistance, BreakOUT!, the Solutions Not Punishment Collaborative, and many other spaces and places across the country do this work daily. We can turn to this work and expand on their work to continue to nurture wholeness, self-determination, and transformation.[21] As the mass movements around the murders of George Floyd, Breonna Taylor, Tony McDade, and other Black people have shown, the time for abolition is now, and defunding police and investing in care—not cops—are avenues to get to a new world without police and cages.

Queering Services

"Basically, end discrimination," said Harper, a twenty-year-old white heteroflexible pansexual non-binary transgender guy. He went on, "Trans women have a lot harder time trying to get jobs. And their housing situation can be a lot more at risk because they have a lot higher risk of being abused or assaulted." A twenty-two-year-old bisexual Black youth, Dante, as well, discussed discrimination in relation to the workplace. He explained, "I know; it is hard for transgender [people] to find jobs. It's hard for lesbians and gays to find jobs. So, if we could open up a specific market—a specific job market for LGBTQ services—that would get more LGBTQ people off of the streets."

Harper's and Dante's quotes suggest that we need to change services, organizations, and society. As shown in chapter 4, heteronormativity and the gender binary shape the public sphere, the streets, and services for people experiencing homelessness. Through gaining what I call queer street smarts—the knowledge of how gender and sexuality shape the public sphere and services for people experiencing homelessness—the youth in this study learned about, navigated, and resisted these heteronormative spaces and places. These queer street smarts and the youth's experiences teach us about what we need to do to change and dismantle the dominant relations of gender and sexuality in US society and how these relations influence the public sphere and other spaces that LGBTQ youth navigate.

For starters, the #MeToo movement to address sexual harassment and assault needs to center the experiences of transgender women of color and gender-expansive people of color. By focusing primarily on white women, the larger movement has often erased more marginalized voices, despite a

Black woman, Tarana Burke, starting the movement. Any solutions to addressing sexual violence need to attend to how transgender women of color and gender-expansive people of color face sexual harassment and violence, especially in the public sphere. This violence harmed many youth in this study. Solutions will mean grappling with how racism, sexism, heterosexism, transphobia, gendered homophobia, and classism are all involved in shaping acts of sexual violence. We need to also wrestle with the fact that most homophobic violence relates to policing expansive expressions of gender in the public sphere, particularly with regard to people of color.[22] Systems of oppression also shape the recourse—or lack thereof—that people have for dealing with experiences of violence. We need better ways for marginalized people to hold accountable people who commit violence against them. This accountability should not rely on prisons or hate crime laws that bolster carceral systems. We need to make the public sphere and all spaces safe for everyone to move freely and without fear.

Furthermore, we need to end gender segregation in services, shelters, and bathrooms. Gender segregation upholds the gender binary and leads to people committing violence toward transgender and gender-expansive people, especially transgender women of color in designated women's spaces.[23] While the dominant narrative for preserving gender-segregated spaces involves a panic about transgender people presenting a danger to women and children, transgender and gender-expansive people are actually the ones who face the most violence and harm in these spaces, as the youth in this study and their experiences showed. Moreover, we need to have more single-stall restrooms publicly available. We should also begin the work of ending gender-segregated public restrooms and making restrooms gender neutral. We also need to respect each person's gender expression and identity when they access services. Gender should only be important in accessing services if a person's gender relates to a specific gendered service, such as needing hormone replacement therapy.

We also do not need gender markers on identification cards and other identification documents, such as passports. Again, the gender marker works to uphold and normalize the gender binary. For the youth in this study, the gender marker generated obstacles in seeking employment in the formal economy, in accessing services, and in encountering authority

figures such as police. While the push to add a third gender marker—X—
to an identification card challenges notions of a gender binary, this solution could still mark people as different and cause further experiences of
discrimination. Removing gender markers can eradicate the barriers and
forms of discrimination that gender markers generate. Furthermore, we
need identification cards to access medical care, to enroll in school, to
apply for a job in the formal economy, to get housing, and so forth.
Therefore, we need to make identification cards free and easy to obtain.
We also need to make changing one's name on identification documents
free and accessible. Having a felony should not function as a barrier for
people to change their name. These steps challenge heteronormativity
and the gender binary, while removing obstacles for LGBTQ youth,
including LGBTQ youth experiencing homelessness.

We also need to invest in safety nets—such as universal health care,
fully funded education, affordable and stable housing, and better food-
assistance programs—and to expand on who can access these safety nets.
As single mothers of color disproportionately experience poverty, we need
more and better targeted programs to assist them. The young parents in
this study should have been able to keep their children in their lives if they
wanted. Having a child should not lead to experiencing housing instability. We need programs that support poor young parents, including better
housing assistance, financial support, and support systems. We also need
to expand programs to support all marginalized people, not only parents.

We also need to find ways to foster intimate, romantic, and platonic
relationships among LGBTQ youth. Relationships functioned as a key
part of support for many youth in this study. Helping LGBTQ youth
develop positive relationships combats feelings of isolation and provides
social support against mental health challenges and other obstacles
LGBTQ youth face. We need better education, social programs, and meeting spaces to foster all types of positive LGBTQ relationships.

Moreover, we need to decriminalize all forms of sex work and end the
profiling of sex workers and transgender women of color. We need to work
to end the violence—including police violence—against sex workers and
reduce the discrimination and stigma that sex workers face.

In the meantime, we need to build on the independence, skills, and
strengths that LGBTQ youth experiencing homelessness gain and learn

through living on the streets. Homelessness services need to support youth, not try to change them. Within the current structure of funding, organizations and services need to find creative sources of money so that funders do not have the power to make services and service providers bound to an agenda of working to change youth.[24] Instead, we need to dismantle or change services. We need to center the youth's voices, skills, and lived experiences in enacting these changes.

Queering Housing

"I told people for a while now—they need a strictly like a gay-friendly shelter. That's ran by gay people. And you have to be gay to stay there," stated Julian, a twenty-two-year-old Hispanic gay youth from Austin, who didn't know about the LGBTQ shelter in San Antonio. He went on, "That way, people will feel comfortable. People will feel safe. People will feel like they belong. People will feel like they don't have to cover themselves in the shower. They can just be around people who know. Yes, a lot of sex will probably happen in there. But you will at least be comfortable."

Although Julian never stayed at a specific LGBTQ shelter, he echoed many things documented in chapter 5. LGBTQ shelters help LGBTQ people feel safe, find belonging, build friendships and families, access safe showers and LGBTQ-specific resources, and serve as a respite from the streets. But shelter regulations, including regulations around gender and sexuality, caused staff to suspend youth—sending the youth back to the streets and perpetuating their experiences of homelessness. At the end of the day, shelters warehouse and manage people, and people staying at shelters still experience homelessness.

We need to prioritize shelter abolition as a way forward. Shelters do not solve homelessness. Indeed, both field sites—the LGBTQ shelter and the drop-in center—had age cutoffs to receive services. Youth approaching their mid-twenties often worried about "aging out" of these programs. Shelters, in general, often only allow people to stay there for a finite amount of time. People need stable housing, as stable housing would not generate these types of instabilities and anxieties about "aging out." We need to divest from and eventually abolish shelters and invest in housing. If we only focus on how shelters serve as a stopgap for people experiencing homelessness, we miss how shelters enact harm, and we fail to invest in actual solutions. Therefore, we need to put funding toward housing and other solutions, while phasing out funding for shelters. We also need to find more humane forms of safety for people experiencing homelessness who prefer not to live in shelters or other forms of housing. We need to invest in people and housing people, not warehousing them.

Many youth in this study also saw housing as a main solution to addressing homelessness. For Sade, a twenty-two-year-old Black lesbian, getting into housing was the foundation of helping her thrive. She exclaimed, "My own place and my job, definitely—as long as I have those two, Brandon, I'm telling you, I can thrive." Minnesota, a twenty-year-old white bisexual woman, saw housing people in abandoned buildings as a start. "There are places in Detroit right now," she stated. "Whole city blocks full—streets of abandoned houses—they could just put every homeless person inside one of those damn houses and everything would be fine." Arthur, a twenty-five-year-old Black gay man, thought that the city should convert the homelessness campus into apartments. He told me, "Make all these places here apartments—like real apartments— where they can live here on campus and be here and get services that they need. Instead of being just a homeless shelter, it can be an apartment. And they can have a certain part be the little part where they can get help." And Silvia, a twenty-two-year-old Hispanic bisexual woman, saw building apartments as essential to helping people experiencing homelessness. "I think they need to start building apartment complexes and allowing homeless people to sleep in those apartment complexes, so that way they can get on their feet," she explained. "And after a while, when that homeless person gets everything ready, they can—like their jobs and stuff like that, get to a certain standpoint in life—they can go ahead and have their own apartment somewhere else. But of course, give them time." Silvia went on, "Instead of arresting these people for being homeless, why don't we build apartments for them or houses. I mean, houses are great. I mean, we are the only species to actually pay to live here."

We need to recognize housing as a human right. Everyone deserves access to safe, secure, habitable, and affordable housing. A stable home provides people assistance in securing other human needs such as basic nutrition, education, privacy, security, and health. The United States needs to recognize housing as a human right and act accordingly.

One immediate solution entails rapid rehousing—getting someone experiencing homelessness into housing as fast as possible. Rapid rehousing works as a strategic plan for delivering services in line with Housing First—the social justice framework predicated on housing as a human right. Importantly, getting a person into housing as quick as possible helps in addressing other things, such as drug use, trauma, and mental health challenges. Indeed, in addition to serving as a humane approach, Housing First works because most people in Housing First maintain their housing, including people who use drugs and experience mental health challenges.[25] As a human right, getting someone experiencing homelessness into housing should not come with any barriers. Barring people who use drugs from housing makes no sense. People using drugs may need housing the most, as they disproportionately experience victimization on the streets. People also take drugs as a response to human suffering. Punishing drug use by barring people who use drugs from accessing housing continues their suffering and marginalization.[26] Likewise, barring people with criminal and/or eviction records also continues the perpetuation of inequalities and marginalization that people with these records already experience. We should not require people to engage in services or treatment to receive housing. Instead, the provider should bear the burden of making services engaging and client directed.[27] We need to also have this housing in communities where people want to live and where they have social support. For some people, getting into housing leads to feelings of loneliness and isolation. We need to invest in marginalized communities and build support systems to go along with housing.

Housing First provides a more cost-effective solution compared to other approaches, yet we continue to jail and punish people experiencing homelessness. As a study in Los Angeles County documents, supportive housing costs about $7,300 a year versus the typical public cost of $35,000 a year for a similar person experiencing homelessness.[28] A study in Central Florida also shows that the cost of someone experiencing homelessness adds up to $31,065 per year versus $10,051 for someone in permanent supportive housing.[29] This is because social service utilization, hospitalization, and carceral systems for people experiencing homelessness cost the taxpayer a lot more money compared to supportive housing. Does disdain for people experiencing homelessness outweigh the US government wanting to be cost effective? We need to reckon with this moral contradiction. We need to begin to view people experiencing homelessness as human beings worthy of respect.

In the longer term, we need more imaginative solutions that would prevent homelessness from ever happening, instead of addressing homelessness once people already live on the streets or in other unstable environments. Countries with more extensive welfare systems and lower levels of poverty such as Denmark have lower levels of homelessness compared to the United States, where homelessness more directly links to poverty and affects a broader group of people.[30] Hence, we need investment in affordable housing. We also need social welfare programs to tackle poverty and economic instability.

We also cannot ignore other forms of inequalities in addressing poverty, housing instability, and homelessness. As structural racism, sexism, heterosexism, and other forms of domination affect people's lives, we need sustained economic investments with certain groups of people. For instance, we need to take seriously the case for reparations and investing in Black communities.[31] We also need to make sure that we provide housing in people's communities. We need to end displacing poor and working-class people of color from their communities through practices such as gentrification. People should not have to pick between housing and living close to their support systems and other social networks. We also need women to get equal pay for equal work. And we need to address the systemic exclusion of LGBTQ people from various aspects of life. Large-scale targeted policies for marginalized people and communities need to happen alongside broader economic changes and investments in housing.

In the end though, we need to question and dismantle the market-driven approach to housing. If housing connects with making a profit, landlords and other people will exploit tenants. Novel ways of changing the market-driven approach to housing needs prioritization. Social housing may be a step in the right direction. We need to imagine more humane ways to support housing for everyone who wants housing.

WHERE THERE'S LOVE OVERFLOWING

"The present is not enough," writes critical theorist José Muñoz. "It is impoverished and toxic for queers and other people who do not feel the privilege of majoritarian belonging, normative tastes, and 'rational' expectations."[32] As Muñoz argues, the here and now—the present—functions as a prison house. And we must look to the past to imagine a future beyond the quagmire of the present moment. In doing so, we can enact new and better pleasures and worlds. We need to actively engage with the present to build these alternative worlds.[33]

While I am not really an optimist, I do know that social change happens and that we can create alternative worlds. The LGBTQ youth in this study inspired me weekly that a new dawn of queer potentiality can arise. As Adelpha, an eighteen-year-old Black, Mexican, and white heterosexual transgender woman, stated, "We have to get all of that hate out, and then the new life to come in." Naomi, an eighteen-year-old bisexual transgender Latina, also imagined a better, more utopian future. "There needs to be something new," she explained. "Something—nothing that has been done before. Something that can help us as people, just like how they help people with cancer and all that. I feel like this is my cancer. I live with it."

We need to continue the radical queer potential of collectively imagining, while centering LGBTQ youth's lives and voices, in envisioning a better tomorrow. We can look to past moments of resistance such as the Compton Cafeteria and Stonewall riots and the AIDS Coalition to Unleash Power to continue to resist the present. We can also look to moments of collective care, love, and support such as the Street Transvestite Action Revolutionaries' STAR House, ballroom communities, and the collective queer work of taking care of one another during the HIV/AIDS crisis to find queer collectivity that propels us forward. Then we will continue the work of making a better future possible. Yes, driving out the hate and letting love be the guide paves a way to a new life. So, let's imagine big. Let's love deeply. Let's envision with the youth and center their voices. Let's get to work to make a new world—a world of love, community, pleasure, and joy—and a world where everyone has a place to call home.

APPENDIX **Compassionate Detachment and Being a Volunteer Researcher**

While sitting at the front desk of the LGBTQ shelter, working an overnight shift as a volunteer and as a researcher, I suddenly heard a loud crash coming from the communal bathroom. I and some youth staying at the shelter ran to the bathroom. We found Obadiah—a twenty-year-old white man who dates transgender women—breaking chairs, throwing trash cans, and kicking over "wet floor" signs. As a volunteer, I had a walkie-talkie on me, and the youth residing at the shelter told me I should dispatch security. But what if security kicked Obadiah, usually a quiet person, out of the shelter for the night? I did not want him on the streets. Yet Obadiah might harm himself or others. What to do?

Eventually, I called security on the homelessness campus and asked them to send an officer. The officer arrived, calmed Obadiah, and asked me whether I wanted to eject him from the shelter for the evening—a punishment staff sometimes imposed when a youth violated shelter rules. I talked with Obadiah, and he agreed to stay in his bed for the evening. I never understood the rule of kicking people out of the shelter, and never enforced it. I found it counterproductive as a way to address homelessness. Later that evening, I learned that Obadiah's anger and hurt came from finding out that his brother had gone back to using crack cocaine.

This incident, and many others like it, captures some conundrums of the volunteer researcher. For instance, how do I conduct research with a marginalized population while also occupying a position of power—as a volunteer—over the youth staying at the shelter? And how do I build rapport with the youth while also being responsible for enforcing shelter and organizational rules? Ethnographers often grapple with ethical methodological quandaries in conducting their work. By volunteering to work for an organization while simultaneously conducting research through it—that is, acting as a volunteer researcher—one faces role conflict. I still think about and wrestle with my ambivalence about calling security on Obadiah, especially since I know that the youth in this study had numerous negative encounters with police and other authority figures. Security could have kicked Obadiah out of the shelter that evening. But I feared for his safety and the safety of the other young people present. Still, I wonder if calling security did more harm than good. I know now that calling security does not often bring about safety. If I had not called security, what would have happened? But also, how can we create alternative solutions to helping the people in our research that do not rely on the dominant ways of responding to situations?

Many ethical questions arose while designing, conducting, and finishing this study. I do not know if all the questions have answers, but in this appendix, I discuss some of these ethical quandaries. I offer up the concept of *compassionate detachment*—that is, having empathy but also enough emotional distance to know that researchers cannot (and should not try to) control or save the people they work with in their studies. As anthropologist Clifford Geertz writes in his discussion of ethics and ethnography, "Detachment comes not from a failure to care, but from a kind of caring resilient enough to withstand an enormous tension between moral reaction and scientific observation, a tension which only grows as moral perception deepens and scientific understanding advances."[1] I hope that this discussion pushes people to think about how to better do research and to continue having conservations about research, ethics, and working with marginalized populations, including marginalized youth.

ACCESS

For this study, I conducted eighteen months of ethnographic fieldwork from January 2015 to June 2016. I conducted this fieldwork mainly at two field sites: a youth drop-in center in Austin, Texas, and an LGBTQ shelter in San Antonio, Texas. I decided during the research design that I wanted to volunteer where I conducted my study. I wanted to give back to the organizations that gave me access. In the introduction to this book, I detail the field sites and my volunteer roles. In this appendix, I present how I gained access to each site and how my engagement with volunteering and accessing each field site unfolded differently.

In Austin, I discussed upfront the purpose of my study. Other researchers had conducted research through this organization, and the staff had protocols in place to approve and support research projects. I had my initial meeting with the director of street outreach and the director of research and evaluation. At this meeting, the three of us discussed my project, how the project could benefit the organization, and how to proceed in implementing the study. I told them I wanted to volunteer while conducting the study. They said I could volunteer in the clothing closet at the drop-in center. As per the organization's memorandum of understanding and policy on collaborating with outside researchers, I agreed to share all data collected through their organization with them. If the organization published anything using the data, I would serve as coauthor and have final veto power on anything written.[2] After my background check and volunteer training, I signed a memorandum of understanding and began fieldwork at this site.

In San Antonio, the LGBTQ shelter opened at the start of my fieldwork. I went to the volunteer training and then began doing overnight volunteer shifts immediately after my background check approval. I volunteered with the organization for three months before I approached the director of the shelter about my study, which she approved. I feel that through my volunteering and the director's contact with me each week, I was able to build trust and rapport with her. This rapport perhaps shaped the director's decision to approve my study at the LGBTQ shelter.

I do believe that institutional gatekeepers influenced which organizations I got access to. The director of street outreach in Austin identified as bisexual, and the director of the shelter in San Antonio identified as a lesbian. I had meetings with other organizations at the initial stages of this study where some staff expressed a lack of interest in my study and/or did not think that their organization served any LGBTQ youth experiencing homelessness. While I do not know the gender and sexual identities of the staff at places I did not get access to, I feel that having non-heterosexual people as institutional gatekeepers probably helped in gaining access to the field sites where I conducted this study.

Professionals at both of my field sites submitted letters to the Institutional Review Board (IRB) at the University of Texas at Austin on my behalf. These letters stated the organizations' support of this study and confirmed that I could conduct research at their organizations. The director of research and evaluation at the Austin field site also gave me federal guidelines—the Regulatory Requirements for a Waiver of Parent/Guardian Permission 45 CFR §46.116—to cite in my IRB proposal to help me get approval to interview youth thirteen to seventeen years old without parental consent. Many youth experiencing homelessness have tenuous relationships with their parents, making getting parental consent difficult and possibly causing further strain between the youth and their parent(s). IRB staff expedited my study and granted me approval to interview youth thirteen to twenty-five years old—all without parental consent. I also got a waiver of written consent so I could get verbal consent from the youth in this study. Many youth experiencing homelessness have nowhere secure to keep paperwork. A written consent form—if discovered by someone else—could also potentially "out" youth as LGBTQ. I saw these waivers of written consent and of parental consent as ways to do the least amount of harm for the youth in this study.

FIELDWORK

I conducted over seven hundred hours of fieldwork, which involved getting to know the people in social settings and their daily routines, developing relationships with them, and observing them. I would take what ethnographers call "jottings" on my phone to record key words and phrases that would remind me of major events and impressions to write up in my field notes after I left the field site.[3] Upon leaving the field, I would turn my jottings into a more systematic and detailed written account of my observations and experiences at the field site for that day. I went to the Austin field site twice a week—roughly eight hours a week. In San Antonio, I did one or two overnight shifts a week. These shifts lasted around nine hours (from 10 p.m. to 7 a.m.).

I also conducted fieldwork at a transitional living program (TLP) associated with the Austin drop-in center. During this study, nine young people lived at the TLP, which housed youth seventeen to twenty-three years old. The TLP provided many of the same services as the drop-in center. The TLP also provided a place to live. The young people residing at the TLP had to work and/or be currently taking GED or higher education classes to stay there.[4] The TLP was in South Austin. Each youth shared a room with one other person. The TLP also had a shared common area, kitchen, bathrooms, laundry room, and outdoor patio and backyard. I visited the TLP four times during fieldwork.

I also conducted some fieldwork at a Child Protective Services (CPS) shelter. Although I had IRB approval to interview youth ages thirteen to twenty-five years of age, I learned early on in fieldwork that youth under the age of eighteen and experiencing homelessness often resided in state child custody systems. Indeed, if social workers found out that a youth was under eighteen and experiencing homelessness, the service provider was required by law to report the youth to the state. For this reason, I wanted to get access to youth currently in CPS. After over six months of bureaucracies and contacting many CPS shelters, I did get access to one CPS shelter. The shelter was in East Austin. Most of what I know about this shelter came from the two youth I interviewed there. The young people stayed in a group-setting transitional living program that housed fourteen youth, aged seventeen to twenty-one. Sometimes the young people residing there had two roommates, sometimes one, and if available, sometimes they had their own private room. The shelter had a curfew based on a person's age and/or whether the person had a night job in the formal economy. The shelter offered mental health services, clothing, food, and transportation. I visited this field site three times.

I also volunteered for the US Department of Housing and Urban Development's (HUD) 2015 point-in-time count in Austin. The point-in-time count involves volunteers across the country counting people experiencing homelessness on a single night in January in their communities. I volunteered, as well, for two youth point-in-time counts in Austin, which counted the population of young people experiencing homelessness in Travis County. Furthermore, I attended the 2015 National Conference on Ending Family and Youth Homelessness, where I got to see the Secretary of HUD, Julián Castro, speak. I also attended three annual Forty to None Summits, a national gathering on ending LGBTQ youth homelessness.[5] These point-in-time counts and conferences helped to contextualize the larger issues and understandings of homelessness, particularly from service providers' and government officials' standpoints.

RECRUITING

As my volunteer role varied at each field site, recruitment at each field site proceeded differently. At the drop-in center in Austin, I mainly volunteered in the clothing closet, where I often made one-on-one contact with youth accessing services at the center. At times, I would also hang out in the common area, but most of my interactions with youth were within the clothing closet.

In doing recruitment, the staff's and my concern involved not "outing" anyone who wanted to participate in this study. To address this concern, I conducted a survey with all youth at the drop-in center who expressed interest in taking the survey. I administered the survey on paper in a private staff office at the drop-in center. I stored all completed surveys in a locked safe in my office. The youth chose either to fill the survey out themselves or to have me read the questions to them. The survey included twenty-five overall questions. Questions covered topics such as health behaviors, resiliency, socioeconomic background, everyday experiences with discrimination, physical and mental health, food scarcity, and demographics. Under the demographic section, if a youth marked transgender man, transgender woman, or wrote in another gender identity that did not include the specific category man or woman, I told them about the interview portion of the study. Likewise, if a youth marked gay, lesbian, bisexual, queer, or wrote in another sexual identity that did not include heterosexual, I told them about the interview portion of the study. Everyone who filled out the survey got a bus pass from the drop-in center. Every LGBTQ youth who did the interview got a $10 gift card to Walmart, which the director of street outreach got Walmart to donate.

In San Antonio, everyone staying at the shelter identified as LGBTQ. There, everyone got to know me for longer periods of time, as I did overnight volunteer shifts. All youth knew me as a person conducting a study with LGBTQ youth experiencing homelessness. I interviewed every youth who stayed at the shelter for longer than two weeks. The director gave some youth gift cards for doing the interview. Most youth at this field site did not receive anything for the interview.

Importantly, I do think building rapport with the youth helped with recruitment. I entered the field in January 2015 but did not begin the interviews until June 2015. I believe that volunteering and researching in the field for a significant amount of time before doing interviews made some youth more receptive to me interviewing them. Youth in this study often had to undergo questioning when trying to access services or in police encounters, so answering questions could be burdensome. But since most of the youth knew me well before the interview portion of this study, their participation in the interviews seemed more enthusiastic and most gave detailed responses to my questions.

INTERVIEWING

I conducted forty in-depth, semi-structured interviews with LGBTQ youth experiencing homelessness and digitally audio-recorded all interviews. I also later transcribed all forty interviews. Most interviews lasted around an hour. The interviews covered four major topics: perceived pathways into homelessness, needs, strengths, and everyday interactions and experiences. I conducted all interviews in-person. Face-to-face interactions helped me to establish rapport with the youth, which usually afforded a more meaningful and in-depth interview.[6] I also wanted to listen to the youth's needs, instead of making assumptions about their needs.[7] Therefore, I chose to do in-depth interviewing to foreground the young people's voices and lived experiences.

At the drop-in center, I conducted the interviews in either a staff member's office or in the choir room located behind the drop-in center. At the TLP, some interviews took place in a conference room and some took place outside at a picnic table or on a swing. At the CPS licensed shelter, both interviews took place in a private room. In San Antonio, I conducted many interviews in a private room— either the staff office or a private room in the main building on campus where people went for counseling, job training, GED classes, and other services. However, some youth wanted me to interview them at their bed or outside at a picnic table.

Fifteen of the forty youth I interviewed came from the Austin drop-in field site. Four interviews came from the TLP. Two interviews came from the CPS shelter. Nineteen of the forty youth I interviewed came from the LGBTQ shelter in San Antonio.

I informed all the young people about all processes of consent, and all voluntarily agreed to the interview. At the end of each interview, I asked each person for demographic characteristics. One youth was seventeen, two were twenty-five, and the rest were eighteen to twenty-four years of age. Generally, nineteen youth identified as Hispanic or Latino/a, eleven youth identified as Black, and ten youth identified as white. Fifteen youth identified as women, fourteen as men, nine as transgender women, and two as transgender men.

At the end of the study, I also conducted ten interviews with service providers to gain a different perspective about LGBTQ youth homelessness. Five came from the Austin field site, and five came from the San Antonio field site. I also conducted these semi-structured interviews in-person and in a private room. The interviews lasted around fifty minutes and covered similar topics and themes as the interviews with the youth. The service providers voluntarily agreed. I also informed them about all processes of consent, and I audio-recorded these interviews as well. As I had grant money during this time of the project, I hired a colleague to transcribe these interviews.

ANALYZING

I uploaded all field notes and interview transcriptions into MAXQDA, a qualitative data analysis software tool. I coded these transcriptions and field notes using techniques adapted from a grounded theory approach. The grounded theory method allowed me to create new insights based on the youth's accounts.[8] I used coding that reflected the action I saw occurring within the data. I coded by first attaching labels to segments of the data, describing what I saw in each segment.[9] This initial line-by-line open coding included codes such as "growing up," "getting kicked out," "feeling unwanted," "perceived as gay," and "experiencing abuse." I also wrote memos about the action I noted occurring within the coding of the data. I then engaged in focused coding to move the analysis to a more conceptual level, while also comparing similarities and differences across the interviews. Focused codes included items such as "abuse," "being LGBTQ," "family," "rejection," and "violence." Finally, I did axial coding to identify the relationship between the focused codes, such as how being LGBTQ within the family related to experiences of abuse, rejection, and violence. I sought to understand the meanings within the young people's accounts to find *how* and *why* LGBTQ youth experiencing homelessness do and experience certain things.

GENDER EMBODIMENT AND RAPPORT

Embodiments shape the interactions that researchers have with the people whom they work with in their studies. People in studies interpret the researcher and their body in particular ways, and researchers interpret the bodies of the people in their studies in particular ways. These interpretations influence how interactions unfold; hence, they influence the data collected.

My gender embodiment remarkably shaped my interactions in the field because my expansive expressions of gender helped in building rapport with the youth. Several youth asked me during fieldwork if I was a boy or a girl. Perhaps because I have long hair and present effeminately, several transgender youth asked me if I was transgender. Some youth acted shocked when I introduced myself as Brandon, and several asked me if I picked Brandon as my "chosen name." I also accrued feminine nicknames, including people calling me "Mary Alice" and "Miss Travis County," and youth told me that I looked like actress Ellen Page and the fictional character Moaning Myrtle from *Harry Potter*. Youth often greeted me with "Hey girl" or called me ma'am, and some youth used feminine pronouns to refer to me. Although I never told anyone my sexuality, during the interviews some youth would mention that I must know what they mean because they knew that I was gay too. Because of my gender embodiment, youth assumed I was non-heterosexual, and this assumption appeared to help many youth want to participate in the study and talk with me about LGBTQ-related experiences in their lives. My expansive expressions of gender helped in building rapport. While researchers who do not embody gender expansiveness can and have studied LGBTQ people, and specifically LGBTQ youth experiencing homelessness, my embodiment helped in building a particular type of rapport, where youth could joke with me and make comments that they believed I would understand through our shared queerness. Youth may not disclose certain things or joke with other researchers in the same way without this queer recognition.

Moreover, my gender presentation helped in gaining access to each site. I wondered if staff read me as visibly queer and, hence, trusted me to work with LGBTQ youth. LGBTQ gatekeepers might find trust in an LGBTQ researcher. As both of my main gatekeepers also identified as non-heterosexual, mutual queer trust may have occurred that helped me to gain access to my sites. Overall, my expansive expressions of gender benefited me in conducting this work. These points, of course, raise methodological questions and conversations about the meaning of visibility for queer researchers and doing LGBTQ research.

CLASS AND ITS INTERSECTIONS

Class shaped a lot of this project as well and raised some methodological quandaries. For instance, the first week in the field, a youth commented on my watch. I took this comment that my watch marked a class difference between the youth and me. I learned to dress in as unassuming a way as possible to avoid creating more obvious differences. I tried to enact what sociologist C. J. Pascoe calls a "least-adult identity" to try to fit in with the youth.[10] However, in working with youth experiencing homelessness, class also shaped this least-adult identity. In this research, least-adult identity meant taking off my watch and only wearing a

T-shirt and jeans while conducting fieldwork; it would look different working with more privileged young adults.

Scheduling interviews proved next to impossible, as the youth in this study had many other necessities to worry about besides meeting me at a specific time. Scheduling interviews is not always the best methodological approach to studying and working with more marginalized populations. Moreover, some youth in this study cycled in and out of jail, making scheduling interviews even more difficult and unpredictable. For example, I had scheduled to interview Adelpha one day. When I arrived at the shelter, the director had not seen Adelpha all day, and we later came to find out that police had arrested her. Youth experiencing homelessness also move around a lot, and staff suspend some youth from services. I learned to interview youth on the spot if they consented. I tried to never postpone or schedule an interview, as I learned that scheduled interviews rarely happened. Researchers need to abandon this conventional notion of scheduling time when working with certain marginalized populations.

How long interviews lasted also varied. I now question the standard methodology that instructs that an interviewer should make the interview last a particular length of time (often an hour) for the in-depth interview to yield important insights. Do white, middle-class standards define this length-of-time benchmark for an in-depth interview? The youth in this study had other things to do, such as making money and finding meals and places to sleep. Some people may not have the luxury to sit for a longer interview. Some youth also battled mental health challenges, including difficulty in focusing. Noticeably, my shorter interviews occurred with youth who shifted a lot in their seats, with youth who acted uninterested in discussing their lives with me, and/or with youth who looked uncomfortable. One youth picked at their skin during the interview. To try to force the interview to go longer because I needed to meet some particular length-of-time benchmark to classify my interview as in-depth might have done harm. Nonetheless, I still learned from these shorter interviews. Researchers need to rethink the length of interviews and to prioritize the needs of the people they work with in their studies.

Notions of a private interview setting fall into a class-based methodological trap as well. While both field sites did offer private rooms to conduct interviews, some youth may not have felt comfortable to do an interview in private. Some youth did not want to leave their bed or preferred interviewing outside so they could smoke during the interview. Other studies might not have an option to conduct interviews in a private space. Privileging a private setting for interviews ignores structural constraints that make interviewing in private difficult or potentially a cause of more harm. Establishing a study around interviewing in a private space also takes power away from the people in the study to decide what interview setting feels safest for them.[11] White, middle-class notions of interviewing may inform notions of a private interview that does not always prioritize the needs of the people whom researchers work with in their studies.

My class status through my educational background as a graduate student also shaped my rapport with gatekeepers and access to my field sites. Staff at the organization in Austin often collaborated with researchers from the University of Texas at Austin. Staff at the shelter in San Antonio seemed impressed that I was working on a dissertation—and eventually a book—on LGBTQ youth homelessness. Neither organization would probably let just any person do research at their organization. As a PhD candidate from a reputable public university in Texas, I was able to gain access and trust with gatekeepers.

Importantly, my race as white, my education background, my age, and other aspects of my embodiments and identities intersected with my class positioning. Most of the service providers at both field sites were also white and college educated. The youth may have seen me as the kind of college-educated, white institutional actor whom they had encountered throughout most of their lives in navigating institutions and services. Notably, the youth in this study often did not explicitly talk about race during the interview portion of the study. This absence of race talk may relate to my being white. The youth may have seen our commonality through being LGBTQ, and hence, focused more on talking about LGBTQ-related experiences. Furthermore, my age—in my late twenties—was closer to the youth's age than the age of some of the service providers. This closer generational connection may have also helped in building rapport, along with being queer and gender expansive.

All in all, class and its intersections with other social categories shape research methods. Researchers need to reflect on these class and other differences in designing and implementing studies. We need to prioritize doing no harm, and this means not always implementing research in ways that academia teaches as the "gold standard." White, middle-class logics shape research methodologies, as white, middle-class men have historically and predominantly enacted and embodied the role of the researcher. This body of thinking hinders us from learning about certain aspects and stories of people's lives. In challenging it and in finding new ways to conduct research, we gain other stories and experiences. We need, then, to continue to center the people in our study when making decisions about how they will participate in the research project. We need to open up new ways of doing research, expanding the researcher position and how we work with more hard-to-reach populations. I end this appendix with an ethical approach of compassionate detachment to try to put people in studies first.

COMPASSIONATE DETACHMENT AS MINDFUL ETHICS

"Strive for objectivity and compassionate detachment," stated the volunteer handbook at one of my field sites. The handbook went on to define what this statement meant. "It is easy to become involved emotionally when working with youth. Remember you fill the role of a professional while at [the organization]." The handbook also outlined what filling a professional role entailed. I needed to act as a positive adult role model and mentor for the youth and had to supervise the youth, enforce the organizational rules, mediate conflicts, and act on behalf of the youth during an emergency. I also had to maintain confidentiality and respect boundaries. These boundaries meant not showing favoritism, not disclosing my address or phone number, not socializing with the youth outside of the organization (including on social media), not giving rides, not keeping secrets, not telling bad jokes, not using drugs and alcohol while volunteering, not discussing my sex life, and not commenting on the youth's bodies.[12] Respectful boundaries also meant limiting my affection with the youth by avoiding physical contact that people might misconstrue and by restricting any touching, such as hugs, to what the youth themselves initiated. The handbook stated that these boundaries helped to maintain a separation of personal and professional life.

How, though, does one supervise and enforce rules as a volunteer while also, as a researcher, wanting to build rapport and do no harm toward the youth? I return to the dilemma I posed in the opening of this appendix to discuss some ethical quandaries of serving as a volunteer and conducting research with marginalized youth.

For instance, one evening, the director of the LGBTQ shelter called me into the staff office when I arrived for my volunteer shift. She told me that Camila and Zoe—two heterosexual transgender women of color staying at the shelter— showed signs of jonesing for drugs because they had recently gone on a methamphetamine binge. The director asked that I keep an eye on Camila and Zoe that evening. After the director left, Camila and Zoe stayed up past the designated shelter bedtime—one rule among many that I did not enforce. Camila kept telling me that I should go to sleep. I stayed up and talked with Zoe and her. Around 2:30 a.m.—well past the 10 p.m. shelter curfew—Camila and Zoe told me that they wanted to leave for the night. Camila asked me if I would write them up for leaving after curfew. I told her that I had an obligation as a volunteer to report if anyone left after curfew. Camila said that she did not like me anymore and that I probably did not even care if she liked me or not. They left. I did not write them up. I never actually wrote anyone up. A few days later, though, a staff person did find them leaving again after curfew. Staff suspended them from the shelter.

As a volunteer, I had to make sure the youth went to bed at "bedtime" and that they followed the other shelter rules, such as the curfew. Knowing the literature on how shelter rules infantilize people experiencing homelessness, however, I did not feel ethically comfortable enforcing rules. If I had tried to enforce a bedtime, would Camila and Zoe not have left that evening? And did I ethically undermine the organizations that allowed me to conduct my study by not enforcing their rules? At times, I worried that if I was not implementing rules, staff might revoke my access to the organization. Access does not occur just one time but involves an ongoing negotiation. As a researcher, my ultimate ethical obligation focused on doing no harm toward the youth in this study. Since I saw rules as infantilizing— and hence, as harmful—I did not implement many of them. Staff either did not notice or did not mind. At one point, the director of the LGBTQ shelter offered me a part-time job. I turned down the offer, as I felt taking on a staff position would have created even more methodological quandaries.

While I do not have all the answers to these quandaries, I did find the notion of compassionate detachment from the volunteer handbook to be a helpful way of confronting some methodological dilemmas. I just approached the concept differently. I tried to enact compassionate detachment as a form of "mindful ethics." As sociologist Gloria González-López writes, mindful ethics involves awareness that people are complex human beings. It involves remaining conscious of the taken-for-granted social contexts that shape people's lives, while also trying to move beyond rigid typologies in understanding the people whom researchers work with in their studies. Mindful ethics also entails acting intentionally in working to alleviate suffering. And researchers need to realize that they often address many ethical questions in the "here and now"—in the field, during the interview, while conducting the study. Resolving all ethical questions ahead of time remains an impossibility. Some ethical questions have no simple answers. Nevertheless, researchers need to recognize, admit, and discuss the complexities of their work.[13]

Compassionate detachment involves a type of mindful ethics, taking an empathetic view, staying aware of the complexities of human lives, and questioning the taken-for-granted social contexts that shape people's lives. Indeed, empathy—the ability to see and feel the world from the perspective of another—functions as a key component of compassionate detachment.[14] Researchers need a balance between emotional engagement and cognitive detachment from trauma.[15] Scientific detachment itself does not mean a moral blankness or not caring, but entails the melding of both engagement and thinking and acting analytically.[16]

Compassionate detachment helps researchers build empathy and see and feel the world through the people they work with in their studies, while not taking on the trauma or trying to control or save the people in the study. Compassionate detachment allows researchers to remain present, to try to feel with the people in their studies, to try to directly minimize harm through their own decisions and actions, and to try to compassionately allow the people in the study to make their own decisions. Yes, I felt deeply for Camila and Zoe. I did not want them to get into trouble or suspended. I could have tried to enforce the bedtime to try to save Camila and Zoe from leaving after curfew and, hence, breaking another rule. But I saw my job as a volunteer researcher as remaining present with them, listening to them, and allowing them to decide how they wanted to live their lives. Of course, no easy way presents itself to know if one is implementing compassionate detachment and mindful ethics in the best way. Researchers can just try their best to care and to be present, but they must not try to change other people's lives or think that they know the best way to help someone else.

I also ponder the applicability of compassionate detachment with the service providers in this study and the larger organizations where I conducted my field-work. I often worried, in writing chapter 5 on the LGBTQ shelter, about depicting the service providers negatively, knowing that the service providers deeply cared about the youth in this study. I tried to frame their behavior within larger structures of shelter life and funding. I also did not want to paint the organizations as horrible. These organizations do important work in addressing LGBTQ youth homelessness—work that most places are not doing. Framing the service providers and the organizations themselves within larger structures helps in enacting compassion toward them and locating them within the larger complexities of the social organization of shelters and service places. But my most ethical obligation remained with the youth in this study and wanting to help them and to address homelessness. I tried to sympathize with the service providers, and even the organizations, and I tried to compassionately understand their actions and mission. I also felt, though, that I had an easier time detaching from the service providers, in that my political commitment remained with the youth in this study.

The goal is for researchers to work *with* the people in the study—through compassionate detachment as mindful ethics—to understand their lives, and to use this knowledge to work toward social change. Alleviating suffering and working toward social change should guide the heart of this work. Compassionate detachment as mindful ethics serves as a way of being present, feeling with the people in the study, centering their needs, minimizing harm, and working with (instead of for) them. This working with, through compassionate detachment, helps us to learn about people's lives and to use this knowledge to try to make the world a more humane place.

Notes

INTRODUCTION

1. While I was writing this book, Congress passed the "Stop Enabling Sex Traffickers Act" and the "Allow States and Victims to Fight Online Sex Trafficking Act." President Donald Trump signed these bills into law. In response, Craigslist removed this section on their website. Although the distinction is beyond the scope of this book, it is important not to conflate sex work with sex trafficking. Also, it should be noted that many academics, sex worker and sex trafficking organizations, and sex workers themselves came out against these bills.

2. "Ts" stands for transsexual, and "t4m" stands for transgender for men. "Party favors" means drugs. "Versatile bottoms" means Camila and Zoe often take the receptive position during sexual intercourse, but they also will take the penetrator position. "Smoke some bud" means smoking weed.

3. Some people perceive transgender youth as gay while growing up because of the youth's expansive expressions of gender during childhood. Also, some transgender youth do identify as gay or bisexual before later identifying as transgender and heterosexual. As *transgender* pertains to gender identity, transgender people can identify their sexuality as lesbian, gay, bisexual, heterosexual, queer, pansexual, asexual, or something else. This sexual identity may change over time and may change as one's gender identity also changes. Essentially, some transgender youth who first came out as gay or bisexual later

identified as heterosexual transgender people, though, at times, they still also say they are gay. Other transgender people identify as bisexual or have another sexual identity.

4. Zoe called her grandfather "Papa." During fieldwork, she showed me the scar on her chest from her Papa shooting her.

5. The description of this program comes from the website of the organization.

6. Beckett and Herbert (2009).

7. Morton et al. (2018).

8. Ray (2006); Durso and Gates (2012).

9. Cochran et al. (2002); Whitbeck et al. (2004); Bruce et al. (2014).

10. Whitbeck et al. (2004).

11. Mottet and Ohle (2006); Keuroghlian, Shtasel, and Bassuk (2014); Shelton (2015).

12. Beauvoir ([1949] 2011); Smith 1987; Collins ([1990] 2000).

13. I use the term *perceived pathways* to mean the youth's perceptions of how and why they are experiencing homelessness. There might be other pathways into homelessness besides what people experiencing homelessness perceive to be their pathways into homelessness; however, *perceived pathways* is a term that captures the meanings that people experiencing homelessness give to their lived experiences.

14. Walters (2014).

15. West and Zimmerman (1987).

16. Paoletti (2012).

17. Warner (1991, 1993); Valocchi (2005).

18. Butler (1990).

19. West and Zimmerman (1987); Schilt and Westbrook (2009).

20. Dwyer (2008).

21. I deliberately use the word *gay*. The heterosexual/homosexual binary often erases other forms of sexual identities and expressions. People often assume a non-heterosexual person is gay.

22. Pascoe (2007).

23. Butler (1993); Pascoe (2007).

24. Meyer (2015).

25. Gray (2009).

26. Stryker (2008).

27. Valentine (2007).

28. Cuthbert (2019: 860).

29. Valentine (2003).

30. Moraga and Anzaldua (1981); Crenshaw (1989, 1991); Collins ([1990] 2000).

31. Collins ([1990] 2000, 2004).

32. Brooks (2010).

33. Collins (2004).

34. Connell (1995).

35. Bettie (2003).

36. Acosta (2013).

37. Meyer (2015).

38. Ferguson (2004); Vidal-Ortiz, Robinson, and Khan (2018).

39. Shepard (2013).

40. Newport (2018).

41. Cray, Miller, and Durso (2013).

42. D'Augelli and Hershberger (1993); Cray, Miller, and Durso (2013).

43. Dunne, Prendergast, and Telford (2002); Russell (2002); Nolan (2006); Institute of Medicine (2011).

44. US Department of Housing and Urban Development's FY2015 Final Fair Market Rents Documentation System determined these rent prices as the fair market rent.

45. The US Department of Housing and Urban Development considers a person who pays more than 30 percent of income on rent to be house burdened.

46. Lee, Tyler, and Wright (2010); Wasserman and Clair (2010); Wright and Donley (2011).

47. Beckett and Herbert (2009); Wright ([1989] 2009); Wasserman and Clair (2010).

48. Hopper (2003); Gowan (2010); Wasserman and Clair (2010); Wright and Donley (2011).

49. Beckett and Herbert (2009); Bourgois and Schonberg (2009); Gowan (2010); Wright and Donley (2011).

50. Wright, Rubin, and Devine (1998).

51. Redlining involves the government and banks denying Black people loans. This discriminatory practice worked systematically to disinvest from Black neighborhoods, furthering the economic decline and underdevelopment of Black neighborhoods and communities.

52. Wright ([1989] 2009).

53. Hays (2004).

54. Desmond (2012).

55. Giroux (2009).

56. Wright ([1989] 2009); Lee, Tyler, and Wright (2010).

57. Cohen (1997).

58. Passaro (1996).

59. U.S. Census Bureau (2013).

60. U.S. Census Bureau (2011).

61. Theis (2015).

62. Flores and Doganer (2010).

63. Culhane (2010).

64. Jamrozy (2007).

65. Martin Prosperity Institute (2015).

66. Quiggin (1998).

67. Funders for LGBTQ Issues (2018).

68. Liamputtong (2007).

69. See Tyler, Akinyemi, and Kort-Butler (2012); Ecker (2016). No study that I know of compares transgender and gender-expansive youth experiencing homelessness and accessing services to other populations that access the same or similar services.

70. By law, staff had to report youth under the age of eighteen to Child Protective Services. Therefore, youth under eighteen and experiencing homelessness resided within CPS and did not access this place, or lied about their age to avoid having staff contact CPS.

71. Gray (2009); Rios (2011).

72. Spivak (1988).

73. Rios (2011).

74. Contreras (2013).

75. Mogul, Ritchie, and Whitlock (2011).

CHAPTER 1. REFRAMING FAMILY REJECTION

1. Many of the gay and bisexual men and transgender women in this study grew up in single-father households. The tension and conflicts brought about by single fathers trying to raise masculine sons, or perceived sons, was often what led many of the transgender women and gender-expansive men in this study to leave their family homes.

2. Morris (2014).

3. Gibbard (2015); Urquhart (2017).

4. Rew et al. (2005).

5. Durso and Gates (2012).

6. Page (2017); Wheeler, Price, and Ellasante (2017); Robinson (2018b, 2018c).

7. Whitbeck and Hoyt (1999); Wasserman and Clair (2010).

8. "Aging out" refers to youth leaving state child custody systems on their eighteenth birthday and the cessation of some or all of CPS benefits. I explore state child custody systems in more detail in chapter 2, as twenty-one of the forty youth in this study discussed going into CPS custody during part of their childhoods.

9. For more on family instability and its effects, see Fomby and Cherlin (2007) and Cavanagh and Huston (2008).

10. Whitbeck and Hoyt (1999); Yoder and Hoyt (2005).

11. Eamon and Kopels (2004).

12. Flatau et al. (2013).

13. Cutuli et al. (2017).

14. Justice was multiracial but identified as Black.

15. Whitbeck and Hoyt (1999); Tyler (2006); Mallett and Rosenthal (2009); Thompson et al. (2010); Gibson (2011).

16. Whitbeck and Hoyt (1999).

17. Mason (2002); Meyer (2015).

18. Flores and Hondagneu-Sotelo (2013).

19. Rubin ([1984] 1993); Bérubé (1990); D'Emilio (1993). See Chauncey (1994) for a history of gay life before World War II.

20. Weston (1991).

21. Herdt and Koff (2000).

22. Decena (2008).

23. Ross (2005); Decena (2011).

24. Whitbeck et al. (2004); Gibson (2011); Durso and Gates (2012).

25. Whitbeck et al. (2004); Durso and Gates (2012).

26. González-López (2015: 184).

27. González-López (2015).

28. Pascoe (2007).

29. Acosta (2013).

30. Collins (2004).

31. Robinson (2018b).

32. Robinson (2018b).

33. Kane (2012).

34. Lareau (2003).

35. Rahilly (2015).

36. Rahilly (2015).

37. Rahilly (2015); Meadow (2018); Travers (2018).

38. Meadow (2018); Travers (2018).

39. See also, Weston (1991) and Bailey (2013).

40. Whitbeck and Hoyt (1999); Burton (2007); Schmitz and Tyler (2016).

CHAPTER 2. QUEER CONTROL COMPLEX

1. When I first met Jessie, he went by masculine pronouns. In the middle of fieldwork, Jessie went by feminine pronouns. By the end of fieldwork, Jessie went by masculine pronouns again. I use the masculine pronouns to respect the pronouns that Jessie wanted people to use to refer to him the last time we met.

2. I found a news story that verified a lot of this experience.

3. According to the school's website, this school offers "a more affordable choice" in boarding school options. Nonetheless, families need economic resources to send a child to boarding school. Although Jessie's dad often experienced unemployment and the family moved around a lot throughout Jessie's childhood, Jessie's mom did appear to make a steady income. However, Jessie's mom had breast cancer—another source of emotional and financial strain on the family. Exactly how Jessie's parents could afford to send Jessie to this school was not made clear in the interview, but he did seem to come from a higher socioeconomic background compared to most youth in this study.

4. Rios (2011: xiv).

5. Foucault (1977).

6. Payne and Smith (2013).

7. Pascoe (2007).

8. Mason (2002).

9. Heitzig (2009); Mitchum and Moodie-Mills (2014).

10. Beadle (2012).

11. Himmelstein and Bruckner (2011).

12. Mitchum and Moodie-Mills (2014); Snapp et al. (2015).

13. Ferguson (2000).

14. Fish et al. (2019).

15. Wilson and Kastanis (2015).

16. More of my interviewees may have had some contact, but during the interviews and fieldwork, only twenty-one mentioned going into state child custody systems.

17. See Goffman (1963) for a discussion of discreditable or concealable stigmas versus discredited or known and visible stigmas.

18. Foucault (1977).

19. In personal correspondence with the Texas Department of Family and Protective Services (DFPS) on June 6, 2017, workers for this department informed me that DFPS does not rank the youth. A third-party organization does the ranking. DFPS also stated that they do not necessarily incentivize foster parents to take foster youth that this third-party organization has labeled as "intense," but they do incentivize some contracted residential childcare providers. Nonetheless, Adelpha's understanding of this ranking system influenced her perspective of and relationship with CPS.

20. Many youth in this study went to jail and/or prison, so they aptly can make this comparison.

21. Ferguson (2000); Casella (2003).

22. The Texas Department of Family and Protective Services' Levels for Care are available at: https://www.dfps.state.tx.us/Child_Protection/Foster_Care /Service_Levels.asp. Accessed October 2, 2019.

23. Robinson (2018a).

24. Personal correspondence with the Texas Department of Family and Protective Services on June 6, 2017.

25. Connell (2015).

26. Connolly (2000); Wasserman and Clair (2010).

27. Barton (2012).

28. Ward (2005); Acosta (2013).

29. Burns and Peyrot (2003).

30. The formal economy consists of work that the government taxes and monitors.

31. Wright ([1989] 2009).

32. Liebow (1993).

33. Fox and Stallworth (2005).

34. Wingfield (2007).

35. Dietert and Dentice (2009); Brewster et al. (2014).

36. Crenshaw (1989).

CHAPTER 3. NEW LAVENDER SCARE

1. The definition of aggressive panhandling varies by city and county ordinances and by state statutes. Some examples include no panhandling at a bus stop, within fifty feet of an automated teller machine, or within three feet of the person solicited. See Duneier (1999); Beckett and Herbert (2009); Wright ([1989] 2009).

2. A date is a sex worker's client.

3. I saw the official police report that Justice filed, confirming what she told me during the interview.

4. Sentencing Project (2017).

5. Travis, Western, and Redburn (2014).

6. Davis (2003); Wacquant (2009); Alexander (2010); Rios (2011).

7. Alexander (2010).

8. Dwyer (2008, 2011).

9. Johnson (2004).

10. I use *gay* and *lesbian* deliberately, not to erase bisexuality, pansexuality, and other forms of sexuality, but to capture how people policing non-heterosexuality often relied on the heterosexual/homosexual binary, and hence, saw non-heterosexual people as gay or lesbian.

11. As lesbians had less access to public spaces, police did not arrest them as much.

12. Johnson (2004).

13. Meyer et al. (2017).

14. Grant et al. (2011).

15. Irvine (2010).

16. Richie (2012: 14).

17. Sociologist Pierre Bourdieu ([1979] 1984) defines economic capital as one's financial resources. Cultural capital consists of one's social assets as related to social mobility, such as education, cultural knowledge, and style of speech and dress. Sociologist Margaret Hunter (2011) defines racial capital as the privileges and resources drawn from having white or light skin within the existing racial hierarchies based on white supremacy.

18. The blue-light system was also along outskirt paths on the San Antonio River Walk—walkways along the San Antonio River. The downtown section of the River Walk is a main tourist attraction of the city. The blue-light boxes on the River Walk were not exactly in a neighborhood but just along the path. The neighborhood of the shelter was the only actual neighborhood where I saw the blue-light boxes.

19. Huey (2012).

20. Huey (2012).

21. Wilson and Kelling (1982).

22. Duneier (1999).

23. Giroux (2009: 78).

24. Giroux (2009); Wacquant (2009); Alexander (2010); Rios (2011).

25. Rios (2011: 35).

26. Huey (2012).

27. Stuart (2016).

28. Dwyer (2008, 2011); Richie (2012).

29. Gibson (2011).

30. Gelman, Fagan, and Kiss (2007).

31. Pager (2003).

32. Thacher (2008).

33. Saperstein and Penner (2010).

34. Dwyer (2008); Mogul, Ritchie, and Whitlock (2011); Daum (2015).

35. Rios (2011).

36. Huey (2012).

37. Huey (2012); Woods et al. (2013).

38. Campbell and Kinnell (2000).

39. Huey (2012).

40. Whitbeck (2009).

41. Daum (2015).

42. Himmelstein and Brückner (2011).

43. Sumner and Jenness (2013).

44. Jenness and Fenstermaker (2014).

45. Potts (2011).

46. Cloud et al. (2015); Reiter (2016).

47. Girshick (2011).

48. Reiter (2016).

49. Arkles (2009).

50. Kunzel (2008).

51. Baus, Hunt, and Williams (2006).

52. Dolovich (2011).

53. Brunson and Miller (2006).

54. Woods et al. (2013).

55. Gurusami (2017).

56. Alexander (2010).

57. Alexander (2010).

58. Robinson (2020).

59. Reck (2009); Orne (2017).

60. Stanley and Smith (2011).

CHAPTER 4. QUEER STREET SMARTS

1. Hatt (2007).

2. Harter et al. (2005); Bender et al. (2007).

3. Hopper (2003); Gowan (2010); Wasserman and Clair (2010); Wright and Donley (2011).

4. Passaro (1996); Wasserman and Clair (2010).

5. Cochran et al. (2002).

6. Ray (2006).

7. Mottet and Ohle (2006); Hunter (2008).

8. Kissling (1991); Davis (1994); Bastomski and Smith (2017).

9. Mason (2002); Meyer (2015).

10. See Cochran et al. (2002). No study, to my knowledge, examines drug use and transgender and gender-expansive youth experiencing homelessness in comparison to their counterparts.

11. Tyler et al. (2004).

12. Buijs, Hekma, and Duyvendak (2011); Meyer (2015).

13. Namaste (2000).

14. Meyer (2015).

15. Witten and Eyler (1999); Lombardi et al. (2002).

16. Kidd and Witten (2008).

17. Taylor (2017).

18. Cavanagh (2010).

19. Mottet and Ohle (2006); Hunter (2008).

20. Gibson (2011); Shelton (2015).

21. Westbrook and Schilt (2014).

22. Bender-Baird (2016).

23. Herman (2013).

24. As detailed in the methodological appendix, a point-in-time count involves, on a particular day, volunteers counting people experiencing homelessness in their communities. During fieldwork, Travis county—where Austin is located—launched two youth point-in-time counts, as county officials and service providers wanted to get a better understanding of the specific population of youth experiencing homelessness.

25. Whitbeck (2009); Smid, Bourgois, and Auerswald (2010).

26. Passaro (1996).

27. Roll, Toro, and Ortola (1999).

28. Roberts (1999); Collins ([1990] 2000).

29. Kidd (2003); Whitbeck (2009).

30. Wasserman and Clair (2010).

31. Whitbeck and Hoyt (1999); Bender et al. (2007); Whitbeck (2009).

32. Pippert (2007).

33. Kruks (1991).

34. Wardhaugh (1999); Radley, Hodgetts, and Cullen (2006).

35. Smith (2008); Whitbeck (2009); Meanwell (2012).

36. Weitzer (2009).

37. Sausa, Keatley, and Operario (2007).

38. Huey and Berndt (2008).

39. Vidal-Ortiz, Robinson, and Khan (2018).

40. Vidal-Ortiz, Robinson, and Khan (2018).

41. Bourgois and Schonberg (2009).

42. Tyler et al. (2004); Tyler (2009).

43. Alliance for a Safe & Diverse DC (2008).

44. Brown and Herman (2015).

45. Bourgois and Schonberg (2009); Gowan (2010); Meanwell (2012).

46. Wardhaugh (1999); Radley, Hodgetts, and Cullen (2006); Huey and Berndt (2008); Watson (2011, 2016).

47. Wardhaugh (1999); Radley, Hodgetts, and Cullen (2006); Huey and Berndt (2008).

48. Huey and Berndt (2008).

49. Prendergast, Dunne, and Telford (2001).

CHAPTER 5. RESPITE, RESOURCES, RULES, AND REGULATIONS

1. Foucault (1994).

2. Williams (1996); Desjarlais (1997); Lyon-Callo (2004); Gowan (2010); Nichols (2014).

3. Warner (1999); Duggan (2002, 2003).

4. Ludwig (2016).

5. Puar (2007).

6. Johnson (2015).

7. Mottet and Ohle (2006); Shelton (2015).

8. By the end of my fieldwork, the youth in Austin still needed safe showers.

9. Hussey (2015).

10. Nichols (2014).

11. Spade (2011).

12. Currah and Mulqueen (2011).

13. Namaste (2000).

14. Shelton (2015).

15. Beauchamp (2009).

16. While many legal, medical, and other policies often reduce and dehumanize transgender and gender-expansive people to their genitals, undergoing legal gender change in Texas did not require sex reassignment surgery.

17. Lombardi (2001); Grossman and D'Augelli (2006); Sanchez, Sanchez, and Danoff (2009).

18. Bradford et al. (2013); Hughto (2017).

19. Grossman and D'Augelli (2006); Sanchez, Sanchez, and Danoff (2009).

20. Meyer (2003); Thoits (2010).

21. Orne (2017).

22. Bérubé (2001); Barrett and Pollack (2005); Han (2007); Robinson (2015).

23. Weston (1991); Nardi (1999); Weeks, Heaphy, and Donovan (2001); Bailey (2013); Orne (2017); Forstie (2018).

24. Pippert (2007).

25. Vidal-Ortiz (2009: 102).

26. Staff made exceptions to curfew and to the requirement of having to leave the shelter during the day for youth who had night jobs in the formal economy. Many people may also see this curfew as fairly late compared to many shelters across the country.

27. US Housing and Urban Development (2006).

28. Hoffman and Coffey (2008).

29. Hurtubise, Babin, and Grimard (2007).

30. Marson and Powell (2014).

31. Field (2014).

32. Walters (1998).

33. Hoffman and Coffey (2008).

34. Connolly (2000).

35. Hopper (2003); Gowan (2010); Wasserman and Clair (2010).

36. Schalet (2000); Elliot (2010, 2012).

37. Raby (2005, 2010).

38. Tori's partner lived across the hall on the adult side of the LGBTQ shelter.

39. Hurtubise, Babin, and Grimard (2007).
40. Liebow (1993); Williams (1996); Donley and Wright (2012).
41. Smith (2002, 2007).
42. Williams (1996); Desjarlais (1997).
43. Mbembe (2003).
44. Puar (2007).
45. See Robinson (2018c) for a further exploration of this topic.

CONCLUSION

1. Cohen (1997).
2. Rubin ([1984] 1993).
3. Moraga and Anzaldúa (1981).
4. Spade (2011).
5. Olivet et al. (2018).
6. Cohen (1997).
7. Robinson (2018c).
8. Olivet et al. (2018).
9. Robinson (2018b).
10. Schmitz and Tyler (2018).
11. See chapters 4 and 5. Also see Abramovich and Shelton (2017).
12. Rios (2011).
13. Meadow (2018); Travers (2018).
14. Crenshaw (1991); Abramovich and Shelton (2017); Robinson (2018a).
15. Mogul, Ritchie, and Whitlock (2011); Rios (2011).
16. Jones and Dugan (2017).
17. Goldstein, Collins, and Halder (2007).
18. The Dutch correctional system organizes more around resocialization and rehabilitation compared to the United States penal system, which organizes more around incapacitation and retribution. The Dutch also imprison far fewer people than the United States. See, for example, Subramanian and Shames (2013). While plenty of critiques exist of the rehabilitation model as well, the main point of this quote showcases Jerico's perception of the two systems and how this perception shapes his views on addressing homelessness.
19. Stuart (2016).
20. Lamble (2013).
21. Mogul, Ritchie, and Whitlock (2011); Bassichis, Lee, and Spade (2011); Lamble (2011); Stanley (2011).
22. Meyer (2015).
23. Westbrook and Schilt (2014).
24. Simões and Adam (2017).

25. Tsemberis, Gulcur, and Nakae (2004).

26. Munro, Reynolds, and Townsend (2017).

27. Cohen et al. (2017).

28. Los Angeles Homeless Services Authority (2009).

29. Shinn (2014).

30. Benjaminsen and Andrade (2015).

31. Coates (2014).

32. Muñoz (2009: 27).

33. Muñoz (2009).

APPENDIX

1. Geertz (2000: 40).

2. As of this writing, the organization has not published anything using the data.

3. Emerson, Fretz, and Shaw (2011).

4. During fieldwork, staff at the drop-in center told me several times that they often did not refer the youth at the street outreach drop-in center to the TLP. The staff said that the street youth often did not or could not follow the TLP rules, so they did not see most of the street youth as a good fit for the TLP.

5. As of this writing, the True Colors Fund has renamed this annual summit as the Impact Summit.

6. Weiss (1994).

7. Talburt (2004).

8. Charmaz (2006); Emerson, Fretz, and Shaw (2011).

9. Charmaz (2006).

10. Pascoe (2007).

11. González-López (2011).

12. The rule on not interacting with the youth outside of the organizations limited the data I could collect to the field sites of the organizations and to the interviews.

13. Wasserman and Clair (2010); González-López (2011).

14. Schell and Kayser-Jones (2007).

15. Rudd and D'Andrea (2015).

16. Geertz (2000).

References

Abramovich, Alex, and Jama Shelton. 2017. *Where Am I Going to Go? Intersectional Approaches to Ending LGBTQ2S Youth Homelessness in Canada and the U.S.* Toronto: Canadian Observatory on Homelessness Press.

Acosta, Katie L. 2013. *Amigas y Amantes: Sexually Nonconforming Latinas Negotiate Family.* New Brunswick, NJ: Rutgers University Press.

Alexander, Michelle. 2010. *The New Jim Crow: Mass Incarceration in the Age of Colorblindness.* New York: The New Press.

Alliance for a Safe & Diverse DC. 2008. *Move Along: Policing Sex Work in Washington, DC.* Washington, DC: Different Avenues.

Arkles, Gabriel. 2009. "Safety and Solidarity across Gender Lines: Rethinking Segregation of Transgender People in Detention." *Temple Political & Civil Rights Law Review* 18(2): 515–60.

Bailey, Marlon M. 2013. *Butch Queens Up in Pumps: Gender, Performance, and Ballroom Culture in Detroit.* Ann Arbor: University of Michigan Press.

Barrett, Donald C., and Lance M. Pollack. 2005. "Whose Gay Community? Social Class, Sexual Self-Expression, and Gay Community Involvement." *The Sociological Quarterly* 46: 437–56.

Barton, Bernadette. 2012. *Pray the Gay Away: The Extraordinary Lives of Bible Belt Gays.* New York: New York University Press.

Bassichis, Morgan, Alexander Lee, and Dean Spade. 2011. "Building an Abolitionist Trans and Queer Movement with Everything We've Got." In *Captive*

Genders: Trans Embodiment and the Prison Industrial Complex, edited by Eric A. Stanley and Nat Smith, 15–40. Oakland: AK Press.

Bastomski, Sara, and Philip Smith. 2017. "Gender, Fear, and Public Places: How Negative Encounters with Strangers Harm Women." *Sex Roles* 76(1–2): 73–88.

Baus, Janet, Dan Hunt, and Reid Williams (dirs.). 2006. *Cruel and Unusual*. Film. Reid Productions.

Beadle, Amanda Peterson. 2012. "Report: Minority Students Face More Disciplinary Actions in Public Schools," ThinkProgress, March 6.

Beauchamp, Toby. 2009. "Artful Concealment and Strategic Visibility: Transgender Bodies and U.S. State Surveillance After 9/11." *Surveillance & Society* 6(4): 356–66.

Beauvoir, Simone De. (1949) 2011. *The Second Sex*. New York: Vintage Books.

Beckett, Katherine, and Steve Herbert. 2009. *Banished: The New Social Control in Urban America*. Oxford: Oxford University Press.

Bender, Kimberly, Sanna J. Thompson, Holly McNanus, Janet Lantry, and Patrick M. Flynn. 2007. "Capacity for Survival: Exploring Strengths of Homeless Street Youth." *Child & Youth Care Forum* 36: 25–42.

Bender-Baird, Kyla. 2016. "Peeing under Surveillance: Bathrooms, Gender Policing, and Hate Violence." *Gender, Place & Culture* 23(7): 983–88.

Benjaminsen, Lars, and Stefan Bastholm Andrade. 2015. "Testing a Typology of Homelessness across Welfare Regimes: Shelter Use in Denmark and the USA." *Housing Studies* 30(6): 858–76.

Bérubé, Allan. 1990. *Coming Out under Fire: The History of Gay Men and Women in World War Two*. New York: The Free Press.

———. 2001. "How Gay Stays White and What Kind of White It Stays." In *The Making and Unmaking of Whiteness*, edited by B. B. Rasmussen, E. Klinenberg, I. J. Nexica, and M. Wray, 234–65. Durham, NC: Duke University Press.

Bettie, Julie. 2003. *Women without Class: Girls, Race, and Identity*. Berkeley: University of California Press.

Bourdieu, Pierre. (1979) 1984. *Distinction: A Social Critique of the Judgement of Taste*. London: Routledge.

Bourgois, Philippe, and Jeff Schonberg. 2009. *Righteous Dopefiend*. Berkeley: University of California Press.

Bradford, Judith, Sari L. Reisner, Julie A. Honnold, and Jessica Xavier. 2013. "Experiences of Transgender-Related Discrimination and Implications for Health: Results from the Virginia Transgender Health Initiative Study." *American Journal of Public Health* 103(10): 1820–29.

Brewster, Melanie E., Brandon L. Velez, Annelise Mennicke, and Elliot Tebbe. 2014. "Voices from Beyond: A Thematic Content Analysis of Transgender

Employees' Workplace Experiences." *Psychology of Sexual Orientation and Gender Diversity* 1(2): 159–69.

Brooks, Siobhan. 2010. "Hypersexualization and the Dark Body: Race and Inequality among Black and Latina Women in the Exotic Dance Industry." *Sexuality Research & Social Policy* 7(2): 70–80.

Brown, Taylor N. T., and Jody Herman. 2015. *Intimate Partner Violence and Sexual Abuse among LGBT People.* Los Angeles: The Williams Institute.

Bruce, Douglas, Ron Stall, Aimee Fata, and Richard T. Campbell. 2014. "Modeling Minority Stress Effects on Homelessness and Health Disparities among Young Men Who Have Sex with Men." *Journal of Urban Health* 91(3): 568–80.

Brunson, Rod K., and Jody Miller. 2006. "Gender, Race, and Urban Policing: The Experience of African American Youths." *Gender & Society* 20(4): 531–52.

Buijs, Laurens, Gert Hekma, and Jan Willem Duyvendak. 2011. "'As Long as They Keep Away from Me': The Paradox of Antigay Violence in a Gay-Friendly Country." *Sexualities* 14(6): 632–52.

Burns, Stacy Lee, and Mark Peyrot. 2003. "Tough Love: Nurturing and Coercing Responsibility and Recovery in California Drug Courts." *Social Problems* 50(3): 416–38.

Burton, Linda. 2007. "Childhood Adultification in Economically Disadvantaged Families: A Conceptual Model." *Family Relations* 56(4): 329–45.

Butler, Judith. 1990. *Gender Trouble: Feminism and the Subversion of Identity.* New York: Routledge.

———. 1993. *Bodies That Matter: On the Discursive Limits of Sex.* New York: Routledge.

Campbell, Rosie, and Hilary Kinnell. 2000. "'We Shouldn't Have to Put Up with This': Street Sex Work and Violence." *Criminal Justice Matters* 1: 12–13.

Casella, Ronnie. 2003. "Punishing Dangerousness through Preventive Detention: Illustrating the Institutional Link between School and Prison." *New Directions for Youth Development* 99: 55–70.

Cavanagh, Shannon E., and Aletha C. Huston. 2008. "The Timing of Family Instability and Children's Social Development." *Journal of Marriage and Family* 70(5): 1258–70.

Cavanagh, Sheila L. 2010. *Queering Bathrooms: Gender, Sexuality, and the Hygienic Imagination.* Toronto: University of Toronto Press.

Charmaz, Kathy. 2006. *Constructing Grounded Theory: A Practical Guide through Qualitative Analysis.* Los Angeles: Sage.

Chauncey, George. 1994. *Gay New York: Gender, Urban Culture, and the Making of the Gay Male World 1890-1940.* New York: Basic Books.

Cloud, David H., Ernest Drucker, Angela Browne, and Jim Parsons. 2015.

"Public Health and Solitary Confinement in the United States." *American Journal of Public Health* 105(1): 18–26.

Coates, Ta-Nehisi. 2014. "The Case for Reparations," *The Atlantic*, June.

Cochran, Bryan N., Angela J. Stewart, Joshua A. Ginzler, and Ana Mari Cauce. 2002. "Challenges Faced by Homeless Sexual Minorities: Comparison of Gay, Lesbian, Bisexual, and Transgender Homeless Adolescents with Their Heterosexual Counterparts." *American Journal of Public Health* 92(5): 773–77.

Cohen, Cathy J. 1997. "Punks, Bulldaggers, and Welfare Queens: The Radical Potential of Queer Politics?" *GLQ* 3: 437–65.

Cohen, Larry, Colin McSwiggen, Ronald Johnson, Kit Cali, and Matthew Montelongo. 2017. "The Youth Homelessness Crisis and a Path to End It: Interventions to Better Serve LGBTQ2S Youth Experiencing Homelessness." In *Where Am I Going to Go? Intersectional Approaches to Ending LGBTQ2S Youth Homelessness in Canada and the U.S.*, edited by Alex Abramovich and Jama Shelton, 115–34. Toronto: Canadian Observatory on Homelessness Press.

Collins, Patricia Hill. (1990) 2000. *Black Feminist Thought: Knowledge, Consciousness, and the Politics of Empowerment*. New York: Routledge.

———. 2004. *Black Sexual Politics: African Americans, Gender, and the New Racism*. New York: Routledge.

Connell, Catherine. 2015. *School's Out: Gay and Lesbian Teachers in the Classrooms*. Oakland: University of California Press.

Connell, R. W. 1995. *Masculinities: Knowledge, Power, and Social Change*. Berkeley: University of California Press.

Connolly, Deborah R. 2000. *Homeless Mothers: Face to Face with Women and Poverty*. Minneapolis: University of Minnesota Press.

Contreras, Randol. 2013. *The Stickup Kids: Race, Drugs, Violence, and the American Dream*. Berkeley: University of California Press.

Cray, Andrew, Katie Miller, and Laura E. Durso. 2013. *Seeking Shelter: The Experiences and Unmet Needs of LGBTQ Homeless Youth*. Washington, DC: Center for American Progress.

Crenshaw, Kimberlé. 1989. "Demarginalizing the Intersection of Race and Sex: A Black Feminist Critique of Antidiscrimination Doctrine, Feminist Theory and Antiracist Politics." *University of Chicago Legal Forum* 1: 139–67.

———. 1991. "Mapping the Margins: Intersectionality, Identity Politics, and Violence against Women of Color." *Stanford Law Review* 43(6): 1241–99.

Culhane, Dennis P. 2010. "Tackling Homelessness in Los Angeles' Skid Row: The Role of Policing Strategies and the Spatial Deconcentration of Homelessness." *Criminology & Public Policy* 9(4): 851–57.

Currah, Paisley, and Tara Mulqueen. 2011. "Securitizing Gender: Identity, Biometrics, and Transgender Bodies at the Airport." *Social Research* 78(2): 557–82.

Cuthbert, Karen. 2019. "'When We Talk about Gender We Talk about Sex': (A)sexuality and (A)gendered Subjectivities." *Gender & Society* 33(6): 841–64.

Cutuli, J. J., Ann Elizabeth Montgomery, Michelle Evans-Chase, and Dennis P. Culhane. 2017. "Childhood Adversity, Adult Homelessness and the Intergenerational Transmission of Risk: A Population-Representative Study of Individuals in Households with Children." *Child & Family Social Work* 22(1): 116–25.

D'Augelli, Anthony R., and Scott L. Hershberger. 1993. "Lesbian, Gay, and Bisexual Youth in Community Settings: Personal Challenges and Mental Health Problems." *American Journal of Community Psychology* 21(4): 421–48.

Daum, Courtenay W. 2015. "The War on Solicitation and Intersectional Subjugation: Quality-of-Life Policing as a Tool to Control Transgender Populations." *New Political Science* 37(4): 562–81.

Davis, Angela Y. 2003. *Are Prisons Obsolete?* New York: Seven Stories Press.

Davis, Deirdre. 1994. "The Harm That Has No Shame: Street Harassment, Embodiment, and African American Women." *UCLA Women's Law Journal* 4(2): 133–78.

Decena, Carlos Ulises. 2008. "Profiles, Compulsory Disclosure and Ethical Sexual Citizenship in the Contemporary USA." *Sexualities* 11(4): 397–413.

———. 2011. *Tacit Subjects: Belonging and Same-Sex Desire among Dominican Immigrant Men*. Durham, NC: Duke University Press.

D'Emilio, John. 1993. "Capitalism and Gay Identity." In *The Lesbian and Gay Studies Reader*, edited by Henry Abelove, Michéle A. Barale, and David M. Halperin, 467–76. New York: Routledge.

Desjarlais, Robert R. 1997. *Shelter Blues: Sanity and Selfhood among the Homeless*. Philadelphia: University of Pennsylvania Press.

Desmond, Matthew. 2012. "Eviction and the Reproduction of Urban Poverty." *American Journal of Sociology* 118(1): 88–133.

Dietert, Michelle, and Dianne Dentice. 2009. "Gender Identity Issues and Workplace Discrimination: The Transgender Experience." *Journal of Workplace Rights* 14(1): 121–40.

Dolovich, Sharon. 2011. "Strategic Segregation in the Modern Prison." *American Criminal Law Review* 48(1): 1–110.

Donley, Amy M., and James D. Wright. 2012. "Safer Outside: A Qualitative Exploration of Homeless People's Resistance to Homeless Shelters." *Journal of Forensic Psychology Practice* 12(4): 288–306.

Duggan, Lisa. 2002. "The New Homonormativity: The Sexual Politics of Neoliberalism." In *Materializing Democracy: Toward a Revitalized Cultural Politics*, edited by Russ Castronovo and Dana D. Nelson, 175–94. Durham, NC: Duke University Press.

———. 2003. *The Twilight of Equality? Neoliberalism, Cultural Politics, and the Attack on Democracy*. Boston: Beacon Press.

Duneier, Mitchell. 1999. *Sidewalk*. New York: Farrar, Strauss, and Giroux.

Dunne, Gillian A., Shirley Prendergast, and David Telford. 2002. "Young, Gay, Homeless and Invisible: A Growing Population?" *Culture, Health & Sexuality* 4(1): 103–15.

Durso, Laura E., and Gary J. Gates. 2012. *Serving Our Youth: Findings from a National Survey of Services Providers Working with Lesbian, Gay, Bisexual and Transgender Youth Who Are Homeless or at Risk of Becoming Homeless*. Los Angeles: The Williams Institute.

Dwyer, Angela. 2008. "Policing Queer Bodies: Focusing on Queer Embodiment in Policing Research as an Ethical Question." *QUT Law Review* 8(2): 414–28.

———. 2011. "'It's Not Like We're Going to Jump Them': How Transgressing Heteronormativity Shapes Police Interactions with LGBT Young People." *Youth Justice* 11(3): 203–20.

Eamon, Mary Keegan, and Sandra Kopels. 2004. "'For Reasons of Poverty': Court Challenges to Child Welfare Practices and Mandated Programs." *Children and Youth Services Review* 26: 821–36.

Ecker, John. 2016. "Queer, Young, and Homeless: A Review of the Literature." *Child & Youth Services* 37(4): 325–61.

Elliot, Sinikka. 2010. "Parents' Construction of Teen Sexuality: Sex Panics, Contradictory Discourses, and Social Inequality." *Symbolic Interaction* 33(2): 191–212.

———. 2012. *Not My Kid: What Parents Believe about the Sex Lives of Their Teenagers*. New York: New York University Press.

Emerson, Robert M., Rachel I. Fretz, and Linda L. Shaw. 2011. *Writing Ethnographic Fieldnotes*, 2nd edition. Chicago: University of Chicago Press.

Ferguson, Ann Arnett. 2000. *Bad Boys: Public Schools in the Making of Black Masculinity*. Ann Arbor: University of Michigan Press.

Ferguson, Roderick. 2004. *Aberrations in Black: Toward a Queer of Color Critique*. Minneapolis: University of Minnesota Press.

Field, Corinne. 2014. *The Struggle for Equal Adulthood: Gender, Race, Age, and the Fight for Citizenship in Antebellum America*. Chapel Hill: University of North Carolina Press.

Fish, Jessica N., Laura Baams, Armeda Stevenson Wojciak, and Stephen T. Russell. 2019. "Are Sexual Minority Youth Overrepresented in Foster Care, Child Welfare, and Out-of-Home Placement? Findings from Nationally Representative Data." *Child Abuse & Neglect* 89: 203–11.

Flatau, Paul, Elizabeth Conroy, Catherine Spooner, Robyn Edwards, Tony Eardley, and Catherine Forbes. 2013. *Lifetime and Intergenerational Experiences of Homelessness in Australia*. Melbourne: Australian Housing and Urban Research Institute.

Flores, Edward Orozco, and Pierrette Hondagneu-Sotelo. 2013. "Chicano Gang Members in Recovery: The Public Talk of Negotiating Chicano Masculinities." *Social Problems* 60(4): 476–90.

Flores, Jennifer, and Sedef Doganer. 2010. "Reducing Urban Sprawl and Revitalizing Historic Downtown San Antonio," The Second International Conference on Sustainable Architecture and Urban Development, July 12–14.

Fomby, Paula, and Andrew J. Cherlin. 2007. "Family Instability and Child Well-Being." *American Sociological Review* 72: 181–204.

Forstie, Clare. 2018. "Ambivalently Post-Lesbian: LGQ Friendships in the Rural Midwest." *Journal of Lesbian Studies* 22(1): 54–66.

Foucault, Michel. 1977. *Discipline & Punish: The Birth of a Prison*. New York: Vintage Books.

———. 1994. *Essential Works of Foucault, 1954–1984: Power*. New York: The New Press.

Fox, Suzy, and Lamont E. Stallworth. 2005. "Racial/Ethnic Bullying: Exploring Links between Bullying and Racism in the US Workplace." *Journal of Vocational Behavior* 66: 438–56.

Funders for LGBTQ Issues. 2018. "An Update on Foundation Funding for LGBTQ Issues in the U.S. South." New York: Funders for LGBTQ Issues.

Geertz, Clifford. 2000. *Available Light: Anthropological Reflections on Philosophical Topics*. Princeton, NJ: Princeton University Press.

Gelman, Andrew, Jeffrey Fagan, and Alex Kiss. 2007. "An Analysis of the New York City Police Department's 'Stop-and-Frisk' Policy in the Context of Claims of Racial Bias." *Journal of the American Statistical Association* 102(479): 813–23.

Gibbard, Megan. 2015. "Young, Gay and Homeless: Why Some Parents Reject Their Children," *Seattle Times*, December 2.

Gibson, Kristina E. 2011. *Street Kids: Homeless Youth, Outreach, and Policing New York's Streets*. New York: New York University Press.

Giroux, Henry A. 2009. *Youth in a Suspect Society: Democracy or Disposability?* New York: Palgrave Macmillan.

Girshick, Lori. 2011. "Out of Compliance: Masculine-Identified People in Women's Prisons." In *Captive Genders: Trans Embodiment and the Prison Industrial Complex*, edited by Eric A. Stanley and Nat Smith, 189–208. Oakland: AK Press.

Goffman, Erving. 1963. *Stigma: Notes on the Management of Spoiled Identity*. New York: Simon & Schuster.

Goldstein, Tara, Anthony Collins, and Michael Halder. 2007. "Anti-Homophobia Education in Public Schooling: A Canadian Case Study of Policy Implementation." *Journal of Gay & Lesbian Social Services* 19(3–4): 47–66.

González-López, Gloria. 2011. "Mindful Ethics: Comments on Informant-Centered Practices in Sociological Research." *Qualitative Sociology* 34: 447–61.

———. 2015. *Family Secrets: Stories of Incest and Sexual Violence in Mexico.* New York: New York University Press.

Gowan, Teresa. 2010. *Hobos, Hustlers, and Backsliders: Homeless in San Francisco.* Minneapolis: University of Minnesota Press.

Grant, Jaime M., Lisa A. Mottet, Justin Tanis, Jack Harrison, Jody L. Herman, and Mara Keisling. 2011. *Injustice at Every Turn: A Report of the National Transgender Discrimination Survey.* Washington, DC: National Center for Transgender Equality and National Gay and Lesbian Task Force.

Gray, Mary L. 2009. *Out in the Country: Youth, Media, and Queer Visibility in Rural America.* New York: New York University Press.

Grossman, Arnold H., and Anthony R. D'Augelli. 2006. "Transgender Youth: Invisible and Vulnerable." *Journal of Homosexuality* 51(1): 111–28.

Gurusami, Susila. 2017. "Working for Redemption: Formerly Incarcerated Black Women and Punishment in the Labor Market." *Gender & Society* 31(4): 433–56.

Han, Chong-suk. 2007. "They Don't Want to Cruise Your Type: Gay Men of Color and the Racial Politics of Exclusion." *Social Identities* 13(1): 51–67.

Harter, Lynn M., Charlene Berquist, B. Scott Titsworth, David Novak, and Tod Brokaw. 2005. "The Structuring of Invisibility among the Hidden Homeless: The Politics of Space, Stigma, and Identity Construction." *Journal of Applied Communication Research* 33(4): 305–27.

Hatt, Beth. 2007. "Street Smarts vs. Book Smarts: The Figured World of Smartness in the Lives of Marginalized, Urban Youth." *The Urban Review* 39(2): 145–66.

Hays, Sharon. 2004. *Flat Broke with Children: Women in the Age of Welfare Reform.* Oxford: Oxford University Press.

Heitzeg, Nancy A. 2009. "Education or Incarceration: Zero Tolerance Policies and the School to Prison Pipeline." *Forum on Public Policy* 9(2): 1–21.

Herdt, Gilbert, and Bruce Koff. 2000. *Something to Tell You: The Road Families Travel When a Child Is Gay.* New York: Columbia University Press.

Herman, Jody L. 2013. "Gendered Restrooms and Minority Stress: The Public Regulation of Gender and Its Impact on Transgender People's Lives." *Journal of Public Management & Social Policy* 19(1): 65–80.

Himmelstein, Kathryn E., and Hannah Brückner. 2011. "Criminal-Justice and School Sanctions against Nonheterosexual Youth: A National Longitudinal Study." *Pediatrics* 127(1): 49–57.

Hoffman, Lisa, and Brian Coffey. 2008. "Dignity and Indignation: How People Experiencing Homelessness View Services and Providers." *The Social Science Journal* 45: 207–22.

Hopper, Kim. 2003. *Reckoning with Homelessness*. Ithaca, NY: Cornell University Press.

Huey, Laura. 2012. *Invisible Victims: Homelessness and the Growing Security Gap*. Toronto: University of Toronto Press.

Huey, Laura, and Eric Berndt. 2008. "'You've Gotta Learn How to Play the Game': Homeless Women's Use of Gender Performance as a Tool for Preventing Victimization." *The Sociological Review* 56(2): 177–94.

Hughto, Jaclyn M. White, Adam J. Rose, John E. Pachankis, and Sari L. Reisner. 2017. "Barriers to Gender Transition-Related Healthcare: Identifying Underserved Transgender Adults in Massachusetts." *Transgender Health* 2(1): 107–18.

Hunter, Ernst. 2008. "What's Good for the Gays Is Good for the Gander: Making Homeless Youth Housing Safer for Lesbian, Gay, Bisexual, and Transgender Youth." *Family Court Review* 46(3): 543–57.

Hunter, Margaret L. 2011. "Buying Racial Capital: Skin-Bleaching and Cosmetic Surgery in a Globalized World." *The Journal of Pan African Studies* 4(4): 142–64.

Hurtubise, Roch, Pierre-Olivier Babin, and Carolyne Grimard. 2007. "Understanding Shelters: An Overview of the Scientific Literature." *Colloque CRI 2007—Shelters at a Crossroads*. Sherbrooke, QC: Departement de service social, Universite de Sherbrooke.

Hussey, Hannah. 2015. *Expanding ID Card Access for LGBT Homeless Youth*. Washington, DC: Center for American Progress.

Institute of Medicine. 2011. *The Health of Lesbian, Gay, Bisexual, and Transgender People: Building a Foundation for Better Understanding*. Washington, DC: The National Academies Press.

Irvine, Angela. 2010. "'We've Had Three of Them': Addressing the Invisibility of Lesbian, Gay, Bisexual, and Gender Nonconforming Youths in the Juvenile Justice System." *Columbia Journal of Gender and Law* 19(3): 675–701.

Jamrozy, Ute. 2007. "Marketing of Tourism: A Paradigm Shift toward Sustainability." *International Journal of Culture, Tourism and Hospitality Research* 1(2): 117–30.

Jenness, Valerie, and Sarah Fenstermaker. 2014. "Agnes Goes to Prison: Gender Authenticity, Transgender Inmates in Prisons for Men, and Pursuit of 'The Real Deal.'" *Gender & Society* 28(1): 5–31.

Johnson, David K. 2004. *The Lavender Scare: The Cold War Persecution of Gays and Lesbians in the Federal Government*. Chicago: University of Chicago Press.

Johnson, Javon. 2015. "Black Joy in the Time of Ferguson." *QED: A Journal in GLBTQ Worldmaking* 2(2): 177–83.

Jones, Natasha, and Michelle Dugan. 2017. "LEAP into Action: Preparing LGBTQ2S Youth for the Workforce." In *Where Am I Going to Go? Intersectional*

Approaches to Ending LGBTQ2S Youth Homelessness in Canada and the U.S., edited by Alex Abramovich and Jama Shelton, 263–72. Toronto: Canadian Observatory on Homelessness Press.

Kane, Emily W. 2012. *The Gender Trap*. New York: New York University Press.

Keuroghlian, Alex S., Derri Shtasel, and Ellen L. Bassuk. 2014. "Out on the Street: A Public Health and Policy Agenda for Lesbian, Gay, Bisexual, and Transgender Youth Who Are Homeless." *American Journal of Orthopsychiatry* 84(1): 66–72.

Kidd, Jeremy D., and Tarynn M. Witten. 2008. "Transgender and Transsexual Identities: The Next Strange Fruit—Hate Crimes, Violence and Genocide against the Global Trans-Communities." *Journal of Hate Studies* 6: 31–63.

Kidd, Sean A. 2003. "Street Youth: Coping and Interventions." *Child and Adolescent Social Work Journal* 20(4): 235–61.

Kissling, Elizabeth Arveda. 1991. "Street Harassment: The Language of Sexual Terrorism." *Discourse & Society* 2(4): 451–60.

Kruks, Gabe. 1991. "Gay and Lesbian Homeless/Street Youth: Special Issues and Concerns." *Journal of Adolescent Health* 12: 515–18.

Kunzel, Regina. 2008. *Criminal Intimacy: Prison and the Uneven History of Modern American Sexuality*. Chicago: University of Chicago Press.

Lamble, Sarah. 2011. "Transforming Carceral Logics: 10 Reasons to Dismantle the Prison Industrial Complex Using a Queer/Trans Analysis." In *Captive Genders: Trans Embodiment and the Prison Industrial Complex*, edited by Eric A. Stanley and Nat Smith, 235–66. Oakland: AK Press.

———. 2013. "Queer Necropolitics and the Expanding Carceral State: Interrogating Sexual Investments in Punishment." *Law Critique* 24: 229–53.

Lareau, Annette. 2003. *Unequal Childhoods: Class, Race, and Family Life*. Berkeley: University of California Press.

Lee, Barrett A., Kimberly A. Tyler, and James D. Wright. 2010. "The New Homelessness Revisited." *Annual Review of Sociology* 36: 501–21.

Liamputtong, Pranee. 2007. *Researching the Vulnerable: A Guide to Sensitive Research Methods*. London: Sage.

Liebow, Elliot. 1993. *Tell Them Who I Am: The Lives of Homeless Women*. New York: Penguin Books.

Lombardi, Emilia. 2001. "Enhancing Transgender Health Care." *American Journal of Public Health* 91(6): 869–72.

Lombardi, Emilia L., Riki Anne Wilchins, Dana Priesing, and Diana Malouf. 2002. "Gender Violence." *Journal of Homosexuality* 42(1): 89–101.

Los Angeles Homeless Services Authority. 2009. *Where We Sleep: Costs When Homeless and Housed in Los Angeles*. Los Angeles: Economic Roundtable.

Ludwig, Gundula. 2016. "Desiring Neoliberalism." *Sexuality Research & Social Policy* 13: 417–27.

Lyon-Callo, Vincent. 2004. *Inequality, Poverty, and Neoliberal Governance: Activist Ethnography in the Homeless Sheltering Industry.* Toronto: University of Toronto Press.

Mallett, Shelley, and Doreen Rosenthal. 2009. "Physically Violent Mothers Are a Reason for Young People's Leaving Home." *Journal of Interpersonal Violence* 24(7): 1165–74.

Marson, Stephen M., and Rasby M. Powell. 2014. "Goffman and Infantilization of Elderly Persons: A Theory in Development." *Journal of Sociology & Social Welfare* 41(4): 143–58.

Martin Prosperity Institute. 2015. *Segregated City: The Geographic of Economic Segregation in America's Metros.* Toronto, ON: Author.

Mason, Gail. 2002. *The Spectacle of Violence: Homophobia, Gender and Knowledge.* London: Routledge.

Mbembe, Achille. 2003. "Necropolitics." *Public Culture* 15(1): 11–40.

Meadow, Tey. 2018. *Trans Kids: Being Gendered in the Twenty-First Century.* Oakland: University of California Press.

Meanwell, Emily. 2012. "Experiencing Homelessness: A Review of Recent Literature." *Sociology Compass* 6(1): 72–85.

Meyer, Doug. 2015. *Violence against Queer People: Race, Class, Gender, and the Persistence of Anti-LGBT Discrimination.* New Brunswick, NJ: Rutgers University Press.

Meyer, Ilan H. 2003. "Prejudice, Social Stress, and Mental Health in Lesbian, Gay, and Bisexual Populations: Conceptual Issues and Research Evidence." *Psychological Bulletin* 129(5): 674–97.

Meyer, Ilan H., Andrew R. Flores, Lara Stemple, Adam P. Romero, Bianca D. M. Wilson, and Jody L. Herman. 2017. "Incarceration Rates and Traits of Sexual Minorities in the United States: National Inmate Survey, 2011–2012." *American Journal of Public Health* 107(2): 234–40.

Mitchum, Preston, and Aisha C. Moodie-Mills. 2014. *Beyond Bullying: How Hostile School Climate Perpetuates the School-to-Prison Pipeline for LGBTQ Youth.* Washington, DC: Center for American Progress.

Mogul, Joey L., Andrea J. Ritchie, and Kay Whitlock. 2011. *Queer (In)Justice: The Criminalization of LGBT People in the United States.* Boston: Beacon Press.

Moraga, Cherríe, and Gloria Anzaldúa. 1981. *This Bridge Called My Back: Writings by Radical Women of Color.* Watertown, MA: Persephone Press.

Morris, Alex. 2014. "The Forsaken: A Rising Number of Homeless Gay Teens Are Being Cast Out by Religious Families," *Rolling Stone*, September 3.

Morton, Matthew H., Amy Dworsky, Jennifer L. Matjasko, Susanna R. Curry, David Schlueter, Raúl Chávez, and Anne F. Farrell. 2018. "Prevalence and Correlates of Youth Homelessness in the United States." *Journal of Adolescent Health* 62: 14–21.

Mottet, Lisa, and John Ohle. 2006. "Transitioning Our Shelters: Making Homeless Shelters Safe for Transgender People." *Journal of Poverty* 10(2): 77–101.

Muñoz, José Esteban. 2009. *Cruising Utopia: The Then and There of Queer Futurity*. New York: New York University Press.

Munro, Aaron, Vikki Reynolds, and Marria Townsend. 2017. "Youth Wisdom, Harm Reduction and Housing First: RainCity Housing's Queer and Trans Youth Housing Project." In *Where Am I Going to Go? Intersectional Approaches to Ending LGBTQ2S Youth Homelessness in Canada and the U.S.*, edited by Alex Abramovich and Jama Shelton, 135–54. Toronto: Canadian Observatory on Homelessness Press.

Namaste, Viviane. 2000. *Invisible Lives: The Erasure of Transsexual and Transgendered People*. Chicago: University of Chicago Press.

Nardi, Peter M. 1999. *Gay Men's Friendships: Invincible Communities*. Chicago: University of Chicago Press.

Newport, Frank. 2018. "In U.S., Estimate of LGBT Population Rises to 4.5%," *Gallup*, May 22.

Nichols, Naomi. 2014. *Youth Work: An Institutional Ethnography of Youth Homelessness*. Toronto: University of Toronto Press.

Nolan, Theresa C. 2006. "Outcomes for a Transitional Living Program Serving LGBTQQ Youth in New York City." *Child Welfare* 85(2): 385–406.

Olivet, Jeffrey, Marc Dones, Molly Richard, Catriona Wiley, Svetlana Yampolskaya, Maya Beit-Arie, and Lunise Joseph. 2018. *Supporting Partnerships for Anti-Racist Communities: Phase One Study Findings*. Needham, MA: Center for Social Innovation.

Orne, Jason. 2017. *Boystown: Sex and Community in Chicago*. Chicago: University of Chicago Press.

Page, Michelle. 2017. "Forgotten Youth: Homeless LGBT Youth of Color and the Runaway and Homeless Youth Act." *Northwestern Journal of Law & Social Policy* 12(2): 17–45.

Pager, Devah. 2003. "The Mark of a Criminal Record." *American Journal of Sociology* 108(5): 937–75.

Paoletti, Jo B. 2012. *Pink and Blue: Telling the Boys from the Girls in America*. Bloomington: Indiana University Press.

Pascoe, C. J. 2007. *Dude, You're a Fag: Masculinity and Sexuality in High School*. Berkeley: University of California Press.

Passaro, Joanne. 1996. *The Unequal Homeless: Men on the Streets, Women in Their Place*. New York: Routledge.

Payne, Elizabethe, and Melissa Smith. 2013. "LGBTQ Kids, School Safety, and Missing the Big Picture: How the Dominant Bullying Discourse Prevents School Professionals from Thinking about Systematic Marginalization or . . . Why We Need to Rethink LGBTQ Bullying." *QED: A Journal in GLBTQ Worldmaking* 1: 1–36.

Pippert, Timothy D. 2007. *Road Dogs and Loners: Family Relationships among Homeless Men.* Lanham, MD: Lexington Books.

Potts, Michelle C. 2011. "Regulatory Sites: Management, Confinement, and HIV/AIDS." In *Captive Genders: Trans Embodiment and the Prison Industrial Complex,* edited by Eric A. Stanley and Nat Smith, 99–112. Oakland: AK Press.

Prendergast, Shirley, Gillian A. Dunne, and David Telford. 2001. "A Story of 'Difference,' A Different Story: Young Homeless Lesbian, Gay and Bisexual People." *International Journal of Sociology and Social Policy* 21(4–6): 64–91.

Puar, Jasbir K. 2007. *Terrorist Assemblages: Homonationalism in Queer Times.* Durham, NC: Duke University Press.

Quiggin, John. 1998. "Homelessness: The Human Face of Economic Imperatives." *Parity* 11(6): 8–9.

Raby, Rebecca. 2005. "Polite, Well-Dressed and on Time: Secondary School Conduct Codes and the Production of Docile Citizens." *Canadian Review of Sociology* 42(1): 71–91.

———. 2010. "'Tank Tops Are OK but I Don't Want to See Her Thong': Girls' Engagement with Secondary School Dress Codes." *Youth & Society* 41(3): 333–56.

Radley, Alan, Darrin Hodgetts, and Andrea Cullen. 2006. "Fear, Romance and Transience in the Lives of Homeless Women." *Social & Cultural Geography* 7(3): 437–61.

Rahilly, Elizabeth P. 2015. "The Gender Binary Meets the Gender-Variant Child: Parents' Negotiations with Childhood Gender Variance." *Gender & Society* 29(3): 338–61.

Ray, Nicholas. 2006. *An Epidemic of Homelessness: Lesbian, Gay, Bisexual, and Transgender Youth.* Washington, DC: National Gay and Lesbian Task Force Policy Institute.

Reck, Jen. 2009. "Homeless Gay and Transgender Youth of Color in San Francisco: 'No One Likes Streets Kids'—Even in the Castro." *Journal of LGBT Youth* 6(2–3): 223–42.

Reiter, Keramet. 2016. *23/7: Pelican Bay Prison and the Rise of Long-Term Solitary Confinement.* New Haven, CT: Yale University Press.

Rew, Lynn, Tiffany A. Whittaker, Margaret A. Taylor-Seehafer, and Lorie R. Smith. 2005. "Sexual Health Risks and Protective Resources in Gay, Lesbian, Bisexual, and Heterosexual Homeless Youth." *Journal for Specialists in Pediatric Nursing* 10(1): 11–19.

Richie, Beth E. 2012. *Arrested Justice: Black Women, Violence, and America's Prison Nation.* New York: New York University Press.

Rios, Victor M. 2011. *Punished: Policing the Lives of Black and Latino Boys.* New York: New York University Press.

Roberts, Dorothy E. 1999. *Killing the Black Body: Race, Reproduction, and the Meaning of Liberty.* New York: Pantheon Books.

Robinson, Brandon Andrew. 2015. "'Personal Preference' as the New Racism: Gay Desire and Racial Cleansing in Cyberspace." *Sociology of Race & Ethnicity* 1(2): 317–30.

———. 2018a. "Child Welfare Systems and LGBTQ Youth Homelessness: Gender Segregation, Instability, and Intersectionality." *Child Welfare* 96(2): 29–45.

———. 2018b. "Conditional Families and Lesbian, Gay, Bisexual, Transgender, and Queer Youth Homelessness: Gender, Sexuality, Family Instability, and Rejection." *Journal of Marriage & Family* 80(2): 383–96.

———. 2018c. "'I Want to Be Happy in Life': Success, Failure, and Addressing LGBTQ Youth Homelessness." In *The Unfinished Queer Agenda after Marriage Equality*, edited by Angela Jones, Joseph DeFilippis, and Michael W. Yarbrough, 117–29. New York: Routledge.

———. 2020. "The Lavender Scare in Homonormative Times: Policing, Hyper-incarceration, and LGBTQ Youth Homelessness." *Gender & Society* 34(2): 219–32.

Roll, Carolyn N., Paul A. Toro, and Gina L. Ortola. 1999. "Characteristics and Experiences of Homeless Adults: A Comparison of Single Men, Single Women, and Women with Children." *Journal of Community Psychology* 27(2): 189–98.

Ross, Marlon B. 2005. "Beyond the Closet as a Raceless Paradigm." In *Black Queer Studies: A Critical Anthology*, edited by E. Patrick Johnson and Mae G. Henderson, 161–89. Durham, NC: Duke University Press.

Rubin, Gayle. S. (1984) 1993. "Thinking Sex: Notes for a Radical Theory of the Politics of Sexuality." In *The Lesbian and Gay Studies Reader*, edited by Henry Abelove, Michéle A. Barale, and David M. Halperin, 3–44. New York: Routledge.

Rudd, Rebecca A., and Livia M. D'Andrea. 2015. "Compassionate Detachment: Managing Professional Stress while Providing Quality Care to Bereaved Parents." *Journal of Workplace Behavioral Health* 30(3): 287–305.

Russell, Stephen T. 2002. "Queer in America: Citizenship for Sexual Minority Youth." *Applied Developmental Science* 6(4): 258–63.

Sanchez, Nelson F., John P. Sanchez, and Ann Danoff. 2009. "Health Care Utilization, Barriers to Care, and Hormone Usage among Male-to-Female Transgender Persons in New York City." *American Journal of Public Health* 99(4): 713–19.

Saperstein, Aliya, and Andrew M. Penner. 2010. "The Race of a Criminal Record: How Incarceration Colors Racial Perceptions." *Social Problems* 57(1): 92–113.

Sausa, Lydia A., JoAnne Keatley, and Don Operario. 2007. "Perceived Risks and Benefits of Sex Work among Transgender Women of Color in San Francisco." *Archives of Sexual Behavior* 36: 768–77.

Schalet, Amy T. 2000. "Raging Hormones, Regulated Love: Adolescent Sexuality and the Constitution of the Modern Individual in the United States and the Netherlands." *Body & Society* 6(1): 75–105.

Schell, Ellen S., and Jeanie Kayser-Jones. 2007. "'Getting into the Skin': Empathy and Role Taking in Certified Nursing Assistants' Care of Dying Residents." *Applied Nursing Research* 20: 146–51.

Schilt, Kristen, and Laurel Westbrook. 2009. "Doing Gender, Doing Heteronormativity: 'Gender Normals,' Transgender People, and the Social Maintenance of Heterosexuality." *Gender & Society* 23(4): 440–464.

Schmitz, Rachel M., and Kimberly A. Tyler. 2016. "Growing Up before Their Time: The Early Adultification Experiences of Homeless Youth People." *Children and Youth Services Review* 64: 15–22.

———. 2018. "LGBTQ+ Young Adults on the Street and on Campus: Identity as a Product of Social Context." *Journal of Homosexuality* 65(2): 197–223.

Sentencing Project. 2017. "Criminal Justice Facts." Accessed June 28, 2018. http://www.sentencingproject.org/criminal-justice-facts/.

Shelton, Jama. 2015. "Transgender Youth Homelessness: Understanding Programmatic Barriers through the Lens of Cisgenderism." *Children and Youth Services Review* 59: 10–18.

Shepard, Benjamin. 2013. "From Community Organization to Direct Services: The Street Trans Action Revolutionaries to Sylvia Rivera Law Project." *Journal of Social Service Research* 39(1): 95–114.

Shinn, Gregory, A. 2014. *The Cost of Long-Term Homelessness in Central Florida: The Current Crisis and the Economic Impact of Providing Sustainable Housing Solutions.* Orlando: Central Florida Commission on Homelessness.

Simões, Raquel (Rocki), and Khalid Adam. 2017. "Messy and Magical: A Closer Look at the GLBT Host Home Program." In *Where Am I Going to Go? Intersectional Approaches to Ending LGBTQ2S Youth Homelessness in Canada and the U.S.*, edited by Alex Abramovich and Jama Shelton, 155–68. Toronto: Canadian Observatory on Homelessness Press.

Smid, Marcela, Philippe Bourgois, and Colette L. Auerswald. 2010. "The Challenge of Pregnancy among Homeless Youth: Reclaiming a Lost Opportunity." *Journal of Health Care for the Poor and Underserved* 21(2): 140–56.

Smith, Anna Marie. 2002. "The Sexual Regulation Dimension of Contemporary Welfare Law: A Fifty State Overview." *Michigan Journal of Gender and Law* 8(2): 121–218.

———. 2007. *Welfare Reform and Sexual Regulation.* Cambridge: Cambridge University Press.

Smith, Dorothy E. 1987. *The Everyday World as Problematic: A Feminist Sociology.* Boston: Northeastern University Press.

Smith, Hilary. 2008. "Searching for Kinship: The Creation of Street Families among Homeless Youth." *American Behavioral Scientist* 51(6): 756–71.

Snapp, Shannon D., Jennifer M. Hoenig, Amanda Fields, and Stephen T. Russell. 2015. "Messy, Butch, and Queer: LGBTQ Youth and the School-to-Prison Pipeline." *Journal of Adolescent Research* 30(1): 57–82.

Spade, Dean. 2011. *Normal Life: Administrative Violence, Critical Trans Politics, and the Limits of the Law.* New York: South End Press.

Spivak, Gayatri. 1988. "Can the Subaltern Speak?" In *Marxism and the Interpretation of Culture*, edited by Cary Nelson and Lawrence Grossberg, 271–313. Basingstoke: Macmillan.

Stanley, Eric A. 2011. "Introduction: Fugitive Flesh: Gender Self-Determination, Queer Abolition, and Trans Resistance." In *Captive Genders: Trans Embodiment and the Prison Industrial Complex*, edited by Eric A. Stanley and Nat Smith, 1–11. Oakland: AK Press.

Stanley, Eric A., and Nat Smith, eds. 2011. *Captive Genders: Trans Embodiment and the Prison Industrial Complex.* Oakland: AK Press.

Stryker, Susan. 2008. "Transgender History, Homonormativity, and Disciplinarity." *Radical History Review* 100: 145–57.

Stuart, Forrest. 2016. *Down, Out, and Under Arrest: Policing and Everyday Life in Skid Row.* Chicago: University of Chicago Press.

Subramanian, Ram, and Alison Shames. 2013. *Sentencing and Prison Practices in Germany and the Netherlands: Implications for the United States.* New York: Vera Institute of Justice.

Sumner, Jennifer, and Valerie Jenness. 2013. "Gender Integration in Sex-Segregated U.S. Prisons: The Paradox of Transgender Correctional Policy." In *Handbook of LGBT Communities, Crime, and Justice*, edited by D. Peterson and V. R. Panfil, 229–59. New York: Springer.

Talburt, Susan. 2004. "Constructions of LGBT Youth: Opening Up Subject Positions." *Theory into Practice* 43(2): 116–21.

Taylor, Jeff. 2017. "Texas Introduces Anti-Transgender Bathroom Bill with Quote from MLK, Jr." *LGBTQ Nation*, January 5.

Thacher, David. 2008. "The Rise of Criminal Background Screening in Rental Housing." *Law & Social Inquiry* 33(1): 5–30.

Theis, Michael. 2015. "Austin Drops on Forbes Fastest-Growing Cities List; Texas Cities Dominate," *Austin Business Journal*, January 28.

Thoits, Peggy A. 2010. "Stress and Health: Major Findings and Policy Implications." *Journal of Health and Social Behavior* 51(S): S41–S53.

Thompson, Sanna J., Kimberly Bender, Lilianne Windsor, Mary S. Cook, and Travonne Williams. 2010. "Homeless Youth: Characteristics, Contributing

Factors, and Service Options." *Journal of Human Behavior in the Social Environment* 20: 193–217.

Travers, Ann. 2018. *The Trans Generation: How Trans Kids (and Their Parents) are Creating a Gender Revolution.* New York: New York University Press.

Travis, Jeremy, Bruce Western, and F. Stevens Redburn. 2014. *The Growth of Incarceration in the United States: Exploring Causes and Consequences.* Washington, DC: The National Academics Press.

Tsemberis, Sam, Leyla Gulcur, and Maria Nakae. 2004. "Housing First, Consumer Choice, and Harm Reduction for Homeless Individuals with a Dual Diagnosis." *American Journal of Public Health* 94(4): 651–56.

Tyler, Kimberly A. 2006. "A Qualitative Study of Early Family Histories and Transitions of Homeless Youth." *Journal of Interpersonal Violence* 21(10): 1385–93.

———. 2009. "Risk Factors for Trading Sex among Homeless Young Adults." *Archives of Sexual Behavior* 38: 290–97.

Tyler, Kimberly A., Sarah L. Akinyemi, and Lisa A. Kort-Butler. 2012. "Correlates of Service Utilization among Homeless Youth." *Children and Youth Services Review* 34: 1344–50.

Tyler, Kimberly A., Les B. Whitbeck, Dan R. Hoyt, and Ana Mari Cauce. 2004. "Risk Factors for Sexual Victimization among Male and Female Homeless and Runaway Youth." *Journal of Interpersonal Violence* 19(5): 503–20.

United States Census Bureau. 2011. "Population Distribution and Change: 2000 to 2010." *2010 Census Briefs.* Accessed February 24, 2015. http://www.census.gov/prod/cen2010/briefs/c2010br-01.pdf.

———. 2013. "Annual Estimates of the Resident Population for Incorporated Places of 50,000 or More, Ranked by July 1, 2013 Population: April 1, 2010 to July 1, 2013." *2013 Population Estimates.* Accessed February 24, 2015.

United States Housing and Urban Development. 2006. *CPD Performance Measurement Training Manual,* Washington, D.C.

Urquhart, Evan. 2017. "Family Rejection Leaves Too Many Transgender Americans Homeless," *Slate,* January 26.

Valentine, David. 2003. "'I Went to Bed with My Own Kind Once': The Erasure of Desire in the Name of Identity." *Language & Communication* 23: 123–38.

———. 2007. *Imagining Transgender: An Ethnography of a Category.* Durham, NC: Duke University Press.

Valocchi, Stephen. 2005. "Not Yet Queer Enough: The Lessons of Queer Theory for the Sociology of Gender and Sexuality." *Gender & Society* 19: 750–70.

Vidal-Ortiz, Salvador. 2009. "The Figure of the Transwoman of Color through the Lens of 'Doing Gender.'" *Gender & Society* 23(1): 99–103.

Vidal-Ortiz, Salvador, Brandon Andrew Robinson, and Cristina Khan. 2018. *Race and Sexuality.* Cambridge: Polity Press.

Wacquant, Loïc. 2009. *Punishing the Poor: The Neoliberal Government of Social Insecurity*. Durham, NC: Duke University Press.

Walters, Suzanna Danuta. 1998. "The Gay Next Door (Now in Prime Time)." *The Harvard Gay & Lesbian Review* 5(2): 39.

———. 2014. *The Tolerance Trap: How God, Genes, and Good Intentions Are Sabotaging Gay Equality*. New York: New York University Press.

Ward, Elijah G. 2005. "Homophobia, Hypermasculinity and the US Black Church." *Culture, Health & Sexuality* 7(5): 493–504.

Wardhaugh, Julia. 1999. "The Unaccommodated Woman: Home, Homelessness, and Identity." *Sociological Review* 47(1): 91–109.

Warner, Michael. 1991. "Introduction: Fear of a Queer Planet." *Social Text* 29: 3–17.

———, ed. 1993. *Fear of a Queer Planet: Queer Politics and Social Theory*. Minneapolis: University of Minnesota Press.

———. 1999. *The Trouble with Normal: Sex, Politics, and the Ethics of Queer Life*. New York: The Free Press.

Wasserman, Jason Adam, and Jeffrey Michael Clair. 2010. *At Home on the Street: People, Poverty, and a Hidden Culture of Homelessness*. Boulder, CO: Lynne Reinner.

Watson, Juliet. 2011. "Understanding Survival Sex: Young Women, Homelessness and Intimate Relationships." *Journal of Youth Studies* 14(6): 639–55.

———. 2016. "Gender-Based Violence and Young Homeless Women: Femininity, Embodiment and Vicarious Physical Capital." *The Sociological Review* 64: 256–73.

Weeks, Jeffrey, Brian Heaphy, and Catherine Donovan. 2001. *Same Sex Intimacies: Families of Choice and Other Life Experiments*. London: Routledge.

Weiss, Robert S. 1994. *Learning from Strangers: The Art and Method of Qualitative Interview Studies*. New York: The Free Press.

Weitzer, Ronald. 2009. "Sociology of Sex Work." *Annual Review of Sociology* 35: 213–34.

West, Candace, and Don H. Zimmerman. 1987. "Doing Gender." *Gender & Society* 1(2): 125–51.

Westbrook, Laurel, and Kristen Schilt. 2014. "Doing Gender, Determining Gender: Transgender People, Gender Panics, and the Maintenance of the Sex/Gender/Sexuality System." *Gender & Society* 28(1): 32–57.

Weston, Kath. 1991. *Families We Choose: Lesbians, Gays, Kinship*. New York: Columbia University Press.

Wheeler, Coco, Christa Price, and Ian Ellasante. 2017. "Pathways into and out of Homelessness for LGBTQ2S Youth." In *Where Am I Going to Go? Intersectional Approaches to Ending LGBTQ2S Youth Homelessness in Canada and the U.S.*, edited by Alex Abramovich and Jama Shelton, 49–61. Toronto: Canadian Observatory on Homelessness Press.

Whitbeck, Les B. 2009. *Mental Health and Emerging Adulthood among Homeless Young People*. New York: Psychology Press.

Whitbeck, Les B., Xiaojin Chen, Dan R. Hoyt, Kimberly A. Tyler, and Kurt D. Johnson. 2004. "Mental Disorder, Subsistence Strategies, and Victimization among Gay, Lesbian, and Bisexual Homeless and Runaway Adolescents." *Journal of Sex Research* 41(4): 329–42.

Whitbeck, Les B., and Dan R. Hoyt. 1999. *Nowhere to Grow: Homeless and Runaway Adolescents and Their Families*. New York: Aldine de Gyuter.

Williams, Jean Calterone. 1996. "Geography of the Homeless Shelter: Staff Surveillance and Resident Resistance." *Urban Anthropology and Studies of Cultural Systems and World Economic Development* 25(1): 75–113.

Wilson, Bianca D. M., and Angeliki A. Kastanis. 2015. "Sexual and Gender Minority Disproportionality and Disparities in Child Welfare: A Population-based Study." *Children and Youth Services Review* 58: 11–17.

Wilson, James Q., and George L. Kelling. 1982. "Broken Windows: The Police and Neighborhood Safety." *The Atlantic*, March.

Wingfield, Adia Harvey. 2007. "The Modern Mammy and the Angry Black Man: African American Professionals' Experiences with Gendered Racism in the Workplace." *Race, Gender & Class* 14(1–2): 196–212.

Witten, Tarynn M., and A. Evan Eyler. 1999. "Hate Crimes and Violence against the Transgendered." *Peace Review* 11(3): 461–68.

Woods, Jordan Blair, Frank H. Galvan, Mohsen Bazargan, Jody L. Herman, and Ying-Tung Chen. 2013. "Latina Transgender Women's Interactions with Law Enforcement in Los Angeles County." *Policing* 7(4): 379–91.

Wright, James D. (1989) 2009. *Address Unknown: The Homeless in America*. New Brunswick, NJ: Aldine Transaction.

Wright, James D., and Amy M. Donley. 2011. *Poor and Homeless in the Sunshine State: Down and Out in Theme Park Nation*. New Brunswick, NJ: Transaction Publishers.

Wright, James D., Beth A. Rubin, and Joel A. Devine. 1998. *Beside the Golden Door: Policy, Politics, and the Homeless*. New York: Aldine de Gruyter.

Yoder, Kevin A., and Dan R. Hoyt. 2005. "Family Economic Pressure and Adolescent Suicidal Ideation: Application of the Family Stress Model." *Suicide and Life-Threatening Behavior* 35(3): 251–64.

Index

Founded in 1893,
UNIVERSITY OF CALIFORNIA PRESS
publishes bold, progressive books and journals
on topics in the arts, humanities, social sciences,
and natural sciences—with a focus on social
justice issues—that inspire thought and action
among readers worldwide.

The UC PRESS FOUNDATION
raises funds to uphold the press's vital role
as an independent, nonprofit publisher, and
receives philanthropic support from a wide
range of individuals and institutions—and from
committed readers like you. To learn more, visit
ucpress.edu/supportus.

64902656R00146